Contents

Women's Leisure Experiences: Ages, Stages and Roles: Editors' Introduction

Sharon Clough and Judy White

The papers collected in this Leisure Studies Association Volume arise from presentations to the LSA Fourth International Conference, "Leisure and Gender: The Big Ghetto", staged at Leeds Metropolitan University in 1998. This volume, one of five, comprises thirteen papers which collectively examine the diversity of leisure experiences of women in different situations, their multiple roles at different stages and ages in their lives. They also illustrate the variety and vibrancy of current research approaches which could loosely be called "feminist". The authors show a common concern with the ways in which women's experiences of leisure continue to be gendered and their lives characterised by constantly changing roles and relationships over which they may feel they have less power and control than they would like.

This volume has been loosely organised around roles related to age, starting with papers concerned with older women, moving through to papers about those in midlife to younger women. There are studies of Australian, African American, British, German, and Native American women. The papers include reflections on the place of leisure in the life situations of women from a number of ethnic backgrounds, women with disabilities, heterosexual women, lesbian women, mothers, lone mothers, married women, single women, schoolgirls, women at home, women in paid employment, and retired women.

Most of the research reported on is qualitative and gives insights into the meanings that leisure holds in women's everyday lives through women's own accounts of their experiences. The women sharing their experiences of leisure view themselves, and are viewed, through the prism of a number of interrelated sexual, social, domestic and age related roles. The women's voices are varied and their stories relate the importance of leisure in challenging common gender narratives in a variety of ways that enrich and empower their lives. This collection recognises and celebrates diversity without dislocating gender narratives from real social processes.

A key central theme in recent feminist research has been the way in which individuals and groups of women negotiate and resist a variety of constraints in different social contexts to find time and space for themselves. Although servicing the leisure needs and caring for others continues to dominate many women's lives, at whatever stage they are in their lives, there is also evidence of sites and acts of resistance. The importance of the sociability and support gained from close personal relationships with networks of women friends is a key element of women's leisure.

The nature, use, and rights to "space" constitute feminist debates in leisure as much as in other parts of women's worlds. The relationships which women have to spaces at work and at home, to "public" and "private" spaces, are explored here, and the exciting prospect that leisure can be used to transform and affirm these relationships is boldly stated, especially in those papers tracing the stories of older women.

Much of the feminist research work undertaken in the 1980s was unable to address complexity and diversity: its task was to set out the frameworks and parameters, and to lay claim to the legitimacy of gender differences, of the sketching out of the territory. Now the territory has been recognised, the task of establishing its complexity continues. Contemporary work advocates sensitivity towards difference and diversity and rejects essentialist theories about patriarchy and masculinity. It takes into account the lived worlds of women: their needs, experiences and interests. It examines the construction of femininities, illustrating the processes of resistance and negotiation needed to develop gendered identities. It contains examples of feminism as praxis; work that goes beyond theorising and is concerned with the improvement of women's lives.

The papers presented in this volume embrace structural, post-structural, and cultural analyses of women's leisure. Several focus on the stories of women who have challenged and overcome social exclusion and marginalisation in their lives. They present descriptions of a prevailing social reality, and convey the possibility of change which is not divorced from power relations or social context. The part played by paid employment and unpaid family obligations, changing caring roles and access to material resources in constructing opportunities for women's increased autonomy in leisure is raised in several papers.

Whilst some of the authors seek to explain the complexity of interrelationships between structural elements in power relations, others reflect the concerns of post-structural feminist discourses in recent years on individualism, subjectivities, and identities. The influence of the sociology of the body on post structural feminist analyses of sexuality, embodiment, and the construction of identity is evident in analyses of the body as a site of contestation and transformation for older and younger women. The deconstructionist approach of a number of authors serves to highlight the dialectic nature of the relationship between gender and leisure.

Josephine Burden presents a vibrant paper which focuses on her work with older women (and men) who are involved in the "purposive activity" of community theatre in Brisbane. She establishes vividly the view that growing older does not inevitably mean a "decline into disability". She elucidates how constraints for the individual is a function of the social construction of the environment; that is, the negotiation of constraint is more or less enabled by the social structures which surround people. She found that although the older people with whom she worked in her study faced some very real constraints, this did not stop them engaging with them and resisting them so that they could develop and change their own social interactions. They used the social world of community theatre to network with their peers and with other groups to show that they could engage with the outside world and negotiate meanings for themselves.

Women's Leisure Experiences: Ages, Stages and Roles

Edited by

Sharon Clough

Judy White

LSA

Publication No. 70

First published in 2001 by

Leisure Studies Association

A catalogue record for this book
is available from the British Library.

ISBN: 0 906337 80 1   2155350s

Layout design and typesetting: Myrene L. McFee
Reproduction: Prontaprint, Eastbourne
Binding: Kensett Ltd., Hove

Burden's work also presents a useful feminist critiques of leisure meanings in older age, and explores the concept of negotiation at three levels: the reflexive negotiation of a sense of self as agent which individuals undertake in the daily construction of meaning in their lives; the negotiation of change in the structuring of the contexts and constraints surrounding leisure, at the community level; the interpersonal negotiations between particular people in a family or group.

The research found that the purposive aspects of leisure became more important for older women, valuing the "purposive busyness" that was associated with them taking control of their own lives and organising their own activities including volunteer work and leisure activities, avoiding boredom, a lack of meaning and the negotiation of a balance between purposive activity and relaxation seen by middle class women as "me time". For the majority of women, community theatre provided a space for personal reflection on experience, social interaction in collaborative creative processes, the development of skills and the public expression of meaning devised in that process.

Burden shows that the model which the research suggests has two avenues of human endeavour in which older women negotiated their sense of self and influenced the nature of social reality : purposive activity, ranging from unpaid housework and caring work within the family, through volunteer work taking place at local community level, to paid work taking place in the wider public arena. She notes that work is defined by Habermas as purposive-rational action. The second avenue was loosely defined as leisure encompassing "freely" chosen activity for the sake of pleasure, ranging from solitary pastimes taking place in the home, through activities and events at the local community level, to the major social gatherings which take place at a wider cultural level.

Jean Carroll uses a group of retired professional women, including herself, who belong, in her words, "to three stigmatised groups- old, never- married, never mothers" to explore their relationships to leisure. The exploration is based on first person accounts from discussions, diaries, and written lifestories of past and present lives. The framework she uses is based around Bourdieu's notion of "capital", mediating between the individual and society and encompassing economic, social, cultural, and symbolic forms. The inadequacy of this analysis made her explore the addition of Bourdieu's other concepts of "habitus" and "field" as well as historicity, place, and discourse.

Although Carroll's material does fit with the suggestion made by Wearing (1995) in Leisure and resistance in an ageing society (*Leisure Studies*, Vol 14, pp. 263–279) that a discourse of leisure would combat the traditional discourse of ageing: "discourses on leisure emphasise a persons abilities and interests, the right to time and space for personal enjoyment and relative freedom of choice", there was a proviso. This was that this group had experiences of resisting discourses and had opportunities to make their own choices in life, so they had developed abilities and reflexivities and flexibilities to bring to retirement. They has place themselves at odds with the then current discourses of class and career, negotiating a path between conformity and resistance, which remained useful in retirement when they had to recreate themselves. The group did not talk of "leisure": "perhaps leisure becomes a surplus concept in retirement, and the secret is a lifeworld which includes "leisureliness" as the qualitative aspect of time that makes for satisfaction in retirement: "In retirement we have to construct a mixture of action and recovery from action; a pattern of variety and repetition; a pattern that accords with the days and the seasons and our own personal rhythms; a pattern that encompasses maintenance and social interaction and a variety of activities".

Karla Henderson and Barbara Ainsworth contribute one of the few pieces of work which has investigated the ways in which women from ethnic minorities ("women of color") articulate their feelings and attitudes towards the feelings they have towards the opportunities they have to be "leisurely". "Sedentary and Busy: physical activity and older women of colour", reflects on a group of women who are neither retired nor necessarily self defined as biologically "older", but whose lives seem to encompass the great variety of caring roles as a result of where they are on their lifetime passages and the complexity of relationships which exist as a result of being in relationships and bearing children. The work chronicled in this paper looks at the "typical days" of 30 African American women and 26 American Indian women who were interviewed about how they perceived and used time and space during typical days and who were all over forty. The premise was that in so doing, it might be possible to show ways that more physical activity might be incorporated into their apparent "sedentary" lives, which it is speculated have some impact on their health. Though sedentary, the women's lives are busy and far from "lazy": "doing nothing" is a definition to which many women aspire, but seldom reach; whilst being able to relax is a perceived reward to which many women feel they are entitled when they are working. Further difficulties are identified over the rights to space, as most women still feel unwelcome or without rights to use public spaces, private spaces in the home are a key resource. But such spaces are work spaces which also have family rights attached and in which leisure cannot take place.

The paper offers an attempt to develop a context for understanding women's perceptions of leisure and physical activity through grounded theory which uses the constantly increasing body of knowledge about space and gender. Few of the women whose views were recorded and discussed had few structured or routinised leisure time physical activities. But they did see that they had relative control of their home spaces, and significant others in their lives did influence what they did — which only infrequently included physical activity.

The plea for further research into the potential of places close to home for freetime structured physical activity, which may be community spaces, echoes the importance of such spaces as found in Burden's work on community theatre, where many participants were clearly looking for "purposive busyness" in the outside world.

Eileen Green links the study of women's experiences of the menopause with researching experiences of leisure at midlife. She explores and deconstructs key theoretical accounts of the menopause and uses post-structural feminist analysis to explore leisure for women. Her view that Hormone Replacement Therapy (HRT) debates have "medicalised" the menopause, and marginalised the "holistic" approach to changes in midlife, is carried vigorously through the paper. She also expresses concern about the negative images which Western cultures have appropriated to the menopause, such as endurance of the hormonal "rollercoaster", the "out of control" bodies, with "leaky hormones, useless-ness and decay". As the menopause "progresses", women become "progressively invisible", losing their youth and femininity. There are complex interconnections between women's identity and their physical health and wellbeing, which the menopause illustrates well : the menopause is a "diverse set of often contradictory experiences". Feminists such as Green are beginning to reclaim the journey into midlife as a positive transitional life stage that is potentially liberating: "a boundary marker and a site of struggle and personal agency". Green illustrates her arguments through women's accounts gathered from other research: they articulate midlife as a time of shifting priorities, of new personal challenges after years of roles of caring for others. Now is the time to turn to caring for themselves, to look to leisure, diet, and physical activities as part of their personal development strategies "in the construction of identities and new roles in midlife". Green urges a new politics of the menopause which recognises its key part of life in which women reclaim time and space for themselves.

Kay Standing investigates the lives of younger women. She shows that many of the attitudes and problems to which older women refer exist from the start of women's adulthood, in negotiating rights to space and time. The lone mothers in her study defined "leisure" in terms of having space and time to oneself, and in terms of social relations, relaxation, and sociability. The 28 mothers varied in age from 22 to 48, with varying degrees of family and kinship support. They are unanimous however in their perceived lack of time for themselves, which was generally compounded by lack of space and opportunity to pursue anything they might consider to be "leisure". Monotonous daily routines and physical tiredness which emanate from the "sheer hard work" of parenting, combine with the mothers' lack of financial security, to provide a situation in which individuals rely on each other and their friends for "a bit of a change" from the "normal" routine. These activities revolve around other routines (e.g. television watching) and children's leisure activities.

There are two strands prominent in this paper which run through all the work collected in this volume: sociability; and the importance of friendship in securing a sense of identity. Sociability seems the key to the women's survival; they use work and education as avenues to time and space for themselves, "thus turning on its head the work/leisure dichotomy, and demonstrating its irrelevance for the lives of many women". Friendship provides a sense of identity, and is also important "to reaffirm and challenge women's formal role positions, as single mothers, depending on the social networks in which they move (Allen 1989; Ribbens 1994). Friends in Standing's study enabled the sharing of childcare as well as "the chats, coffees and cigarettes, the time and spaces for themselves".

These papers reinforce the notion which feminists have been exploring for at least three decades, that leisure is intricately and intimately bound up the everyday, the dailiness, the small and boring repetitive activities which form the landscapes of many women's days.

Gertrude Pfister looks at the conundrums of the social roles of "motherhood" and the desires of some women to maintain their mental and physical fitness through sport, either ones which they had enjoyed before the birth of children (e.g. tennis), or one they had newly discovered (e.g. aerobics). The paper reports on a small sample of German mothers interviewed as part of the four European nation study concerned with women who were active in some sport. For this group, sport had clearly been important before they became mothers, and they continued their commitment, for their health and wellbeing, to regain a positive body feeling, contributing to their empowerment, but not necessarily to regaining their overall self confidence. Using physical activities as resistance and empowerment is therefore limited; as has been pointed out more than once, empowerment through leisure and sport does not necessarily overall have a transformative influence on women's lives; though it may affect their bodies and their identities, it is unlikely to make their work less monotonous, give them more money, or change their relationships.

The German mothers' major preoccupation was to organise childcare whilst they were playing sport, as it was acknowledged, covertly usually, that if they wanted to "do something for themselves", they had to organise who looked after the children. In this way, their leisure was a continuation of work, for which they were also responsible for childcare. Although some women embraced leisure with their family, it was clear that this was only a surrogate for their own leisure and own ways of celebrating their needs.

Laurene Rehman supports the approaches which fit together to develop a coherent picture of gender as a process of social construction, a system of social stratification, and an institution that structures every aspects of our lives because of its embeddedness in the family, the workplace and the state, as well as in sexuality, language, and culture. Rehman's focus is on the gendered nature of the family and its leisure. After some debate about the rigidity of pre-feminist research on what constituted "the family", she recognises the increasing understandings of family diversity, and within that, the diversity of family leisure experiences. She sees that leisure for women can be a form of resistance to traditional socialised gender roles. Leisure allows mothers with a chance to "focus on self" particularly at the end of their roles as "active" mothers, when the children "have left the nest", and could bring the focus back to themselves, where it had been before they had become mothers.

Rehman also notes that family research has been almost exclusively concerned with "privileged" families from white backgrounds and cultures, and that it is still rare to find any work looking at other family types and cultures, or at the roles and expectations of fathers. Finally, she suggests that it is vital to recognise the original argument of Eichler in 1983 that a multi-dimensional approach to family research is needed, using "feminist science", or as Henderson might term it, "feminist empiricism" which recognises the subjectivities involved in roles in the family, and the place of space in including or excluding individuals.

Jenny Anderson uses the "traditional" family group, with two resident parents, as her research focus, and attempts to explore the impact of particular types of "family" holidays on participants, assessing how perceptions may be different for each. Of particular interest was the extent to which mothers' attitudes toward their own personal leisure and caring for children at home are similar to their attitudes whilst on holiday. In this survey, both mothers and fathers were professionals in paid employment, and children of such parents were used at home to having their leisure "programmed", rather in the same way as child care, and it was suggested that parents were deciding how their children's leisure is spent. The research found that this pattern was mirrored on sailing and windsurfing "activity holidays" overseas, where there was separate provision for parents and children. Both parents and children liked the fun and good competent instructors which both groups had independently of each other.

In terms of the genderedness of such activity holidays, it was clear that mothers always initially mentioned the safety and happiness of their families; the "ethic of care" was paramount. Their own needs and satisfactions were invariably seen as secondary; holidays were a continuation of their nurturing roles, and it was a bonus if they did things for themselves. For fathers, the reverse was true: primarily for developing their skills, being on holiday with their children was a pleasant bonus. Anderson's view is that as each parent had different aspirations and expectations, it is not possible to say who was more or less satisfied, but "the main motivation for these mothers seemed to be first to ensure the happiness of their families".

Tess Kay echoes some of these themes in her paper in gender stereotyping in dual income households. She undertook in depth interviews with 11 women who were in full time employment, were either married or in a permanent relationship with a man, and had at least one pre-school child. Each described their relationships to work, mothering, and leisure; and each identified distinct differences ("divides") between their perceptions and those of their partners. The women saw the inequitability of entitlement to leisure as being the crux of the divides: men always accessed personal time in ways that the women did not, because of the responsibilities the mothers thought they had primarily with childcare and domestic tasks. The overriding ability of women to "sustain this burden, however reluctantly ... allowed household activity patterns to remain so inequitable".

Another useful finding (which has echoes in work on organisational effectiveness and commitment) was that although professional and highly work oriented, the women had made practical adjustment to their work activities to accommodate mothering, their male partners had not done so: "work was contained within fewer hours and within a narrower range of activities than previously". Clearly, parenthood created sites of gender differentiation in work behaviour, in domestic tasks, and in leisure, and there is no evidence that their high employment status "posed a substantial challenge to traditional gendered distinctions in couples' lifestyles".

Although the mothers felt they had rights to their own leisure, they were often in conflict with themselves over the time debt they felt they owed their children through working full-time, hence felt they should put their children's needs first when they were with them. "Leisure" was for themselves, no-one else in the family; it was in counterpoint with other domesticity, as a relief from mothering ... and indeed for a number, paid work time represented time to themselves, free from the intrusions of family needs, and the place where they have their strongest sense of self confidence and self identity.

Sharon Clough talked to another group of 12 professional women, some of whom had a partner and a child, but this was not a necessary condition of their inclusion. The focus for her Ph.D. research has been women academics in UK universities in an attempt to reassess the boundaries between paid employment, unpaid domestic work and leisure, and their relative importance in the lives of an apparently homogenous group of women. She has examined the motifs which have emerged from using grounded theory from their narratives about balancing work and family responsibilities with their own leisure needs. She notes the relative lack of research about this group, reflecting perhaps a tendency for the group itself to regard themselves as an elite rather than a disadvantaged group; but it may also be a reflection of their low status within the academy as well as relative to other professional women, and their relative lack of influence over the research agenda in social sciences.

The women with pre-school or young school children felt quite "stuck", with their caring responsibilities, and perhaps their relative geographic immobility. Their commitment to their work was as strong as those without children; they felt very much that their work provided them with a site of relative freedom which added to rather than detracted from their self esteem, in similar terms to Kay's group. Those with older children or without them at all felt less pressured, but still encountered huge time and role conflicts, and felt that their gender *per se* disadvantaged them in terms of career progression.

Clough suggests a useful typology. Her group categorised themselves and their leisure according to whom they were with, rather than the types of activity they undertook, or when or where they happened. Hence she evolved four types, which may be applicable to other groups and situations: family orientated, partner orientated, work orientated, and personal. Personal leisure was that most highly sought for, and the most precious, probably as it was the "most difficult to organise and preserve, particularly for those with children and partners to satisfy"; "personal leisure planes were the first to be cancelled or postponed, demonstrating a lower priority than either work or family commitments". So the themes continue: the difficulties of women acting autonomously remain greater and seemingly more complex than those of men, despite apparent strides in knowledge about each individual's needs for personal space and time, whatever their gender.

Diane Samdahl, Sharon Jacobson and Susan Hutchinson share some of the results of two postgraduate pieces of work about women who felt "marginalised", either by their sexuality or as the result of severe brain injury. The paper argues that leisure is a particularly gendered space as it is "a site where the ideology of personal freedom comes into direct confrontation with the constraints of gendered expectations". In the course of their research, the authors realised that they were unable to separate leisure form other aspects of these women's lives, and that they could only understand leisure in relation to "the broad cultural discourses that create meanings in a person's life". The analysis of how these women viewed themselves was based on a framework of negotiation, in which resistance is made visible through interactive processes, and in which for some women it is possible to reinforce their desire to remain within their familiar domains rather than change them. The paper's conclusion is that using a negotiation framework allows better understanding of the interactive processes mediating between agency and structure, and hence highlighting how leisure is embedded in our lives. It also contends that this approach to theory is exciting, as, unlike traditional feminist or leisure theory, it recognises that many of leisure's attributes (self-expression, self-determination, flow) are a result of the "self" feeling comfortable; thus providing a "more dynamic and integrative view of leisure".

Eleanor Peters and Diana Woodward contribute one of the two papers concerned with how young women resist and negotiate the cultural discourses around healthy living and exercise as promulgated by central government agencies. Based on participant observation in youth clubs and schools, a grounded-theory approach enabled fieldwork to inform theory. It was clear that the young women watched and chatted with were very adept at resistance; they used tools of femininity to subvert rules about sexualised appearance and behaviour. Whilst this does not jeopardise femininity, ironically as a strategy for resistance, as the authors argue, it is limited: it does not (unless it is lesbian sexuality) free such young women from the regulation of boys, but rather serves to bind them more tightly to their subordination as women. As well as these rituals of "looking good", they avoided any physical activity, but particularly that regulated and taught at school, which might involve getting sweaty and dirty, and so contravening the "cool" glamorous norms of their femininity. The only physical activity which fitted their "cool" criteria was dancing, formal and informal: it was something they regulated, and controlled, from which boys were generally excluded, and in which they could mark out their own space and develop their own skills. This model may be a more appropriate one to use to encourage young women in the enjoyment of activity than the traditional school sports.

Laura Hill's paper reinforces these findings and theories of resistance; and her work amongst a group of girls of about the same age, or slightly younger than those in Peters and Woodward's study, catches the same concerns and diversities of gender difference. Her analysis of the experiences and self-perceptions of the girls in her ethnographic study, including British Asian and African Caribbean girls, in the context of gender segregated physical education (PE) in an inter city school, focuses on how physical activities both reinforce and contradict their conceptions of femininity. Hills finds opposition to the traditional norms of gender and the institutional differentiating practices in PE: for example, the exclusion of girls from football, perceived as "sexist and unfair". She concludes that PE continues to "serve to limit, devalue and demean girls' participation", hence echoing and reaffirming Scraton's findings of a decade earlier.

Hill draws on post structural feminism to analyse the reflections of the girls about their physicality, their developing bodies, their competence and bodily confidence, in a range of sports in relation to gender ideologies. The girls tended to rely on stereotypical gender dualisms of masculinity and femininity that "recognise female participation as oppositional rather than a part of a broader definition of femininity". The "sporty" girls were "uncool" in the sport that they took seriously, but not if they were exploratory or reluctant; the author suggested that most "normal" girls' experiences in physical activity "need to be conceptualised in a way that does not blur them into a broad undifferentiated understanding of sporty or not sporty, feminine or not feminine". Although it is difficult to draw comparisons, it appears that the young women and girls in both the Peters and Woodward and Hills studies continue to struggle with a "cult of femininity", a gender stereotyping particularly in relation to physical activities, as least as much, if not more than, older women.

The past three decades have seen feminist theories and methodologies become increasingly complex, and sometimes more rarified. The LSA's 1998 conference highlighted the continuing need for research that is reflexive — both within and outwith leisure studies — which does not lose sight of the wider research agendas of other related areas of study. The papers published here demonstrate that the discourse does not have to be a "ghetto" fraught with incomprehensible internal factions, but can be a safe place for sisterly debate, acknowledging the necessity for and legitimacy of contributions from a range of theoretical perspectives.

Sharon Clough
Judy White
April 2001

About the Contribuors

Barbara E. Ainsworth is on the faculty in the Department of Epidemiology and Biostatistics and the Department of Exercise Science at the University of South Carolina. Dr. Ainsworth is also the Director of the USC Prevention Center. Ainsworth has conducted extensive research on physical activity patterns of women in the United States.

Jenny Anderson is Head of Marketing and Leisure at Southampton Institute which offers a range of sport, leisure and tourism courses including Maritime Leisure Management. Her research interests include demand and participation in watersports, leisure life styles and family leisure. She has been involved in several consultancies concerning maritime leisure.

Josephine Burden convenes a major in Community Cultural Development in the School of Leisure Studies at Griffith University, Brisbane, Australia. Her research approach is constructivist and she favours action research as a process whereby leisure research can facilitate social change. Most recently Josephine's research has explored the meanings of volunteering and she has begun a team research programme investigating young people's leisure interactions in public space. Her research is informed by a feminist perspective and she is Chair of the Women and Gender Commission of World Leisure.

Jean Carroll retired as principal of Dunfermline College in 1987 to live in SW Scotland. She began her studies of retirement at Lancaster in 1993 and completed her doctorate in 1998. In 2000 she moved to South Lakeland where she has been developing a further stage in her own retirement. Her extensive gardening has been replaced by additional social and cultural life; her jogging has been replaced by regular visits to a local fitness centre; her academic reading has been replaced by modern novels and she is a member of a reading group. She continues her daily swim and reflects that there is scope for much more research into retirement.

Sharon Clough is a Senior Lecturer in Sport and Leisure Management at the University of Edinburgh and she previously lectured at Brunel University and the University of North London, prior to which she managed one of the first community sports development projects specifically for women and girls in London. Her main research interests are gender issues in sport and leisure and the strategic management of sports organisations. She has been a member of the LSA executive committee for four years.

Eileen Green is Professor of Sociology and Director of the Centre for Social and Policy Research at the University of Teesside. She has longstanding research interests in gender and leisure which includes collaborating on an ESRC/Sports Council funded project with Diana Woodward and Sandra Hebron between 1983–7, and more recent research on young women, risk and leisure. Her most recent work includes an ESRC/MRC funded project on Midlife Women and Health technologies with colleagues from Warwick University and a DETR funded project on Enhancing Asian Women's Opportunities for

Health and Well-being on Teesside. Co-authored publications include Women's Leisure, What Leisure? (Macmillan, 1990); Gendered by Design? (Taylor and Francis, 1993); Through the Wardrobe; Women's relationships with their Clothes (Berg, 2001) and Virtual Gender (Routledge, 2001). She served as Chair of the Lesiure Studies Association (1999–2001) and a managing editor of Leisure Studies.

Karla A. Henderson is Professor and Chair in the Department of Recreation and Leisure Studies at the University of North Carolina at Chapel Hill. Professor Henderson with her colleagues has been studying various aspects of women's leisure including physical activity and outdoor involvement for the past 20 years.

Laura Hills currently lectures in Sociology and Psychology on the Sport, Health and Exercise course at the University of Durham. Her current research focus involves using ethnographic methods to explore relationships between physicality and physical activity experiences within the context of Physical Education. Related areas of interest include gender, theories of the body, and sexuality and physical activity contexts.

Susan Hutchinson is originally from Canada, where she had worked as a Recreation Therapist for a number of years. In her first year as a doctoral student at the University of Georgia, Susan was exposed for the first time to feminist writing and thought in a "Women and Leisure" course taught by Diane Samdahl. It was this course that shaped much of the thinking about the women who had acquired traumatic brain injuries in her study. Susan is currently an assistant professor in Recreation and Parks Management at The Pennsylvania State University.

Sharon Jacobson is affiliated with the Women's Studies program and co-director of the Women's Center at SUNY College at Brockport, New York. Jacobson completed her doctoral studies at the University of Georgia (1996) with concentrations in gerontology and women's studies. While her doctoral research established her expertise in the leisure of lesbians and qualitative methodology and analysis, her current research has drawn on cultural studies and post-structural feminist theories to examines the creation of physical, metaphorical, and metaphysical leisure spaces in women's lives, specifically those that experience multiple sources of social sanctioning. Jacobson has contributed to a number of books and journals including *The Forgotten Aged: Ethnic, Psychiatric And Societal Minorities* edited by T. L. Brink (1993), *Lesbian Social Services; Research Issues* edited by C. Tully (1995), *The Lives Of Lesbians, Gays And Bisexuals: Children To Adults* edited by R. C. Savin-Williams and K.M. Cohen (1995), *Journal of Gerontological Social Work, Journal of Gay and Lesbian Social Services, Therapeutic Recreation Journal, Journal of Leisurability* and *Journal of Leisure Research.*

Tess Kay is a Senior Lecturer in the Institute of Sport and Leisure Policy at Loughborough University. Her research into leisure and social relations has focussed on leisure and gender, leisure and the labour market, leisure and social inclusion, and leisure and social policy. She has been a member of a number of European research initiatives on the reconciliation of work and family life and is currently overseeing research into family life in Europe for the European Commission's project on Improving Policy Responses to Social and Economic Change. Her book *Leisure and Welfare: A Social Policy Analysis* will be published by Routledge in 2002.

Ellie Peters is currently Research Manager at The Children's Society, working on its Youth Justice Programme. Prior to this post, Dr. Peters worked as a post-doctoral researcher on a series of health-related projects at the Queen's Medical Centre, Nottingham University, and before that held a research post in the Scottish Office. This paper is based on part of her PhD project, on young women's health-related beliefs and behaviour, working with Diana Woodward at Cheltenham and Gloucester College of Higher Education.

Gertrud Pfister studied Latin, physical education, history and sociology in Munich and Regensburg. PhD in history at the University of Regensburg in 1976; PhD in sociology at Ruhr-Universität Bochum in 1980. 1981–2001 professor for sport history at the Free University in Berlin; and since 2001 professor at the University Copenhagen. President of the International Society for the History of Physical Education and Sport, Vice President of the German Gymnastic Federation, Head of the Scientific Committee of the International Association for Physical Education and Sport for Girls and Women. She has published several books and more than 200 articles. Her main areas of research are gender and sport. Loves all kinds of sport activities, namely skiing, tennis, long-distance running.

Laurene Rehman is an Assistant Professor in the School of Health and Human Performance at Dalhousie University, Halifax, Nova Scotia, Canada, where she teaches in the recreation and leisure studies program. Her research interests include: gender, entrepreneurship, work-life negotiation, access to the Internet and its relationship to income status, and leisure. The work and research for this paper was completed while Dr. Rehman was completing her doctorate under the supervision of Dr. Susan Shaw at the University of Waterloo, located in Waterloo, Ontario.

Diane M. Samdahl is an Associate Professor in the Department of Recreation and Leisure Studies and an Affiliate Faculty in the Women's Studies Program at the University of Georgia (USA). Her interests include the sociology of leisure and the social construction of gender, with particular emphasis on the ways leisure is shaped by normative cultural discourse. Dr. Samdahl hosted the First International Conference on Women and Leisure at the University of Georgia in 1995.

Kay Standing is Programme Leader for Women's Studies and a lecturer in Sociology at Liverpool John Moores University. She has an MA in Women's Studies (Canterbury University) and recently completed her Ph.D on lone mothers' involvement in their children's schooling (South Bank University) Her main research interests are in lone motherhood and education and feminist methodology. Kay has published articles in *Critical Social Policy, Gender and Education, Feminst Legal Studies* and *Journal of Social Policy*. She is a single mother with a daughter (and little leisure time!) who enjoys jazz dance and long walks on the beach with her dog.

Judy White is Reader in Leisure Management in CELTS at the University of North London, where she works on issues of current concern which are shaping leisure policy in the public sector. Recent consultancy work with the National Tourist Boards and the DCMS to develop models for the measurement of local tourism statistics has continued the relationship with local authorities and policy makers established whilst

Judy was a member of the Centre for Urban and Regional Studies at the University of Birmingham. During her 23 years there, she worked with all of the agencies involved in leisure and tourism policies as well as undertaking extensive management development work for a large range of local authorities. She was also involved with developing and convening some of the earliest postgraduate taught and research degrees in leisure and tourism in universities. Her current research interests involve the impacts of lotteries and gambling on individuals and communities in different countries, particularly the UK, Australia and North America. She is working on the ways in which women have developed "the lottery habit" in the UK and the cultural implications of the National Lottery on their leisure lives.

Diana Woodward is is Dean of the Graduate School at Cheltenham and Gloucester College of Higher Education. After working on the Sheffield study of women's leisure in the 1980s, with Eileen Green and Sandra Hebron, Professor Woodward moved into research on women academics' careers and equal opportunities issues in higher education. Recently she has been combining these research interests, looking at how women managers in higher education use leisure to manage the home/work interface.

Leisure, Change and Social Capital: Making the Personal Political

Josephine Burden

School of Leisure Studies, Griffith University, Brisbane

Introduction

Until the late seventies, older women remained almost invisible in both the gerontological and feminist literatures (Fennell *et al.*, 1988; Arber and Ginn, 1991). In the leisure literature, the assumption that women's experience was simply a reflection of men's continued to dominate until well into the eighties (Brattain Rogers, 1995). This paper draws on research carried out during three cycles of community theatre involving older people over a period of five years. Community theatre contextualised the research, was the focus for participant observation and constituted research data which triangulated interview data. The participants ranged in age from 45 years to 85, and were from diverse class and cultural backgrounds. They were predominantly women, but some men became engaged with the second cycle of theatre building. The processes of participant observation used in the community theatre studies revealed changes in the ways in which participants and audiences viewed themselves and older people in general, and interviews conducted with participants following their involvement documented some of the changes that participants perceived in themselves.

The location of the research in the setting of community theatre supported the view that growing older is not necessarily an inevitable decline into disability. Whilst constraints such as a decline in physical abilities were common for many people who participated in this research, constraint for the individual was also a function of the social construction of the environment. In other words, the negotiation of a constraint is more or less enabled by the social structures which surround people. Sometimes the social environment is structured to maximise the disempowering elements of life circumstances. For example, people whose eyesight has changed with age are constrained in their access to public space by the privileging of the motor car at the expense of public transport; people whose pace of life has slowed are constrained by social imperatives to live life at a faster pace. The people in this study faced some very real constraints in their lives, yet they continued to engage with the negotiation of those constraints and in doing that resisted the constraining influences of their worlds, and thus influenced social change. Many constraints were negotiated through contact with other people and it was the social world of community theatre which was one window to this aspect of people's lives in the research reported here. Community theatre is a social process which seeks to maximise the enabling aspects of social interaction. The negotiation of constraint which many older people were undertaking through networking with other older and younger people was facilitated for the people in this study through their engagement with community theatre. In this paper, the processes of community theatre are examined to show how they facilitate the negotiation of constraint for older people.

Community theatre is usually group devised and is based on the stories and experiences of the people involved. Arts workers may be employed to assist the process of building and performing the theatre piece but the aim is to allow the shape of the production to remain in the control of the participants (see for example Fuoss, 1995; Mda, 1993; Diamond, 1992; Pflanzer, 1992; George, 1984). In this way, community theatre has been developed as a means of empowerment for marginalised groups and as a tool for social and political change (Boal, 1995).

Rojek (1995) points out that times, spaces and activities of leisure are contested sites under constant negotiation between self and social environment. Whilst Kelly (1987, 1983, 1983a) emphasises personal agency in this negotiation process, Clarke and Critcher (1985) emphasise social control. Some classic leisure theorists (Dumazedier, 1967) have proposed the virtues of leisure as opportunity for individuals to influence the construction of culture, and humanistic psychology with its emphasis on self-actualization (Maslow, 1968) has been influential in philosophical interpretations of leisure as a process of personal growth. However, few leisure theorists have concerned themselves with the exploration of the processes whereby some leisure opportunities may facilitate both personal agency and social change, although Henderson (1993) makes the case for leisure researchers to begin to take on the role of creating social change. This paper examines how community theatre facilitates change at both personal and social levels.

Agency and purposiveness

The term agency implies taking action as an engagement with life and with the negotiation of meaning. Negotiation is necessarily purposive, and whilst leisure in this research was defined by participants as enjoyment, a second essential characteristic was self-direction which again implies agency and purposiveness. Community theatre is purposive activity in that it moves towards a product which is the public performance of a work created by the participants. However, in shaping that public performance, the emphasis is on a self-directed yet collaborative process which raises personal awareness, raises consciousness of common constraints and develops skills. Process is as important as product.

In this way, community theatre blurs the boundaries between work which is purposive and product oriented and leisure which is expressive and process oriented. There was strong evidence in the research reported here, that in older age when the paid workforce and/or the raising of a family diminish in importance as a purposive, product-oriented source of meaning, leisure does not take on a central role in meaning making unless it incorporates purposive elements. As one research participant, Sarah, who was in her 70s, expressed it, it did not take long after retirement before she realised that the hedonistic lifestyle was not for her.

Leisure meanings in older age

The concept of 'free' time did not sit comfortably with the older people in this study. Many of them took pride in being busy, and many took on volunteer work. The search for meaning in older age remained as important as it had been in earlier life phases when meaning had been determined by a capitalist economy which privileged paid work as the major determinant of meaning for men, and family as central for women. The imperative of capitalism to highlight paid work as the most significant element in the construction of the self, contributes to a blurring of the boundaries between leisure and unpaid work for those who are outside the paid work system, including people who are retired. In a society where leisure is framed by the paid workforce, those unpaid work activities often undertaken by women and older people are regarded as leisure, and volunteer work often takes the place of leisure as an avenue for the negotiation of self outside of the home. When all of human endeavour is regarded as either paid work or something else, then the endeavours of those who are not involved with paid work are lumped together and trivialised as not purposive. The people who took part in the research reported here were often actively engaged in the work associated with negotiating the constraints to their involvement and were also organising their own opportunities to be part of a community. They often found as much meaning in these endeavours as they did in the activities which some of the less active described as 'pastimes'. The dichotomy between work and leisure, which has been constructed in modern capitalist society, has as a major dimension the association of purposiveness with work and non-purposiveness with leisure. The research reported here indicates how this denies those who are outside the paid workforce the acknowledgement that they continue to be active in the construction of meaning in their lives. Purposive engagement with creative activity such as community theatre is one avenue for restoring a sense of worth and meaning.

Kelly (1983a) suggests that when we are most free to be ourselves, we experience our lives as 'leisure'. Paradoxically, freedom to be ourselves is contingent upon the social negotiation of a balance between the expression of self and our relationship with others. It is also contingent upon the negotiation of a balance between purposive activity which in our culture we have limited to paid work, and expressive activity which we have devalued as leisure, hobbies or pastimes. It is these balances, between self and other and between purposive and expressive, that we are in a constant process of negotiating, rather than the balance between work, leisure and family which is traditionally constructed as the pathway to 'life satisfaction'. Processes of community theatre offer an arena within which people can explore changing relationships between self and other in a way that encourages personal reflection and collaborative decision-making. Community theatre is also an opportunity for meaning making which enables people who are outside the paid workforce to negotiate a balance between purposive and expressive activity. Both these processes facilitate heightened self-esteem and confidence in abilities to negotiate constraint. Community theatre as a process enabled individual agency through collaborative action.

Feminist leisure theory has demonstrated the need for change in the ways we conceptualise leisure (Bella, 1989), and leisure theorists such as Kelly (1983) and the Rapoports (1975) have suggested that our experience of leisure changes as we move through our life cycle. In these processes of change at both the macro and the micro levels, the concept of negotiation is pertinent in three ways. Firstly, there is the reflexive negotiation of a sense of self as agent which individuals undertake in the daily construction of meaning in their lives. This negotiation of meaning at the personal level contributes to our sense of identity and may challenge the dominant discursive practice existing at the macro level. Secondly, there is the negotiation of change at this macro or broad social level, bringing about changes in the structuring of the contexts and constraints surrounding leisure. I refer to this level as the community level. Thirdly, there are the negotiations which go on at a micro level and involve interactions between particular people in a family, friendship or community grouping. I refer to these negotiations as interpersonal. Although I have separated out these different levels for the sake of clarity, negotiations at one level are assumed to influence negotiations at other levels.

Agency and the negotiation of identity

Several writers have attempted to link leisure and the negotiation of identity. Wearing and Wearing (1992) argue that the commodification of leisure in a market economy acts as a restrictive rather than a liberalizing influence on identity. Wearing (1991, 1991a), in a qualitative study of the relationship between leisure experiences and the construction of gender identity at different stages of the life cycle, found that leisure experiences may reinforce traditional gender identities but they may also provide a space for challenging the traditional and creating liberating individual identities for women (Wearing, 1991: p. 575).

The definition of leisure as a quality of experience has led to research which focuses on the ways in which the experience of leisure at levels of intense involvement may eliminate awareness of external factors such as time and space, as well as internal factors such as awareness of self (Harper, 1986; Tinsley and Tinsley, 1986). Loss of self awareness has been identified as fundamental to the intense levels of leisure involvement which Csikszentmihalyi (1975) describes as 'flow'. Samdahl and Kleiber (1989: p. 8) however, in their study of quality of leisure and non-leisure experience using a pager method of research, found that social interaction in any context is associated with increased self-awareness but that self-awareness in a leisure context is associated with positive affect, whilst self-awareness in a non-leisure context is associated with negative affect. They conclude that a definition of leisure which stresses lack of self-awareness is limiting and there is no consistent association between objective self-focusing and the realization of leisure. They argue that their research points to more research on the processes of self-development in leisure and 'serious' leisure (Stebbins, 1982). When leisure involvement is strategic, purposeful or analytic, or when leisure requires planning and evaluation, self-awareness is inevitable (Samdahl and Kleiber, 1989: p. 9). But a particularly significant implication of Samdahl and Kleiber's work lies in its questioning of the masculine bias of leisure theory which overemphasises the individual rather than social nature of leisure experience and undervalues the role of self reflection. Awareness of self is an inevitable aspect of awareness of others, and fundamental to the self reflection which contributes to a sense of identity and supports agency.

A central theme in the research reported here is that self-awareness is also necessary in challenging the social stereotypes of 'normality' in terms of gender or age, and that community theatre is one way in which self-awareness may be developed and challenges made. All of the participants in this study, including myself, had at least forty years of experience in the world and continued to actively construct their sense of who they were through their actions in the wider community. Part of our individual experience includes how the wider community reacts to our presence in the world and seeks to construct a generalised representation of who we are based largely on our physicality. Our physical appearance in the world changes as a result both of natural processes such as aging and our changing sense of who we are. Gender and age are significant factors in shaping our physical appearance in the world, as are class and ethnicity. Indeed, Freysinger (1995: p. 31) points out that cognitive psychologists maintain that the social constructs of age, gender, race and social class are automatically and often unconsciously activated in social perception. Thus awareness of our own changing experience of ourselves and of the social responses to our presence in the world are fundamental to the construction of identity. However, it is the act of speaking out about our own perceptions of who we are which may challenge a dominant, stereotyped construction.

Thus there are both concrete (physical or bodily) and cognitive components in the negotiation of meanings about ourselves. Our gender and ethnicity do not change for most of us as we move through the life cycle, but our age certainly does, and so may our class position. However, the social representation of those factors may also change as a result of social and cultural changes in the way these factors are constructed. For example, women who are in their later years at this point in time, have experienced remarkable changes in the ways in which gender is represented in the world. So what in earlier life may have been experienced as a contradiction between their own sense of self and representations of their sex in the wider community, may now be experienced as less of a contradiction. Women who are now older and who in their younger lives may have repressed their desire to express their sense of self in public arenas because of the social expectation that they should devote themselves to home and family, now live in a world where it is somewhat more acceptable for women to express themselves in public. On the other hand, an older woman's excursions into the public arena may now be experienced in terms of the invisibility which many older women report as they move into their later years. In today's world, women may enter the public arena but are still subject to a male gaze and a world where women are primarily valued for their reproductive and sexual qualities.

However, there is also a growing body of work (Greer, 1991; Sheehey, 1992) which indicates that as women move beyond menopause they move into a new phase of independence and self awareness. So in both social and personal terms, there is some indication that women move towards greater independence as they grow older. Whether or not this independence leads to happiness or dissatisfaction may be associated with the extent to which women explore social relationships outside of the family during the course of their lives and particularly as they grow older and the extent to which they are enabled to develop a sense of agency in the negotiation of their sense of identity.

Gilligan (1982, 1987) has explored the different positions of women and men as they negotiate identity and relationship. She suggests that it is women who have traditionally attended to relationships and that this aspect of women's role has been undervalued. Although Kelly (1983, 1983a) maintains the significance of relationships in leisure and life satisfaction, the discourse surrounding leisure in general continues to emphasise freedom, autonomy and self. The discourse of freedom of choice, individuation and natural rights which surrounds leisure sits most readily with a construction of masculinity. Belenky *et al.* (1986) suggest that we develop our sense of self through our relationships to others, that we cannot conceptualise self except in relationship to others. The different constructions of masculinity and femininity in early adulthood constitute differing foundations of self in relationship to others for men and women. One of the primary expressions of this difference is through the private world of the family. As people move into older age, there is evidence of a gender crossover in terms of public and private expressions of self as the relationship of women and men to the private and public worlds of family and paid work changes.

For men in early adulthood, marriage allows the negotiation of a life style which encompasses both the expression of autonomy in leisure pursuits and paid work whilst the development of relationships is managed through the social networking undertaken by wives. Hence Kelly's (1987a) finding in his research with older Americans, that balanced investors and family-focused tend to be men. For women, however, the discourse on freedom in leisure does not sit comfortably with views on femininity except where leisure is seen as enhancing social and familial relationships. So for many women, particularly those who marry, leisure is solely a space for negotiating relationship rather than negotiating identity and autonomy. As women grow older, some may stay in this mode of thinking which Belenky *et al.* (1986) describe as placing authority outside of themselves. These become what Kelly (1987a) described as passive adaptors, who, in his study of older people in a small North American town, were mostly women. Other women who may experience independence earlier in life, have their sense of self strengthened as they move beyond 50 and these become Kelly's (1987a) self-sufficients. Those women who are able to maintain a sense of self-in-relationship (Porter, 1991) during earlier phases of family life, may find they can use their skills of relationship building to enhance their growing sense of autonomy and independence as they grow older. Leisure for these women would then become a space for both relationships and for self expression and these may be most closely compared with Kelly's balanced investors. In his study, balanced investors were mainly men who balanced work, family and leisure. However, the women whom he classified in this category were women who built associations with other women.

Kelly's description of passive adaptors would suggest that not all people are active negotiators of their own life cycle; that for some, the external shapers of life experience become dominant and as Belenky *et al.* (1986) describe it, the self is never discovered as an active agent of intention and reflection on action. Other people, and Kelly's data would suggest that these are more often men than women, are able to develop a sense of agency in negotiating the givens of life circumstance and these people are able to use leisure and other spheres of living to negotiate relationships which strengthen their sense of self and make the traumas of life easier to handle. For men, a sense of self as active agent is part of what it means to become a man, and for many men, marriage provides a partner who will take care of relationship building whilst allowing them to continue asserting their own agency in their work and leisure. For women, however, whose sense of self is embedded in relationship (Porter, 1991), the development of the self as an actively negotiating subject in the progression of life is not encouraged either by her socialisation as a woman or by the 20th century institution of marriage. Some women negotiate this dilemma by focusing on self rather than relationship — Kelly's self-sufficients. Others move beyond marriage to the support of other women as a mirror of their own self as an active agent. Entry to the paid workforce is one avenue of seeking out this support, volunteer work is another, and leisure may be another.

The action of self-awareness and speaking up about our understanding of ourselves is fundamental to a personal sense of agency and I argue in this paper that certain forms of leisure activity such as community theatre may facilitate both the development of self-awareness, and the action of speaking up.

Interpersonal negotiations, the personal becomes political

Structuring discourses such as those of gender and age are mediated through our interpersonal relationships as well as more impersonal institutions such as the media. Yet at the same time, meanings of gender and age are social in that they are the products of relational involvements. Stokowski (1994: p. 95) claims that the processes by which meanings become adopted, and later institutionalised, by members of a society are social processes arising from engagement in interpersonal relationships. In the previous sections I have examined the concept of negotiation at the personal level of agency and identity, pointing out how wider social constructs such as age and gender intersect with individual constructs. However, it is at the interpersonal level that many of the tensions between macro and micro constructs are played out. For example, patriarchy as a system of gender relations influences individual women's negotiation of a sense of self by privileging certain actions over others. Whilst it may be difficult for women to negotiate with the threat of violence which some feminist theorists such as Brownmiller (1986) have identified as underpinning the power imbalance of gender relations, the ways in which individual women negotiate their relationships with male partners or work colleagues is fundamental to the negotiation of a new gender order as well as to personal identity. Lather (1991) points to the manner in which the now commonplace concept of the personal as political has obvious implications for the praxis of emancipation.

Rojek (1985) has written about the historical processes whereby capitalism has played a significant role in the control of men's behaviour in relation to their leisure. In Althusser's (1977) construction, leisure is an ideological apparatus for social control which confers an illusion of freedom and choice on the participant consumer and 'recreates' them for their primary role as fodder for the workplace. In this construction, women who are outside the paid workforce are also excluded from leisure. Hargreaves (1982, 1986) has suggested that for women the role of social control, their reward system, has been taken on by the family. Some feminist leisure studies academics (Deem, 1986; Green *et al.*, 1990) demonstrate how the family is deemed to serve as women's 'expressive' arena and this has led to a tendency to conflate the family and leisure for women, to the extent that undertaking family obligations may be regarded as leisure for women by both women themselves and by men. The controlling function of the family for women is itself negotiable, but for those women who marry, husbands and other family members take on a particularly significant role in negotiating their leisure since family structures focus the patriarchal control of women's lives.

However, Walby (1990) argues that the form of patriarchy in Western capitalism of the late 20th century demonstrates a movement from private to public patriarchy in that women are moving away from private control by men in the home to a more public control of women outside the home. Walby suggests that the movement of women into the public arena of work and political influence has been accompanied by an increase in pornography and violence against women which Brownmiller (1986) identifies as a means whereby men control the public activity of women. Wolf (1990) further argues that this is also associated with increasing pressure on women to conform to a public norm of appearance. This may be one of the shifts which is facilitating the increase in participation rates by women in physical leisure activities such as aerobics as women go to increasing lengths to maintain youthful body shapes that are regarded as physically attractive to men.

Bittman (1991) also subscribes to the notion of a shift from private to public patriarchy intersecting with the constraints of capitalism. He suggests that the price women have paid for increased participation in the public world of paid work is a slight reduction in leisure time since the demands of unpaid work remain unnegotiable to a large extent. However, I maintain in this paper that the nexus between paid and unpaid work, between purposive and expressive activity and between public and private negotiations of identity change in several critical dimensions as people grow older.

Leisure, community theatre and purposive activity

This research found that the purposive aspects of leisure became more important for older people, even though some such as Lottie, who was in her sixties, joked that life is supposed to be more relaxing as we grow older. Whereas relaxation aspects of leisure were important for people in this study who were still pursuing paid work, people who had moved beyond the paid workforce emphasised purposive aspects of leisure as well as relaxation. Purposive activity was valued in terms of self-direction which was identified by participants in this study as defining leisure and as contributing to the independence which the men in particular sought in life. Many of the women also talked about 'me time', or time alone when they could pursue their own interests. For many women, this sense of a 'right' to think of themselves as well as others had only been expressed in their later years.

Thus many people valued highly the purposive busyness that was associated with taking control of their own lives and organising their own activities including volunteer work and leisure activities. For some, this was also expressed as an avoidance of boredom, or the feeling of lack of meaning. They endeavoured to negotiate a balance between purposive activity and the relaxation that for the middle class women in particular was expressed in 'me time'. The theatre projects with which people were involved, contributed to both their full lives and their sense of control over their activities. However, the creative nature of community theatre also meant a high level of stimulation and change. Participants in this research were constantly negotiating for themselves an appropriate balance between the purposive, demanding, social, changing aspects of their busy lives, and the relaxing 'me-time' which they also enjoyed. For some people such as Dot, 60s, the level of change in community theatre was higher than she could cope with at that time of her life and she withdrew. The processes of reflection and discussion used in the creative work of building a theatre piece were too stimulating for Dot who was keen to negotiate social interaction in her life, but could not manage the creative instability as well. She found creative social interaction excited her to the point where she was unable to disengage into the relaxation of 'me-time'.

Nevertheless, for many others, community theatre offered the space for personal reflection on experience, social interaction in collaborative creative processes, the development of skills and the public expression of meaning devised in that process.

In this way, community theatre offers a synthesis which is not found in many other leisure activities. The nature of this synthesis, or the processes of community theatre, can enable older people in negotiating a meaningful life. Community theatre facilitates an awareness of self in relationship with others and the public expression of that awareness in a performance that may also influence the wider social environment. In this way, the personal becomes political.

Communicative action

Habermas (1991) posits a dimension beyond the socioeconomic in the definition of self or the making of meaning, and he describes this in his theory of Communicative Action. According to Habermas, the public realm of social interaction, including for example the social interaction which takes place at some leisure venues, both shapes and is shaped by the individual contributions of people negotiating their own understandings of their world. In this analysis, language plays a significant role in the construction of our understanding of self. Social philosophers such as Foucault (Kelly, 1994) describe how discursive practices, or the ways in which people interact with each other, operate to sustain a particular group in power and exclude others. Feminist critiques such as those of Pateman (1988) have pointed out that women have been excluded from this public arena of communicative action in which men negotiate their understanding of the world and their own place in it. In this analysis, the exclusion of women from public leisure events and activities has excluded them from an important area of meaning making.

The model which emerged from the research reported here suggested that there are two avenues of human endeavour in which people negotiated their sense of self and influenced the nature of social reality. The first was purposive activity ranging from unpaid housework and caring work within the family, through volunteer work taking place at local community level, to paid work taking place in the wider public arena. Work is defined by Habermas (cited in Outhwaite, 1994: p. 17) as purposive-rational action.

The second avenue was loosely defined as leisure encompassing 'freely' chosen activity for the sake of pleasure and ranging from solitary pastimes taking place in the home, through activities and events at the local community level, to the major social gatherings which take place at a wider cultural level.

However, for the older people who took part in this research, there was often a blurring of the boundaries between work and leisure. Although at least two of the participants talked about their whole lives now in terms of leisure because they were now free to do the things they wanted to do, many study participants also said that they were 'too busy' to do the relaxing activities which they regarded as leisure. Participants also resisted terms such as hobbies and pastimes because they felt they trivialised important activities which constructed meaning in their lives.

However, participants continued to operate across a range of activities from private to public. They resisted the social constraints which acted to confine older people to the privacy of their homes and adopted 'busy' lifestyles which took them out into the public arena.

The gendering of public and private worlds

The fuzzy boundary between some forms of work and leisure, and between some forms of leisure and work, is also associated with the separation and gendering of private and public spheres. Imray and Middleton (1983) suggest that the avenues for social interaction which are made available to people in a capitalist system associated with patriarchy, tend to be clearly separated into the private and the public with the latter valued over the former. Since women have been and continue to be more frequently associated with the private rather than the public world this in turn has tended to devalue the work and leisure undertaken by women at the private and community levels and once again these activities are lumped together as 'not work'. Smith (1990, 1991) amongst others, points out how the silencing of the private and of women has led to a distorted and one-sided view of the social reality of the public world.

Participants in this research negotiated their sense of self across a range of social relationships available to them through the family, the community and the wider cultural context. Work and leisure were two areas of human activity which ranged across these concentric circles of social relationship and offered avenues for people to increase their social contact. Whilst the social structures of modern capitalist cultures have gendered the concentric spheres such that women are more associated with work and leisure activities taking place around the home and community, and men's work and leisure has been more associated with wider, more public arenas that take them away from home and local community, the gendered nature of these spheres of social interaction has changed to some extent during the life times of people who participated in this research. At the close of the twentieth century, women are now more strongly represented in the paid workforce, and men are taking a little more responsibility for household, caring and volunteer work.

For the older people in this study who were outside of the paid workforce, there was evidence of the gender crossover with age, with women becoming much more active in the public sphere, whilst men were inclined to locate themselves more firmly at home. Community theatre served as a powerful social medium for facilitating women's ventures into the public arena by providing both a safe and supportive environment within which to explore shared meanings with others, and a public platform to represent those shared meanings to a wider audience. For men, Community Theatre offered an opportunity to build social networks which had previously been limited to the paid work environment, or had been left to the social skills of a wife.

Community theatre draws on the private world of personal experience and then uses reflective, collaborative and creative practices to construct a public presentation. Boal (1995, 1979) adds to the work of Moreno who suggests that in the process of acting out through theatre ways of being in the world, people can bring about personal change. Boal (1995, 1979) maintains that the public presentation of work in which people have been active in creating alternatives can also lead to political change. In this way, community theatre facilitates the negotiation of self across the spectrum of private to public, helping to bring about change at the personal as well as the political level. Participants in the research reported here constructed theatrical pieces from their own experience for public performance. The work was built collaboratively using the stories and experiences of the people involved and participants were also performers. Some participants were able to articulate this powerful sense of self-realisation as being profoundly associated with public expression

... the excitement of seeing people who, not so much undervalued themselves, but didn't realise their full value suddenly come to an awareness of it. I think that is the most exciting thing you can be around, to find someone absolutely astonished at their ability and their credibility to others too, y'know that they are believable and have something that they can share. Sharing's very important. (May, 50s)

Community theatre and community development

In bringing about this change at both the personal and the social levels, community theatre uses a community development model of leisure service. In recent years, community development processes have been recognised as an appropriate way for leisure professionals to work with communities at a time when we are moving beyond a consumer society where leisure programmes are consumed, towards a more co-operative society where people negotiate their own leisure experiences (Goodale, 1991). Barnes *et al.* (1997) refer to Hutchison and McGill (1992) in linking community development with the concept of empowerment. They suggest that "The purpose of community development is to bring people in the community together to increase co-operation and collaboration, which in turn builds a stronger sense of community" (Barnes *et al.*, 1997: p. 47). Montuori and Conti (1993: p. 60) emphasise the creative nature of empowerment when they write, "when we talk of 'empowering' people these days we are talking in a very real sense about allowing people to be creative, to create their own world, their own circumstances, rather than to conform to a pre-existing pattern". In this way, the concept of empowerment supports agency in challenging the normalising influences of the social structures, yet encourages individuals to link up with others to develop their own supportive infrastructures.

Arai (1997: p. 8), again drawing on Hutchison and McGill (1992) as well as Pedlar (1996), suggests that a community paradigm, which includes avenues for inclusion of individuals in community, and development of social relations, must be in place before personal empowerment can be effected. Arai (1997: p. 5), drawing on personal experience with a disabled sister, identifies four stages in personal empowerment: awareness; connecting and learning; mobilization or taking action; and meaningful contribution. Community theatre cycles through all of these stages. By drawing on personal stories it raises awareness; by working collaboratively with others through skills development workshops, it facilitates connection with others and learning; by building and presenting a theatre piece based on personal stories people are mobilized and take action; and by presenting the theatre piece publicly participants make a meaningful contribution.

Community development approaches to social work have been in place in many developed countries for several decades (see for example Ward, 1978, Stevens, 1978, Vasoo, 1984). In recent years, it has assumed increased significance in leisure service delivery, particularly in Canada (Hutchison and McGill, 1992; Labonte, 1996). The approach often underpins projects which seek to integrate communities with unequal power bases. Hill (1996) works with mainstream and marginalised groups to build networks between communities so that more members from different communities may come together for mutual learning and problem solving.

Stevens (1978) and Vasoo (1984), however, note that the term is often misunderstood because its definition frequently depends on the sector of the community which is constructing it. When governments act to 'develop' communities, the processes may in fact be those of community control (Stevens, 1978). Vasoo (1984: p. 17), in discussing community development in Singapore, writes that the term may be used to denote an activity directed towards organising services or programmes for people living in a specific community rather than as a planned process to encourage people living in a community themselves to initiate services or programmes to meet their felt needs.

Labonte (1996: p. 8) writing about community health in Canada confirms a twin responsibility held by community groups themselves and professional agencies in defining problems and working to resolve them. Community development is seen as a collaborative process whereby communities and government instrumentalities work together to identify and find solutions to their problems.

Writing in the Australian context, McArdles (1995) defines community development in terms of change at personal and social levels. Disempowerment of individuals or groups is associated with lack of choice resulting from economic factors, isolation (particularly from decision-making), cultural prejudice and myths, and internalised oppression such as feelings of guilt, fear or shame. Lack of choice may be compared with leisure constraints where the two most frequently mentioned leisure-related problems are financial and time constraints (Kay and Jackson, 1991). Community development as a strategy to overcome disempowerment, works on two fronts to bring about change in both the individual and the community. McArdles' (1995) seven "tools" of community development may be compared with Scott's (1991) three strategies for negotiating constraints in leisure although only two are obviously similar. Where Scott talks about acquisition of information, McArdles lists information gathering and giving, and where Scott identifies skill development, McArdles discusses personal growth through networking, self-help and the development of resources. However, the major contrast between the reporting of leisure research on the negotiation of leisure constraints, and the literature about community development as an enabling process is that the former describes the negotiations which people undertake, whereas the latter seeks to enable people to negotiate change. McArdles identifies three aims of community development; firstly decision making by those most affected by outcome, secondly the assistance of individuals to develop an ongoing set of structures to meet their own needs, and thirdly, personal empowerment through greater control over one's own life. The dream for McArdles is to move towards a self-directed community through the development of alternative power structures, the reform of existing structures and better utilisation of the democratic process. Yet at the same time, his vision includes what he terms, following Maslow (1968), self-actualised individuals through breaking down a sense of isolation, increased confidence, self esteem, assertiveness and more informed people capable of overthrowing myths about self or society. The mutual support developed through individuals working collaboratively to build their own set of structures contributes to both a more self-directed community and more self-actualised individuals.

Power, personal change and social change

Following McArdles (1995), I maintain in this paper that we need to develop in both personal and social terms simultaneously. The conceptualisation of self in relationship indicates that one cannot change independently of the other. McArdles (1995, 1989:

p. 2) suggests that the use of the term 'empowerment' is problematic because disempowerment may be attributed to such a complex and broad range of factors including lack of information, skills or confidence; disempowering attitudes; 'structural' inequalities used by society to keep people in their place; the attitudes of bureaucracy; isolation and so on. McArdles emphasises the need to work on both personal growth and social change in moving towards the dream of both self-actualized individuals and self directed communities. In the model which has been developed in this research, 'disempowering' factors may be compared with the constraints to leisure, identified as personal (fear, health, fitness), material (transport, money) and social (family, work, lack of companions, cultural difference). In a one-way hierarchical model of power these constraints act to isolate people in their homes and thus 'disempower' them. Social structures such as community theatre which facilitate interaction between people in the public arena enable engagement with others in addressing constraining influences and thus open up avenues for a more equitable, two-way operation of power whereby people may influence the constraining structures.

McArdles (1995, 1989: p. 2) defines empowerment as "The process whereby decisions are made by the people who have to wear the consequences of those decisions". He associates this with community development which he defines as "The development and utilisation of a set of ongoing structures which allow the community to meet its own needs". The development of these ongoing social structures may be compared with Cox's (1995: p. 15) construction of social capital which "refers to the processes between people which establish networks, norms and social trust and facilitate co-ordination and co-operation for mutual benefit". Cox (1995: p. 16) goes on to suggest that "We increase social capital by working together in egalitarian organisations". Cox draws on the work of Robert Putnam (1995) to suggest that social capital is built through co-operation rather than competition because it requires reciprocity and the equalisation of power relations. However she extends Putnam's work beyond a focus on definable organisations which work formally in the public arena, and includes the household and informal sectors, "extended household operations, neighbourliness and community support, all of which informally link people" (Cox, 1995: p. 22). Thus Cox builds on the feminist critiques of Habermas and Foucault to increase the visibility of the contributions made by women in building social capital at the household and community levels. Cox (1995: p. 23) maintains that the elements of social structures which facilitate social capital involve space, time, opportunities, precedent and the valuing of processes, all of which enable interactions between people.

Cox's work is a clear expression of the exploration of alternative social structures which constitutes one theme of academic writing in the last decade of the twentieth century. The theme is further evidenced in the work of Dalmau and Dick (1994) whose concept of collaborative individualism implies social structures which value the individual over the collective and collaborative over competitive relationships between people. The research reported here explored how social capital may be built up by older people through the collaborative processes used in community theatre. The research throws light on both the individual and the social facets of the debate about alternative social structures. Firstly, many older women do not find public spaces welcoming particularly at nights. The creation of women only spaces through community theatre was enabling in that a 'safe' place in the public arena was constructed. Secondly, women, who have been socialised to the collaborative processes of an ethic of care rather than the competitive ethos of the paid workforce are in a stronger position to build social capital as they grow older than are men. Many older women who were engaged with community theatre were guided by an ethic of care in their own interactions with one another. In so doing, they were not only discovering new ways to provide for their own needs but also new ways of working with other women to help each other. Community theatre presented an opportunity to express this advantage in the public arena. Third, community theatre offered a social structure which operated as an informal link for people in a community. And fourth, community theatre used processes which placed decision-making in the hands of participants and maximised opportunities to reflect on personal stories and construct a public voice which could influence the social environment.

This research indicated that it was the element of self direction in community development models of leisure provision which led to an enhanced sense of agency and consequently a stronger experience of enjoyment and freedom. When leisure is defined as enjoyment and self-direction but negotiated along continua which include dimensions of purposiveness, change, and social interaction in public and private arenas, then the social structure in which a leisure opportunity occurs assumes significance. This research has shown that the community development model used by community theatre serves to build social connections between people, develop a shared awareness of constraints operating in people's lives, increase public awareness of the ways in which a particular section of the community, namely older people, experience their lives, and heighten individuals' sense of agency by facilitating strategies to negotiate constraint. In the next section this latter process will be delineated.

Community theatre and agency

Community theatre offered a particular opportunity for older women to renegotiate and demonstrate their changing sense of self. In previous sections community theatre processes were discussed and shown to rely on reflection about personal experience and collaborative development of a publicly presented piece about that experience. It is a stage upon which older women can demonstrate that they are active people and, for some, it allows the exploration of new ways of negotiating life pathways.

Women who are older at this point in time have grown up in an era when the construction of the gendered self was different for women and men. Women were not expected to regard themselves as an active agent of choice but rather as someone who found life satisfaction in the service and support of others, particularly husbands and children. Older women and men now live in a world that has changed substantially in its expectations of gendered roles. They have also seen many personal changes in their lives. These changes alter the context within which people negotiate their lives. Older women and men experience change points in their own lives where the imperatives of caring for others or providing for others are lessened. Separation from a partner through death or divorce, children leaving home, and retirement from paid work, are key change points that bring pain, but also bring the possibility of renegotiating a sense of self. For some older women, this renegotiation of themselves as active agents is expressed in taking up new activities in the public arena where their changing sense of self may contribute to the construction of a changing social world. Changes in the rights of access of women to the public arena which have been negotiated in the past by feminists, some of whom are now older women themselves, has altered the context within which today's older women may negotiate their personal rights.

In the process of growing older, women experience significant change points which influence their sense of self. These change points include children leaving home, menopause and living without a partner. Those women who become actively engaged with leisure activities such as community theatre are able to negotiate their decreasing orientation towards the care of others by expressing, sometimes for the first time in their lives, a sense of themselves as an active agent in the construction of their own experience. Older women do experience constraints to their leisure participation, but the active negotiation of those constraints contributes to their self-construction as a person who breaks the stereotypes of age and gender and for many of the women in this study community theatre allowed the public expression of this new sense of self.

Women who are now in their later years have not been encouraged to express themselves as independent and active. Often their social and communication skills are well developed, but the 'selfish' skills of reflection and decision-making are not. Community theatre adopts processes which encourage self-reflection, group decision-making and the social construction of meaning. Participants are actively involved in all stages of the construction of the leisure experience and in this way the process of community theatre itself contributes to the heightened self concept of older women.

> ... the idea of creating a script out of our own lives really that's very creative, and it's very freeing somehow — freeing. It gives your spirit a chance to grow somehow and expand — I suppose it's the creative thing in it — I find that really exciting and even seeing it happening to other people and being part of it happening to the group that's always really great fun. (Vera, 50s)

> I don't know, I think it's to do with optimism, and I can see the value and benefit I get out of it. And the pleasure of other people too. And job satisfaction really, the pleasure of finding that there are skills that I still have. (Barbara, 60s)

Many research participants using different forms of expression identified the twin faces of involvement in community theatre, the expression of self and the collaboration with others:

> And you got a group of people there, all of us and not one of us was the same as each other, and it's really — although we're not the same as each other we finished up like a round ball, a circle — that's what I'm trying to get at. (Eric, 60s)

> I suppose because it's different, it gives you an opportunity to express yourself, doesn't it, through the singing and whatever. I like the group of women. I was standing here thinking last night after Sunday, different again to other groups of friends, it was just something, something, you know, a nice group. (Tania, 60s)

> It's a very good idea. I think it's marvellous to get people, for people to get to know each other. I know it's basically what it's all about, isn't it — getting to know each other. Yes I think it's a wonderful idea. So I've enjoyed it, I really have. (Jackie, 60s)

Community theatre, community development and negotiation

> Theatre is action!... perhaps the theatre is not revolutionary in itself; but have no doubts, it is a rehearsal for revolution. (Boal, 1979: p. 155)

I have suggested that community theatre is about participants working together in a collaborative process. In this case, the end product is a theatre performance using the life experiences of participants as building blocks. Many of the outcomes of community theatre are similar to those described by McArdles, and like community development, the processes used may lead to both political and personal change (Boal, 1995).

The idea of a link between arts practice and community development has emerged quite strongly in the late eighties and nineties in Australia. Government funding bodies and other arts agencies now use the term "community cultural development" to describe the processes associated with a particular way of working in the arts. The process usually involves a community artist or artists working collaboratively with a community to produce artworks which are relevant to that particular community. Whilst the role of the arts worker varies in ways which can be compared with that of the action researcher (Moroney, 1985), generally the arts worker employs democratic, consultative techniques which allow problems and solutions to emerge from the community involved. Workshopping is also used for skills development and the creative exploration and construction of the work. The process allows for people involved to negotiate a meaning for their own work, and in so doing to challenge the meanings structured for them by the dominant culture. For example, aging is frequently represented in the dominant culture as a rapid deterioration into dependency, yet the simple act of a group of older people coming together to build an artwork representing a different view of their own aging process is in itself a challenge to the stereotype.

It is the process of devising and performing which is personally transformative for the participants involved in community theatre. In traditional mainstream, including amateur theatre, the actors experience the certainties associated with a script written by someone else (Tait, 1994: p. 45). But the actors in community theatre are also the source of the script, and in acting out their personal experience, they are able to reflect on that experience and also rehearse alternative ways of being. The collaborative processes involved in negotiating and workshopping the script raises awareness in that people are able to compare their own stories with those of other participants. Collaborating to build performance work also develops skills in working creatively with others. In addition, the performance of the script is the point at which both personal and social change become possible. In writing about women's circus, Tait (1994: p. 17) suggests that "An emphasis on doing in physical theatre removes the performer from the confusion of acting "self' (female self) and transforms self into a demonstration of physical presence through action".

This "demonstration of physical presence through action" challenges the invisibility conferred on marginalised groups of people by a dominant culture, and so increases self esteem as well as challenging the status quo. A group of older women performing their own work in a public space are claiming a right to be seen and heard, and that act enhances agency and is both personally transformative and socially disruptive. Referring to the work of Foucault, Tait (1994: p. 132) writes that "Spatial location is crucial to the formulation of a performative identity because society orchestrates and structures space to control, contain, exclude and imprison".

Community theatre, then, is a collaborative process that builds theatrical performances based on the personal experiences of a group of people. The collaborative process involves negotiation at several different levels. At the personal level it allows the reflection, skills development and acting out which contributes to the development of agency. At the interpersonal level, community theatre uses processes which call for collaborative ways of working which may be compared with the consciousness raising of liberation politics. And at the community level, the public performance of alternative points of view opens a dialectic which may bring about social change.

Kershaw (1992) identifies community as the significant link between personal change and social change and emphasises "the importance of actual communities and forms of association as the necessary mediating element between individuals and large society" (Williams, 1965: p. 95, cited in Kershaw, 1992: p. 29). From this perspective, community is seen as "the concrete medium of face–to-face interaction through which we transact ideological business with the wider social structures" (Kershaw, 1992: p. 29). This may be compared with Stebbins (1993a) efforts to develop a mesostructural analysis of serious leisure, and there are echoes of Habermas' theory of communicative action in Kershaw's (1992: p. 35) view of "... community as a process of ideological meaning-making...". In this view, theatre performance becomes a powerful tool in negotiating a sense of self and of our surrounding worlds. "Community is thus a potential site of ideological opposition to the status quo, and a performance which engages with the ideological identity of a particular community may enlist powerful forces for change" (Kershaw, 1992: pp. 29–30).

Fuoss (1995: p. 79) argues further that community is not a fixed, stable construct, nor a social structure, but rather is a process that is constructed, contested and negotiated in cultural performances and other symbolic forms. Theatre performance is part of a dialectical process which articulates divisions within a community by constructing and negotiating relations among members. Since the community itself produces the cultural performance that constructs community, the theatre performance represents some of the competing interests operating to subvert or sustain social relations.

Since it is the participants in community theatre who are themselves engaged in building the structure of the play and shaping the messages for communication to an audience, community theatre may be conceptualised as a process rather than an established social structure, and this is where its strength lies in bringing about personal and social change. For this reason, community theatre has been recognised as a valuable tool in working with under developed communities where centralised systems of communication have failed (Mda, 1993: p. 2). Mda maintains that community theatre can be effective because it uses interpersonal channels found to have more impact than mediated channels of electronic and print media. However, "[f]or theatre to be effective, it needs informed intervention" (Mda, 1993: p. 186) in order to extract underdeveloped communities from the "culture of silence" (Freire, 1972) resulting from the internalisation of oppression and domination. In the research reported here, informed intervention was undertaken by the community arts workers engaged on the projects and by myself as a researcher. However, it was also evident in the work of community development workers over the previous ten years in the Inala community where two of the projects took place, and in some of the participants themselves who took a leadership role in planning the theatre projects.

Conclusion

The research study reported here was about the ways in which older women negotiated their leisure. But the location of the research in the context of community theatre opened up an arena in which older women negotiated the issues that were significant in their own lives and expressed their views about those issues on the public stage, thus raising both individual self awareness and the potential for social change.

In this paper, the established paradigm of 'ideal' lifestyles as balanced between work, leisure and family was problematised and it was suggested that there is a much more fundamental balance to be negotiated, that between self and relationship, or agency and social structure. Work, leisure and family may offer contexts within which to negotiate this balance, but the significance of these contexts in any one person's life changes according to many factors, including age, gender, marital or family situation and socio-economic status. It is the complex interaction between identity and relationship, between agency and structure, that was explored in this paper. The development of a sense of self as active agent coupled with the negotiation of connection with other people through a collaborative process is fundamental to community theatre. By grounding the research in community theatre, the analysis of older women's negotiation of these basic tensions was informed both by individual stories and through collaborative creative processes. The research enabled some older people, including myself, to speak out about their standpoint in the world. The negotiation by older women of constraints surrounding their leisure is in itself an emancipatory action and the public expression of ideas and experiences through community theatre may bring about social change, including change in the theoretical construction of leisure.

References

Althusser, L. (1977) 'Ideology and ideological state apparatuses', In his *Lenin and philosophy and other essays*. London: New Left Books.

Arai, S. M. (1996) 'Benefits of citizen participation in a Healthy Communities initiative: Linking community development and empowerment', *Journal of Applied Recreation Research* Vol. 21, No. 1: pp. 25–44.

—— (1997) 'Empowerment: From the Theoretical to the Personal', Journal of Leisurability Vol. 24, No. 1 (special issue on empowerment): pp. 3–11.

Arber, S. and J. Ginn 'The invisibility of age: Gender and class in later life', *The Sociological Review* Vol. 39, No. 2: pp. 260–291.

Arber, S. and J. Ginn, eds. (1995) Connecting Gender and Ageing. Milton Keynes: Open University Press.

Barnes, M., *et al.* (1997) 'Empowerment Through Community Development in Recreation and Leisure', *Journal of Leisurability* Vol. 24, No. 1 (special issue on empowerment): pp. 47–52.

Belenky, M. F., Clinchy, B. M., Goldberger, N. R. and Tarule, J. M. (1986) *Women's ways of knowing: The development of self, voice and mind*. New York: Basic Books.

Bella, L (1989) 'Women and leisure: Beyond androcentrism', in E. Jackson and T. Burton (eds) *Understanding leisure and recreation: Mapping the past, charting the future*. State College, PA: Venture, pp. 151–179.

Bittman, M. (1991) *Juggling time: How Australian families use time.* Canberra: CPN.

Boal, A. (1979) *Theatre of the oppressed.* London: Pluto Press.

——— (1995) *The Rainbow of Desire: The Boal method of theatre and therapy.* London, New York: Routledge.

Brattain Rogers, N. (1992) 'A qualitative analysis of leisure in the lives of older, middle-class women', Paper presented at Leisure and Mental Health International Conference Salt Lake City, Utah.

Brownmiller, S. (1986) *Against our will: Men, women and rape.* Harmondsworth: Pelican.

Clarke, J. and C. Critcher (1985) *The devil makes work: Leisure in capitalist Britain.* London: Macmillan.

Cox, E. (1995) *A truly civil society.* Sydney: ABC.

Czikszentmihalyi, M. (1975) *Beyond boredom and anxiety.* San Franscisco: Jossey-Bass.

Dalmau, T. and Dick, B. (1994) *From the profane to the sacred. Small groups as vehicles for cultural change* (Revised). Brisbane: Interchange.

Deem, R. (1986) *All work and no play? A study of women and leisure in Milton Keynes.* London: Routledge and Kegan Paul.

Diamond, D. (1992) *This is my life?.* Vancouver, BC: Headlines Theatre.

Dumazedier, J. (1967) *Toward a society of leisure.* Amsterdam: Elsevier.

Fennell, G., Phillipson, C. and Evers, H. (1988) The Sociology of Old Age Milton Keynes: Open University Press.

Freire, P. (1973) *Pedagogy of the oppressed.* London: Penguin Education.

Freysinger, V. J. (1995) 'Studying gender and leisure in later life: Current issues and future directions', Paper presented at International Conference on Women and Leisure: Toward a New Understanding. Athens, GA: University of Georgia.

Fuoss, K. W. (1995) '"Community" contested, imagined, and performed: Cultural performance, contestation and community in an organized-labor social drama', Text and Performance Quarterly Vol. 15, No. 2 (April): pp. 79–98.

George, V. (1984) 'Community Theatre as a strategy in rural community development: The case of New Market, Jamaica', *Community Development Journal* Vol. 19, No.3: pp. 142–150.

Gilligan, C. (1982) *In a different voice. Cambridge*, MA: Harvard University Press.

——— (1987) 'Woman's place in man's life cycle', in S. Harding, (ed) *Feminism and methodology.* Indiana: Indiana University Press: pp. 57–73.

Goodale, T. (1991) 'Prevailing winds and bending mandates', in T. Goodale and P. Witt (eds) *Recreation and leisure: Issues in an era of change.* State College, PA: Venture Publishing, pp. 231–242.

Green, E., Hebron, S. and Woodward, D. (1990) *Women's leisure, what leisure?.* London: Macmillan Education.

Greer, G. (1991) *The change: Women, ageing and the menopause.* London: Hamish Hamilton.

Habermas, J. (1991) *Communication and the evolution of society. Cambridge*: Polity Press.

Hargreaves, J. (ed) (1982) *Sport, culture and ideology.* London: Routledge and Kegan Paul.

——— (1986) *Sport, power and culture.* London: Polity Press.

Harper, W. (1986) 'Freedom in the experience of leisure', *Leisure Sciences* Vol. 8, No. 2: pp. 115–130.

Henderson, K. A. (1993) 'The changer and the changed: Leisure research in the 1990s', *Journal of Applied Recreation Research* Vol.18, No. 1: pp. 1–18.

Hill, L. (1996) *Rebuilding fun into life facilitator's manual*. Duncan, BC: Building Bridges Across Differences.

Hutchison, P. and J. McGill (1992) *Leisure, integration and community*. Concord: Leisurability Publications Inc.

Imray, L. and A. Middleton (1983) 'Public and private: Marking the boundaries', in E. Gamarrikow, *et al.* (eds) *The public and the private*. London: Heinemann Education, pp. 12–28.

Kay, T. and E. Jackson (1991) 'Leisure despite constraint: The impact of leisure constraints on leisure participation', *Journal of Leisure Research* No. 23: pp. 301–313.

Kelly, J. R. (1983) *Sources of leisure styles*. Footscray: Department of Physical Education and Recreation, Footscray Institute of Technology.

———— (1983a) *Leisure identities and interactions*. London: George Allen and Unwin.

———— (1987) *Freedom to be: A new sociology of leisure*. New York: Macmillan.

———— (1987a) *Peoria winter: Styles and resources in later life*. Lexington, Mass: Lexington Books.

Kelly, M. (ed) (1994) *Critique and power: Recasting the Foucault/Habermas debate*. Cambridge, MA: MIT.

Kershaw, B. (1992) *The politics of performance: Radical theatre as cultural intervention*. London and New York: Routledge.

Labonte, R. (1996) 'Community empowerment and leisure', *Leisurability* Vol. 23, No. 1: pp. 4–20.

Lather, P. (1991) *Getting smart: Feminist research and pedagogy within the postmodern*. New York: Routledge.

Maslow, A. H. (1968) *Toward a psychology of being*. New York: Van Nostrand Reinhold.

McArdles, J. (1989) 'Community development — Tools of the trade', *Community Quarterly* No. 16: pp. 47–54.

———— (1995) *Resource manual for facilitators in community development*. St Kilda, Victoria: Vista

Mda, Z. (1993) *When people play people: Development communication through theatre*. Durban: Witwatersand University Press.

Montuori, A. and Conti, I. (1993) *From power to partnership. Creating the future of love, work and community*. San Francisco: Harper.

Moroney, B. J. (1985) *Four approaches to community arts*. Melbourne: Victorian Ministry for the Arts.

Outhwaite, W. (1994) *Habermas: A critical introduction*. London: Polity Press.

Pateman, C. (1988) *The sexual contract*. Cambridge: Polity Press.

Pedlar, A. (1996) Community development: What does it mean for recreation and leisure?', *Journal of Applied Recreation Research* Vol. 21, No. 1: pp. 5–23.

Pflanzer, H. (1992) 'Older people act out: Making the ordinary extraordinary', *The Drama Review* Vol. 36, No. 1 (Spring): pp. 115–123.

Porter, E. J. (1991) *Women and moral identity*. Sydney: Allen and Unwin.

Putnam, R (1995) 'Bowling alone: America's declining social capital', *Journal of Democracy* Vol. 6, No. 1: pp. 65–78.

Rapoport, R. and R. Rapoport (1975) *Leisure and the family lifecycle*. Boston: Routledge and Kegan Paul.

Ristock, J. L. and J. Pennell (1996) *Community research as empowerment: Feminist links, postmodern interruptions*. Don Mills, Ontario: Oxford University Press.

Rojek, C. (1985) *Capitalism and leisure theory*. New York: Tavistock Press.

―――― (1995) *Decentring leisure: Rethinking leisure theory*. London: Sage.

Samdahl, D. and D. Kleiber (1989) 'Self-awareness and leisure experience', *Leisure Sciences* No. 11: pp. 1–10.

Scott. D. (1991) 'The problematic nature of participation in Contract Bridge: A qualitative study of group-related constraints', *Leisure Sciences* No. 13: pp. 321–336.

Sheehey, G. (1992) *The silent passage: Menopause*. New York: Random House.

Smith, D. E. (1990) *Texts, facts and femininity*. New York: Routledge.

―――― (1991) 'Writing women's experience into social science', *Feminism and Psychology* Vol. 1, No. 1: pp. 155–169.

Stebbins, R. A. (1982) 'Serious leisure: A conceptual statement', *Pacific Sociological Review* Vol. 25, No. 2: pp. 251–272.

―――― (1993a) 'Social world, life-style, and serious leisure: Toward a mesostructural analysis', *World Leisure and Recreation* Vol. 35, No. 1, Spring): pp. 23–26.

Stevens, B. (1978) 'A fourth model of community work', *Community Development Journal* Vol. 13, No. 2: pp. 86–94.

Stokowski, P. A. (1994) *Leisure in society: A network structural perspective*. London: Mansell.

Tait, P., ed. (1994) *Converging realities: Feminism in Australian theatre*. Sydney: Currency Press.

Tinsley, H. E. A and D. J. Tinsley (1986) 'A theory of the attributes, benefits and causes of leisure experience', *Leisure Sciences* Vol. 8, No. 1: pp. 1–45.

Vasoo, S. (1984) 'Reviewing the direction of community development in Singapore', *Community Development Journal* Vol. 19, No. 1: pp. 7–19.

Walby, S. (1990) *Theorising patriarchy*. Oxford: Basil Blackwell.

Ward, J. (1978) 'Creative conflict? A perspective on the relations between Government, Statutory Agencies, the voluntary movement and community work', *Community Development Journal* Vol. 13, No. 2: pp. 79–85.

Wearing, B. (1991) 'Leisure and women's identity: Conformity or individuality', *Society and Leisure* Vol. 14, No. 2: pp. 575–586.

―――― (1991a) 'Leisure and women's identity in late adolescence: Constraints and opportunities', Paper presented at the Congress of the World Leisure and Recreation Association, Leisure and Tourism: Social and Environmental Change held in Sydney.

Wearing, B. and S. Wearing (1992) 'Identity and the commodification of leisure', *Leisure Studies* Vol. 11, No. 1: pp. 3–18.

Wolf, N. (1990) *The beauty myth*. Sydney: Griffin.

Rejecting the Ghetto: The Retired Spinsteratae

Jean Carroll

Institute for Women's Studies, Lancaster University

Introduction

This paper examines the lives of a group of retired professional women, of which I am a member. All of us belong to three stigmatised groups — old, never-married, never-mothers. The thesis from which the data are drawn brings together first person accounts from discussions, diaries, and written life-stories in an interrogation of our past and present lives. The relationship of our retirements to leisure, as addressed in this paper, is problematised in a former colleague's anecdote of a child's response to her question about retirement; the child's reply was — it's the holiday you have before you die!

But I must start from the ghetto, which, in this instance, is the place constructed for older women by our society — the place of poverty, of illness, of loneliness. Ever since the systematic studies of Charles Booth in 1894 we have known that older people comprise a large proportion of those living in poverty in Britain and that the majority of these are women. This is confirmed by recent work (Walker 1992; Braid 1995; Social Trends 1995). It is the place reinforced by stereotypes and jokes and images (Featherstone and Hepworth 1991). It is also the place reinforced by academic studies which focus on age as a 'problem'. It is the place for elderly spinsters, widows and the childless.

A positive approach to ageing has, however, begun to develop. Positive ageing attacks the belief that ageing is a disease and puts forward new norms. This new approach was signalled in Britain by Miriam Bernard (1987) at a seminar in conjunction with the Leisure Studies Association; and developed by Bernard and Meade (1993), Johnson and Slater (1993) and Arber and Ginn (1995). Positive ageing also gained momentum with Betty Friedan's The Fountain of Age published in 1993, just 30 years after The Feminine Mystique; she asserted that the mystique of ageism was a much more difficult mystique to crack than that of sexism. The examination of the leisure of retired spinsters involves ageism, sexism, and homophobia.

In the paper I examine the resources of the group in retirement using Bourdieu's notion of 'capital' which mediates between the individual and society and encompasses economic, cultural, social, and symbolic forms. Then I note the inadequacies of this analysis in relation to my group and indicate how the addition of Bourdieu's other concepts of 'habitus' and 'field' are required along with historicity, place, and discourse. Finally I return to the relationship of leisure to retirement.

Resources in retirement

How do the members of my group stand in relation to the ghetto in which many older women exist? How helpful is it to explore their resources against Bourdieu's four forms of capital?

(1) Economic capital

> Economic power is first and foremost a power to keep economic necessity at arm's length. (Bourdieu, 1984: p. 55)

The seven women in my research group all retired from posts in Higher Education and so throughout their working lives have contributed to occupational pensions (of approximately half their final salary) which they now have in addition to DHSS pensions. As well as her pension each person had received a lump sum on retirement (equivalent to her final annual salary multiplied by her years of service divided by 30).

An important factor in looking at anyone's economic resources is the nature of her household. Does the person live alone and meet all house-owner expenses; or does she share these; in short, what is the income of the household? Two of the women live alone. These two clearly shoulder the financial responsibilities of their homes. In 1971 there were approximately 10% of households occupied by single females; this rose to 12% by 1993 and constituted the largest group of people living alone (Social Trends, 1995). It is forecast that this will be nearer 20% at the Millennium. The other five women share financial responsibilities with same-sex partners. One said:

> Financially I feel secure. In the past I have had good advice about savings and investments and on the whole I've been lucky. I live within my pension allowance, this includes Crombie of course, and my interest provides for extras such as holidays etc. (Marjorie, first meeting)

Two members of the group, Dorothy and Jill, still do part-time remunerated jobs in that they supervise students, mark and examine post-graduate work, act as external examiners or consultants. Similarly, for ten years after retiring from her full-time post, Marjorie also did a considerable amount of part-time work, but did not continue with this when her partner retired.

Comments, however, indicated that the deployment of this economic capital varied considerably along with the disposition of individuals towards money. Some were more careful:

> Checked possibility of paying in advance for more oil to 'beat' VAT after March 31st. (Barbara, Diary)

Others more casual:

> ... we don't have any fixed rules ... we don't even have any rules over money ... (Harriet, Second Meeting)

In general there was a certain ambivalence; a sense of comfort with some, but also anxiety about a volatile economy and a deteriorating health service; others wished for more money, but recognised that they were relatively well off. Some were more careful and austere about what they spent than others who were more consumer oriented. They have different priorities in the way they spend money; some are more expensively dressed than others; some spend more on food and drink and entertaining; three have invested in Holiday Property Bonds and take regular holidays with them; one has not had a holiday since she retired. I did not get the impression that anyone was totally unconcerned about money, but most of them were aware that, in comparison with other women of the same age in our society, and certainly in comparison with many other cultures, we were well off and some distance from the state of "necessity" referred to by Bourdieu in the next section. In this sense the seven women are part of a fairly elite group among older women in that they have adequate independent incomes and so we look next at their life-styles.

(2) Cultural capital

As the objective distance from necessity grows, life-style increasingly becomes the product of what Weber calls a 'stylization of life', a systematic commitment which orientates and organizes the most diverse practices — the choice of a vintage wine or cheese or the decoration of a holiday home in the country. (Bourdieu, 1984: pp. 55–6)

Within these 'systems of taste' Bourdieu variously refers to literary, scientific, and artistic areas and includes clothing, cinema, radio, and photography and the 'uses of the body' (1984: 191). Here, Bourdieu tangles with a mixture of information, taste, knowledge and values and accepts the complexity of his concept of cultural capital in his endeavours to show variations in class factions. Bourdieu also emphasises the importance of cultural capital in relation to production (in terms of life chances on the labour market through knowledge, language, titles, qualifications) and in relation to consumption (through the ability to appreciate works of art, music etc.) From modest beginnings in the 'respectable' working class and lower middle class of the 1920s the women developed their skills and interests, took advantage of new educational opportunities which enhanced their life chances and resulted in varied careers and retirement from senior posts. This provided them not only with occupational pensions but also with knowledge and interests that now seem to make life in retirement purposeful and satisfying. What cultural resources do they draw upon in retirement?

My own opportunity to pursue this research project in my retirement is clearly dependent on Bourdieu's (1984: p. 54) "distance from necessity' as it is one of the "activities which are an end in themselves, such as scholastic exercises or the contemplation of works of art".

There are other examples among my collaborators:

... I knew what I particularly wanted to do, that was that I knew I wanted to paint and it was something I'd always intended to do and in fact I had meant all my life since I left school and left college to keep it up but I never had time ... (Harriet First Meeting)

This person spends one whole day each week at a local art centre. She also visits exhibitions regularly. The same person attends weekly classes in Italian as well as art and is a regular theatre goer. The theatre visits like the exhibitions are long term interests, but the Italian classes only started after retirement and were prompted by holidays in Italy. She is also politically active and at the time of data collection was canvassing before the general election.

Another member:

[a neighbour is] taking a class on the history of the symphony, so I'm going
to that and I'm trying to join the Lakeland Symphonia group, but they're full
up at the moment but I get return tickets so I mean we go quite regularly to
(town) to the music concerts. I keep in touch with (friend) because of the
concerts back in (city) so I go back there once a month ... we've a very good
cinema and so we see good films almost once a fortnight. (Marjorie First
Meeting)

I go to these sessions that are either philosophy seminars ... or something
organised by the philosophy department on the environment and values. This
is something that's been going on for quite a number of years. I go to concerts
and plays occasionally, very very rarely to the cinema ... (Barbara First Meeting)

The above quotations are all instances of interests that the women have developed now
that they have the opportunity to pursue them; they have the time and the economic
resources to engage in activities of which they became aware through educational
opportunities earlier in life. They are as Bourdieu remarks, 'legitimate areas', areas
inculcated by the dominant group.

Another group of interests were relaxing, generally undemanding and centred on
the media.

... I do a lot of listening to the radio and there are certain fixed things ... Poetry
Please on Sunday ... Kaleidoscope ... In the evenings quite often a concert on
Radio 3 and the interval talks ... (Barbara First Meeting)

This person lived alone and the radio, in particular, seemed to provide both congenial
company for her and a certain structure to her days. Another person often used the
radio as a background:

Listened to radio 4 for the news and then went down for breakfast. Shopped
quickly for a few essentials after washing up to Melvin Bragg ... listened to 'With
Great Pleasure ' (Gwen Diary)

They mentioned television:

I've never watched so many first week matches at Wimbledon (Marjorie Second
Meeting)

Literary interests formed another group:

... went to bed, fortified with Ovaltine and dipped into 'How To Be Ridiculously
Well Read In One Evening' ... and now I'm going to finish 'Ties Of Blood' ...
(Harriet Diary)

These instances, within a very small group of women, range quite widely; it would be
difficult to identify specific social class factions in the way that Bourdieu did with his
1960s French data; but this particular range does seem to fall within a generally middle-
class band though there is some support for the postmodern view that high and mass
culture are no longer distinct (Rojek, 1995).

Bourdieu identifies the importance of the body and physical activities as markers
of class and taste within his concept of cultural capital. The importance of physicality
in the early years and in the careers of the group has been a feature of the study; they
all experienced active childhoods in the 1920s and 1930s when freedom of play in home
environments was possible; they developed careers in physical education which extended

over approximately forty years and so encountered changing curricular approaches. But do they continue to take part in, as well as watch, any physical activities?

They all garden and some are very keen gardeners:

I loved the garden and was growing more knowledgeable all the time. I attended several courses and was helped enormously by Bill, the gardener next door ... We negotiated an allotment in the purchase price ... (Marjorie Life-story)

It's one of the really my main interests since I retired although I recognise that it's something that lots of elderly people do you know it isn't on the whole it's not a young person's interest I don't think, it's for the time when you've actually got more time to give to it ... so that's been a great joy since I retired, I must say I, I very much enjoy it ... (Harriet First Meeting)

Across age groups and social classes gardening is recorded as a home-based leisure activity by approximately 2% of the population (Social Trends 1995). From the comments made I tend to think that the popularity of gardening comes more from its mix as an experience rather than its physical aspects alone. Inhetveen (1994) suggested that gardening as a productive, active and sensory experience also provided a connection with the seasonal patterns of nature.

Other forms of physical activity are mentioned:

Swimming, ... I go swimming at the local baths, I try to go regularly but I'm bad about it, I haven't been lately, I stopped going because they were redoing the bath ... but I've got a ticket for the year ... and you get reduced fees of course if you're an O.A.P. so I usually go once a week before my Italian class because I do so many things that I have to try to fit them in so I don't muck up every day ... I love being in the water and I always feel that I'm very very at home in the water, just turning around in it. (Harriet First Meeting)

And there are several references in Jean's diaries:

We had a swim and then an early meal in order to be ready for the skating on TV.

Swimming is the second most popular physical and sporting activity amongst the population at large although involvement drops after the age of 60. Only 8% of the over 60s record participation (Social Trends 1995).

The most popular activity is walking in the general population and among the over 60s where 44% record their participation. All but one of my collaborators mention walking. One walks on most days and makes diary entries such as:

13.45 hrs. Brisk, invigorating constitutional round the block. (Jill Diary)

Barbara is a very keen fell walker and engages in this activity whenever the weather is suitable; she counts this activity as her main priority — indeed the reason for retiring to Cumbria. On days she is not on the fells she walks locally. Harriet had joined a Tai Chi class, but was thinking of giving it up because she thought the teacher was inadequate.

An underlying feeling that people should have some regular exercise is undoubtedly a shared characteristic in the group and is more likely to be as a result of our careers than the influence of modern marketing. Those who do not engage in some activity or other feel obliged to justify it, perhaps especially to myself whose connection with them was professional and who shared with them an interest in engagement in physical activity:

> I'd like to play tennis but my shoulder plays up as soon as I get to play tennis
> ... (Gwen First Meeting)

The life-stories come to an end with an account of lives in retirement and formulate afresh the material of the diaries. For instance Harriet writes:

> I am fortunate to have such a good life and to be fit. (When I have time I try to swim regularly, but it's constantly pushed out of the schedule by more urgent matters, however delivering leaflets and canvassing are good exercise!).

Associated with physicality is, of course, health. In the literature on ageing the dominance of the medical model asserts itself; the ageing of the body is seen as a completely negative process. Phillipson (1982) noted that it is used as a justification to move people from employment to unemployment; Germaine Greer (1991) that it changed the ability of women to have children; Dittman-Kohli (1990) that rewards and satisfactions diminished; Kathryn Woodward (1991) that the body registered the successive subtraction of meaning; Biggs (1993) that the physical characteristics of ageing seem to eclipse all other forms of meaning and that images and surfaces have come to dominate. Much of this negative thinking focuses on dysfunctional bodies. The origins of such thinking can be found in the medical model of health (Linda Jones, 1994). What do the personal accounts reveal about dysfunctional bodies? What do members of my group say about this?

One collaborator had a cold during the week she kept a diary for the study and this curtailed her activities as she stayed in bed later than usual and did not attend her weekly art class. The life-stories contained more examples.

Harriet wrote:

> ... the only problem I have experienced since I retired ... That was that I nearly lost the sight in one eye ... I had suffered detached retinas in both eyes and for about a week I thought I would be blind and I was very distressed and became very reliant on [partner] — we listened to a lot of music — I shall ask for Beethoven's Violin Concerto when I am interviewed on Desert Island Discs! I could not believe that this was happening to me. But after a miraculous duo of operations ... my sight was restored. I had not been in hospital since I had an appendix operation when I was six and it was a salutary and interesting experience.

Barbara:

> In 1991, too, it was discovered that I have angina which luckily, however, does not prevent me from climbing mountains.

Gwen, in an appendix to her life-story, writes about having cancer.

> It is odd that this period of my life was omitted from my earlier account — I am still not sure why ... The treatment at the Marsden was superb but I realised how lucky I was compared with many of the people we saw waiting for treatment. I have now had four years of checkups and, touch wood, everything, so far, has gone well.

As Gwen herself commented it was an 'odd' omission; I read it as a silence of anxiety as I was collecting the research material during the four years of checkups.

There is awareness and concern about health, about participation in exercise but there is a refusal to recognise an inevitable deterioration because of their age. Even in the cases of serious illness there is a positive attitude.

In general, the category of cultural capital tapped a rich source of data and indicated that the seven women were engaged in a range of activities that interested them, that they had encountered during their careers, that they could afford to engage in because of their pensions, and that also involved social interactions, which is the focus of the next section.

(3) Social capital

Bourdieu (1984) wrote of social capital consisting of "resources based on connections and group membership" (pp. 3–4). This very sparse definition strikes one as that of the traditional middle aged professional man whose main interest in people is as 'contacts' for the furtherance of careers. And this is far removed from the traditional parts that women play in affective relations, in the harmonisation of relationships, and in supportive networks (Fishman, 1978; Bernard, 1981) though these also can be seen to have exchange value which is cumulative.

The basic social interactions of my group took place in the household. Rosemary Deem (1995) comments on the:

> ... little if any work which tells us about divisions of labour amongst same sex couples in western societies, information which would allow us to assess at least some of the significance of gender relations. (p. 14)

An interesting aspect of these same-sex partnerships is the sense of sharing that comes across. In some cases the sharing of some responsibilities seems to be of a rather ad hoc kind:

> Well [partner] likes to do, you know like for example she'll have done the first course ... whilst I do a lot of the actual cooking like making casseroles and they go into the freezer and I do all that kind of thing and soups and I do the salads usually. We spread it out, you know. It depends who's around and who's doing something. (Gwen First Meeting)

In other cases the division of labour is very systematised:

> Cooking we take, we do three days, three days and then alternate Sundays ... (Marjorie First Meeting)

The division of labour had been negotiated, was flexible, and was reviewed. Marjorie captures this in her life-story:

> Our domestic arrangements have been 'sorted out' quite amicably each of us taking our share of cooking and housework. Big jobs in the garden too have been negotiated — I undertook to look after the lawn and herbaceous — [partner] the pond and other beds, mainly alpine. I handle all our joint finances!!
> ...

The women with partners all referred to shared activities e. g. attending a wedding, shopping expeditions, visiting friends for a meal, as well as joint activities in the home and discussions. They also saw friends and engaged in activities independently — one had friends from her art class; another from a gardening group; one met a former colleague regularly, three took holidays with former colleagues. Askam (1994) remarked on the possibility with couples both to maintain stability and individuality and this seemed to apply in different degrees with these partnerships.

The social interactions took place face-to-face in ones or twos; in group situations; by telephone; by fax; by e-mail; by letter.

The overall impression is of a group involved in a considerable amount of social interaction. The people with whom the interaction took place included friends (of long and short standing; close or more casual); relatives; neighbours; past and present colleagues; acquaintances in their communities. Jessie Bernard (1981) pointed to the changes taking place in women's social relations; the extension from kin and locale-based relations to friendship networks. Certainly kin are not prominent in the daily lives of most members of the group, though several do keep in touch with kin, but then most of the kin from previous generations have died as have some of their own generation. Perhaps the fact that they all have brothers and not sisters is important here as research suggests that contact with brothers becomes more tenuous as people age. Although none have children of their own three of them have regular contact with nephews and nieces. The contacts with neighbours varies. Barbara lives alone and seems to engage in reciprocal action with her neighbours; looking after each others' cats; walking dogs; giving lifts to and from the local railway station; attending classes. Harriet has the greatest number of neighbourhood contacts and finds much satisfaction in this; at our first meeting she said:

> ... I feel, well one of the things that took me a long time to become accustomed to was actually having friends in the area because when I was at college most of my friends were professional friends ... and now I'm sort of really into ... I have made so many friends through going to the art centre and through being involved in the Lib. Dems. you know and it's so nice because they're friends that live near and I can just walk round the corner to see Joan and Bert who are Liberal Democrats and up the road to see Barbara and Harold ...

Dorothy recorded the highest number of encounters with colleagues and acquaintances as she was still most heavily involved with professional work and semi-professional groups. At our first meeting, about her continued professional involvement, she said:

> ... very wide ranging and at times it does become a bit daunting ... it's a bit more than I'd anticipated

In reviewing the literature, Clare Wenger (1992) found that friendship, confidant relationships, social support, marital status and social isolation were all related to morale and quality of life in old age and my material contributes to this view. The distinction was made between social and support networks; support networks are part of larger social networks (Wenger 1984); then Anne Scott and Clare Wenger (1995) developed a typology of support networks that operates in later life, but does not encompass the networks of my group. The nearest category is that of the wider community-focused network, but the description of it does not cover the relationships that emerge from the diaries. It is not distant relatives, but former friends and colleagues who comprise the networks. There is also a high level of community involvement with most members, for instance Marjorie wrote of three such groups: a fuchsia growing group of which she became secretary within twelve months; a music club on which she was a committee member; and a walking group. Marjorie shows a recognition of the importance she gives to the establishment of local connections in a new place:

Over Xmas at one of the neighbour's parties I was persuaded (reluctantly I must admit) to join the local W. I. and last week went to their first meeting. It's really not my 'scene' but I do accept that it's a good method of getting to know the local farmers' wives and of also getting known oneself and I'm going to regard it as just that.

And many new friends have been made in retirement. Probably this is another indication of the special nature of the group, but it does also demonstrate the inadequacy of the Scott and Wenger typology which takes for granted the traditional role of women as married with children and women as family centred. O'Connor (1992) emphasised the complexity of analysing the friendships of elderly women and the continuing ambiguity in the definition of friendship. This was certainly the case as I tried to categorise my material. A typology based on range and variety over the life-course and showing stage-based and continuing relationships would more accurately describe the social capital of the group. Retirement brought into sharp relief the contacts maintained from previous stages, the ones resuscitated after lapsing, and the new ones made.

Social relationships are important capital. They provide interactions and exchanges that give a sense of belonging; that often extend interests in other cultural activities; that can be called upon in need or crisis; and as Eileen Green (1998) argues, can be "a site of identity construction, empowerment and resistance" (p. 171). Some social contacts give a certain prestige and this leads to the fourth and final category of Bourdieu's concept of capital.

(4) Symbolic capital

Bourdieu wrote of symbolic capital:

> ...that is, with the acquisition of a reputation for competence and an image of respectability and honourability that are easily converted into political positions as a local or national notable. (1984: p. 291)

In the main, women have traditionally enjoyed the reflected symbolic capital of fathers, husbands and other male members of their families rather than their own. This was not the case with members of this group who forged independent lives and gained their own reputations for competence etc. during their working lives. At that stage, their career stage, symbolic capital was important. They improved their qualifications by obtaining degrees and publications; they moved into higher status posts. But I doubt the applicability of Bourdieu's concept to my group in retirement, except perhaps as public self-confidence. My observations are that people are not interested in what older women (or men) did in their working lives and indeed find such 'harking back' very tedious. This is, I think, what makes the adjustment to retirement, in this particular historical period, more difficult for professional men than for professional women; the identities of the former have been built on their public lives far more exclusively than have the identities of the latter. And it is the symbolic capital that they enjoyed in their later professional lives that so quickly drains away in a rapidly changing world; no longer are they sought as sponsors, no longer asked for references, consulted about posts, etc. They lose professional power. This does not seem important to most women, though two members of the group retain professional contacts. Why? Is the prestige still important to them or the social contacts? It is unlikely to be the small amount of money involved. Does the notion of leisure frighten them or have they a different notion of leisure?

Capital in context

Although Bourdieu's analysis gives both an insightful picture of group characteristics and a way of identifying individual differences, it does have some limitations, particularly in relation to women. There are aspects of the lives of the group members recorded in the personal accounts that did not fall easily into Bourdieu's categories and one of these related to domestic work. The women frequently cited domestic tasks in their diaries:

> Did two washes — one load one half load ... A very good drying day ... Sawed off the long planks of wood from the fence outside ... and chopped sticks ... Did the ironing ... (Barbara)

> ... followed by a few domestic chores ... hoover and dust house ... First load of washing in machine; wheelie bin out ... Ironing ... shopping completed ... (Jill)

> ... shopped for bread etc. ... cleared up a bit ... Froze all the raspberries ... shopped for vegetables in the village and prepared them for lunch ... put the washing in ... did some ironing ... (Gwen)

Another characteristic of the life-styles in retirement is the engagement in voluntary work in the community. All the retired women cited voluntary work they did in the community: with Cancer Care; distributing meals and books on wheels; giving help each week at a local horticultural centre; involvement with an international association for child dance and with a local youth dance group; party political activities; weekly help with archival materials; and serving on a regional sports council. Similarly caring does not feature, yet one woman was caring for her very elderly mother at the time of the data collection and all had been so involved earlier in their lives. The omission of these activities are instances of the gender blindness of Bourdieu's work and instances of the classic unpaid labour that feminists brought to prominence (Vanek, 1980; Stacey, 1981; Allin and Hunt, 1982; Martin and Roberts, 1984). There is no place in Bourdieu's scheme for these activities unless they are distorted; for example, some domestic work, like cooking, can be regarded as a cultural activity, and presenting an elaborate dinner party as a symbolic display; caring and voluntary work can be re-cast as social activities. And although one of Bourdieu's main concerns is that of social class he does not refer to the problematics of placing women in class categories (Dale *et al.*, 1985; Payne and Abbott, 1990; Roberts, 1993; Lampard, 1995).

The metaphor of capital with its four components and their movement through social space does provide a general model of class and enables an analysis of the micropolitics of power (Skeggs, 1997). The economically comfortable lives in retirement, the culturally diverse activities, the wide social contacts, and the confidence and adaptability displayed point to middle class life-styles, but the appreciation of life-style probably resides in the changes in life-style that have taken place over the life-courses of the group. In these ways we meet the weaknesses of Bourdieu's schema, but also its strengths. He insists on the fluidity and vagueness of his categories so that they can be interpreted in innumerable ways. The categories themselves are not precisely defined and between them there is considerable overlap not only between the four categories within the concept of capital, but between his other concepts of habitus and field. A detailed picture of people's lives can be gained only by complementary analyses of these, as is possible with auto/biographical material.

There has been criticism of Bourdieu's stress on cultural reproduction rather than cultural change (Lash, 1993) and on his lack of cultural and historical specificity (LiPuma, 1993). The life-stories have enabled us to examine the previous lives of the women and so we can place their resources in retirement within their life-courses and also identify the importance of historical time and place and their accompanying discourses.

The women wrote much about their childhoods after World War 1, in the depression of the 20s and 30s, and during World War 2 and I argue that these events and the social conditions and discourses contributed to the early formation of their dispositions, their 'habitus'. In particular the freedom they had in play developed physical skills and confidence that then enabled them to take up the educational opportunities that were available after World War 2. So from very modest beginnings in working class or lower middle class families they became first generation higher education — in general teacher training or specialist physical education colleges. They also wrote much about their careers — the gendered 'field' in which they worked and the ideological conflicts within it; their rejection of marriage and their varied and varying sexualities; their regular attendance at courses and conferences; their movements from place to place which necessitated judgements and adjustments and promoted reflection; their systematic promotion through schools and colleges; and the effects of economic and political changes during their adult lives. Finally their retirements into very different circumstances from their childhoods; their relatively comfortable positions because of their occupational pensions; their varied cultural and social lives; their enjoyment of the present.

Leisure and retirement

So what can we say about leisure in retirement?

The standard definition of leisure is encapsulated in Betsy Wearing's (1995) suggestion that a discourse of leisure would combat the traditional discourse of ageing.

> ... discourses on leisure emphasize a person's abilities and interests, the right to time and space for personal enjoyment and relative freedom of choice. (p. 263)

Similarly Rojek (1995) contends that leisure:

> is about what freedom, choice, flexibility and satisfaction mean in relation to determinate social formations. (p. 1)

My material does fit with this vision of leisure, but there is a proviso: my group of women had experiences of resisting discourses and had opportunities to make their own choices in life, so they had developed abilities and reflexivities and flexibilities to bring to retirement. The women deviated from the expected form of a woman's life in the earlier part of the century; this constituted a short period of paid work, marriage, family, widowhood, and old age spent in children's family. The women in the research group placed themselves at odds with the then current discourses of marriage and motherhood and their ambition involved resistance to discourses of both class and career. Throughout their lives the women have negotiated a path between conformity and resistance. This has not necessarily been a conscious strategy, but can account for the way in which they achieved authority in their particular careers. They have also made choices, of jobs, of places, of social interactions. These experiences were useful in retirement, when we have to re-create ourselves as retired people without the constraints of childhood and employment. The ability to do this is helped by previous experiences of meeting new people in different places, at different times, in different roles and so re-constituting ourselves throughout the life-course. Harriet makes it clear that, of course, there are differences:

> ... so you could just go on living and enjoying life as it is. But I am kind of conscious that most of life is gone so there can't be a lot left, which is unfortunate because there are still quite a lot of books left to read and pictures to paint.

Leisure is not a word used by the women in the research yet clearly they are enjoying their retirement. Perhaps leisure becomes a surplus concept in retirement. And the secret is to build a life-world which includes, but is not restricted to Roche's (1989) postulation that 'leisureliness' is the qualitative aspect of time that makes for satisfaction in retirement. In retirement we have to construct our lives more radically than at any other stage. We have to construct a mixture of action and recovery from action; a pattern of variety and repetition; a pattern that accords with the days and the seasons and our own personal rhythms; a pattern that encompasses maintenance and social interaction and a variety of activities. But we have had to accumulate the resources with which to construct retirement. Then retirement really can be a holiday!

References

Allin, P. and Hunt, A. (1982) 'Women in official statistics' in E. Whiteless, M. Arnot, E. Bartels, V. Beechey, L. Birke, S. Himmelweit, D. Leonard, S. Ruel, M. Speakman (eds) *The changing experience of women*. Oxford: Blackwell and Open University.

Arber, S. and Ginn, J. (eds) (1995) *Connecting gender and ageing: A sociological approach*. Buckingham: Open University Press.

Askam, J. (1994) *Identity and stability in marriage*. Cambridge: Cambridge University Press.

Bernard,. J. (1981) *The female world*. New York: The Free Press.

Bernard, M. and Meade, K. (eds) (1993) *Women come of age: Perspectives on the lives of older women*. London: Edward Arnold.

Biggs, S. (1993) *Understanding ageing*. Buckingham: Open University Press.

Bourdieu, P. (1984) *Distinction: A social critique of the judgement of taste*. London: Routledge.

Braid, M. (1995) 'Tomorrow belongs to them', *The Independent on Sunday*, 1 October.

Dale, A., Gilbert, G. N., Arber, S. (1985) 'Integrating women with class theory', *Sociology* Vol. 19, No. 3: pp. 384–408.

Deem, R. (1995) 'No time for a rest? Women's work, engendered leisure and holidays', paper presented to the Association for the Social Studies of Time Annual Conference.

Dittman-Kohli, F. (1990) 'The construction of meaning in old age: possibilities and constraints', *Ageing and Society* Vol. 10, No. 3: pp. 279–294.

Featherstone, M. and Hepworth, M. (1990) 'Images of ageing' in J. Bond and P. Coleman (eds) *Ageing and society: An introduction to social gerontology*. London: Sage.

Fishman, P. (1978) 'Interaction: the work women do', *Social Problems* Vol. 25, No. 4: pp. 397–406.

Friedan, B. (1963) *The feminine mystique*. London: Victor Gollancz Ltd.

———— (1993) *The fountain of age*. London: Jonathan Cape Ltd.

Green, E. (1998) 'Women doing friendship: An analysis of women's leisure as a site of identity, construction, empowerment and resistance', *Leisure Studies* Vol. 17: pp. 171–185.

Greer, G. (1992) *The change*. London: Penguin Books.

Inhetveen, H. (1994) 'Farming women, time and the "re-agrarianization" of consciousness, *Time and Society* Vol. 3, No. 3: pp. 259–276.

Johnson, J. and Slater, R. (eds) (1993) *Ageing and later life*. London: Sage.

Jones, L. (1994) *The social context of health and health work*. London: Macmillan.

Lampard, R. (1995) 'Parents' occupations and their children's occupational attainment: A contribution to the debate on the class assignment of families', *Sociology* Vol. 29, No. 4: pp. 715–728.

Lash, S. (1993) 'Pierre Bourdieu: Cultural economy and social change', in C. Calhoun *et al.* (eds) *Bourdieu: Critical perspectives*. Cambridge: Polity Press.

LiPuma, E. (1993) 'Culture and the concept of culture in a theory of practice', in C. Calhoun *et al.* (eds) *Bourdieu: Critical perspectives*. Cambridge: Polity Press.

Martoin, J. and Roberts, C. (1984) *Women and employment: A lifetime perspective*. London: HMSO.

O'Connor, P. (1992) *Friendships between women*. Hemel Hempstead: Harvester Wheatsheaf.

Payne, G. and Abbott, P. (eds) (1990) *The social mobility of women: Beyond male mobility models*. London: Falmer Press.

Phillipson, C. (1982) *Capitalism and the construction of old age*. London: Macmillan.

Roberts, H. (1993) 'The women and class debate' in D. Morgan and L. Stanley (eds) *Debates in sociology*. Manchester: Manchester University Press.

Roche, M. (1989) 'Lived time, leisure and retirement', in T. Winnifrith and C. Barrett (eds) *The philosophy of leisure*. London: Macmillan.

Rojek, C. (1995) *Decentring leisure*. London: Sage.

Scott, A. and Wenger, G. C. (1995) 'Gender and social support networks in later life', in S. Arber and J. Ginn (eds) *Connecting gender and ageing*. Buckingham: Open University Press.

Skeggs, B. (1997) *Formations of class and gender*. London: Sage.

Social Trends (1995) London: HMSO.

Stacey, M. (1981) 'The division of labour revisited or overcoming the two Adams', in P. Abrams, R. Deem, J. Finch, P. Rock (eds) *Practice and progress: British sociology 1950–1980*. London: Allen and Unwin.

Vanek, J. (1980) 'Time spent in housework', in A. Amsden (ed) *The economics of women's work*. London: Penguin Books.

Walker, A. (1992) 'The poor relation: Poverty among older women', in C. Glendinning and J. Millar (eds) *Women and poverty in Britain in the 1990s*. Hemel Hempstead: Harvester Wheatsheaf.

Wearing, B. (1995) 'Leisure and resistance in an ageing society', *Leisure Studies* Vol. 14: pp. 263–279.

Wenger, G. C. (1984) *The supportive network: Coping with old age*. London: Allen and Unwin.

———— (1992) *Help in old age — facing up to change: A longitudinal network study*. Liverpool: Liverpool University Press.

Woodward, K. (ed) (1997) *Identity and difference*. London: Sage/Open University.

Sedentary and Busy: Physical Activity and Older Women of Color*

Karla A. Henderson
Recreation and Leisure Studies, University of North Carolina
at Chapel Hil

Barbara E. Ainsworth
Prevention Center, University of South Carolina

Louise, a 41 year old educated professional African American woman living in South Carolina, married with children still at home and a grandchild, described her "typical" weekend:

> Starting on Fridays, it's usually wind down family [time]. We usually go out for pizza. The kids look forward to pizza on Friday, so we usually do that. And then we just get some videos and let them think they're going to stay up all night. Of course they fall asleep after about an hour. Saturday, in the winter, wake up and take [child] to bowling in the morning. And he bowls until about 11. And then it's usually going out and grocery shopping. Just the usual work — weekend clean-up work type things. Saturday just eat leftover pizza, look at some more videos, and that's it Saturday evening. Sunday starts all over with church. After church I usually try and do something with 'em maybe that's when we would usually drive somewhere. Or go to the museum or the mall or the movies, something to do different. And wash clothes, look at TV.

Nashanta, a 42 year old educated married African American woman with a family income above average and children in the household, described a typical weekday:

> Rush, rush, rush. It's like it's not enough hours in the day, okay. This morning we got up at 6:30. We need to leave home no later than about 7:15, 7:20, but we didn't leave until 7:30 this morning and we were rushing around there ... breakfast is not big deal at our house. When I get there [work] it's pretty much like a normal routine. And then I get off, I have to get her [daughter] by six so I normally pick her up...and we always have to stop someplace. I gotta go into Wal-mart to get this, I go to the grocery store to get that, so we usually go by some store every day and we usually get home about 6:15. And then I start my thing — the cookin' and my son goes to karate, and then I go back to pick him up if my husband's not there to get him. And tonight I have a church meeting so I'll get my daughter a burger at Wendy's or something and go straight to the church. My husband and son have to fend for themselves...leftovers from

last night or whatever. And then I get back in — it's pickin' up, fussin' [giggles], gettin' ready for the next day to come to work. About 11 o'clock I'm ready for bed. I like to be ready for bed when the 11 o'clock news comes on.

Emmie, a 40 year old married worker with children, middle income American Indian described her typical day as:

> Get up at 6 in the morning, go to the kitchen, fix breakfast, lunch. Get ready for work, come to work, stay here all day, go home, fix supper, if it's not already fixed. Eat supper, watch TV for a little while, get ready to go walk, go walk. We [she and husband] usually stop and visit my mother and father-in-law, check to see how they are, about every day. And then go home and stretch out some more and watch some more TV, get ready for bed.

Grace, a 69 year old divorced lower income American Indian living alone described her typical weekend as:

> I usually spend my day [Saturday] at home, like cooking. Sometimes my family comes in from town, my brothers, my brother and sisters that live away from here, and so they come in so I try to give them a home cooked meal, a traditional meal or something like that. Then on Sundays I usually go to church over here and then after that sometimes I go to bingo, and meet some old friends there, you know, and all that. And then crochet. Sometimes I go to town when I feel like it.

All of these women lead active lives although, except maybe for Emmie, would be considered sedentary according to a Mortality and Morbidity Weekly Report (cited by Wells, 1996). A sedentary lifestyle was defined as reported participation in fewer than three 20-minute sessions of "leisure time physical activity" (LTPA) per week excluding usual job related physical activity. According to these statistics in the United States, more than half of all women are sedentary in their lives. Among women of color this percentage nears 65%. Yeager, Macera, and Merritt (1993) found that being sedentary decreased for individuals as socioeconomic income went up, but socioeconomic income level alone did not eliminate racial differences. They also found that being sedentary related to age with older people being less active than younger women.

We know little, however, about women's physical activity patterns and how to measure involvement by taking into account home and family responsibilities, ethnicity, marital, economic, and other situational factors. Yeager *et al.* (1993) suggested that perhaps the instruments used to measure leisure time physical activity have not been sensitive enough. Further, some of the terminology typically used in measuring "leisure time physical activity" may not be appropriate for women of color (Masse *et al.*, 1998). Wells (1996) stated that "Research and educational efforts must focus on conceptually-based programs in schools and communities that are culturally-sensitive and ethnic-specific" (p. 6). Shaw (1985) also suggested that it is necessary to be concerned with attitudes and perceptions surrounding particular situations rather than just describing types of activities that women may do.

The purpose of this paper, therefore, is to provide information about life situations and "typical days" as defined by a sample of African American and American Indian women over the age of 40 years. We were interested in how people made sense of their lives and the priorities that existed on an "everyday" basis. The statistics show that many women of color are sedentary so we wanted to know what they were doing with their time. How did they use the space around them? As the examples above illustrate, the everyday lives of these women of color were filled with many activities that seemed to provide subjective meanings in their lives. Though sedentary by definition, their lives were busy. This study is a part of an ongoing larger study to determine what African American and American Indian women do as physical activity and how this activity contributes to making their lives healthier.

Background

The activities of everyday life epitomize the way that most people define living. Although many of us go on vacations and have holidays, most of our lives consist of routine day to day activities, or what might be referred to as "typical days". Most days revolve around work and home life. This everyday life, however, is sometimes invisible in the research done within leisure studies. As Bloch (1987) suggested, people have different ways of coping with the unstaged settings of everyday lives based on conditions including the social division of labor, age, sex, and race. For many women, everyday life is also infused with addressing the needs of others before addressing their own needs. Free time is often co-opted by others. It is in this everyday life, however, that researchers can attempt to capture the interplay between economic, political, and ideocultural institutions and the ways that people cope with their lives and the gendered space that surrounds them. As Bloch further stated, it is within this everyday life that conflicts exist among wage labor, demands of family, and the potential for personal leisure and opportunities for free time physical activity. Leisure and how it is embodied is an experience of this everyday life (Allen and Chin-Sang, 1990; Shaw, 1985).

With the changes that have occurred in US women's lives over the past 30 years (Henderson, Bialeschki, Shaw, and Freysinger, 1996), we would expect most women to be more liberated from traditional gender role expectations with the potential to increase their involvement in leisure and physical activities. Further, with the burgeoning information about the importance of physical activity in maintaining one's health (US Dept. of Health and Human Services, 1996), we would expect that more women would see physical activity as an important dimension of their everyday lives. Unfortunately, physically active lifestyles related to leisure involvement do not seem to be the case among many women, and particularly among women of color. Robinson and Godbey (1993) found that major gaps are occurring between males and females related to physical activity and confirmed that this gap was even greater when African American women and men were studied. They attributed this gap to lower levels of education and income, urban residence, large family size, and other factors negatively associated with exercise. They concluded overall that exercise is declining and the gender gap regarding physical activity is widening.

Physical activity encompasses a variety of potential involvements. Traditional sports, however, have not been common in the everyday lives of most women (Deem, 1987; Lenskyj, 1988; Henderson *et al.*, 1996). Deem (1987) found that those sports or activities that were most popular had to be free or inexpensive, flexible, and easily combined with children's activities and interests (e.g., walking and swimming). These activities were more likely to occur when done on short notice or when combined with household duties. Most were done either from home or in a place and at a time that fit with women's other roles and responsibilities. Deem also found that women said they had little energy left for sport at the end of most days. Henderson and Bialeschki (1994) concluded that women who participated regularly in some type of physical activity made it a part of their routine each day or else it was not likely to happen. Based on the US statistics on physical activity, however, regular structured physical activity is obviously not part of most women's lives, and less so for women of color (US Dept. of Health and Human Services, 1996).

In the industrial world, we have created the dichotomy of the week as composed of weekdays and weekends. Many of us think in terms of weekly rhythms (Zuzanek and Mannell, 1993). We have "productive" time during the week and then Friday (as Louise suggested above) is a transition into the weekend. Saturdays are typically days to catch up and Sundays are reserved for worship or family relaxation. Many Americans spend much of the week either in anticipation of or in recollection of the weekends. Rybczynski (1991) described how a history of leisure has unfolded around the weekend as a break from work. Rybczynski suggested that the weekend often creates its own demands and many feel obliged to fill it. One of the problems with the weekend for many women is that they still are responsible for unpaid work that although different from waged work, still requires energy and often confines them to their home.

In addition to the rhythms of time associated with leisure, the aspects of space are being discussed in a number of situations (e.g., Deem, 1996; Mowl and Towner, 1995; Scraton and Watson, 1998; Wearing, 1996). The thesis of these analyses suggests the need to create an environment where women's leisure includes physical and metaphysical space. In the private sphere of the home as well as in public spaces as they relate to everyday, women often do not have spaces of their own. Mowl and Towner (1995) suggested that is only through developing a deeper understanding of the way individuals and groups perceive different places, that a more complete and contextual representation of women's leisure can emerge. The analysis of everyday life provided a way to further understand the social processes that underlie the way people organize their lives.

Despite the statistics that indicate that the majority of both white women and women of color are physically inactive during their leisure, most of them are not "doing nothing". Studies by both Deem (1987) and Henderson and Bialeschki (1991) found that doing nothing was a definition of leisure that many women aspired to, but was seldom reached. On the other hand, being able to relax was a perceived reward to which many women felt they were entitled when they were working.

Examining how women perceived their use of time and space during the day may show ways that more physical activity might be incorporated into their "sedentary", but no less busy lives. More is yet to be learned about physical activity for women in general, but because of the high incidence of health problems and the apparent sedentary lifestyles of a majority of women of color, much can be learned that may be helpful in addressing physical activity issues for all women.

Methods

Deem (1996) noted that abstract theorizing without reference to empirical research is a feature of current social theory. To aid in the development of further social theory about the geography of leisure, we collected data to examine the meanings of everyday life related to time and space. We used an interpretive paradigm (Henderson, 1991) in this study along with the collection of data using in-depth qualitative interviews. Human beings are conscious, feeling, thinking, and reflective subjects and people impute meanings about what is happening to them and how they interact with others.

Data were collected using a semi-structured or interview guide approach. The women interviewed were part of a larger study examining African American women from South Carolina and American Indians from New Mexico. The women interviewed were a subset of the women who volunteered to participate in the first phases of the project where the physical activity patterns were measured through surveys, daily physical activity records, and mechanical devices (Henderson, Ainsworth, Stolarzcyk, Hootman and Levin, 1998). Indigenous interviewers were trained to conduct the interviews and were instructed to ask additional probing questions to supplement the interview guide. Because of the oral traditions of African Americans and American Indians, (Baldwin and Hopkins, 1990; McDonald and McAvoy, 1997), qualitative data seemed to be particularly useful. Usually the in-depth interviews took 45–75 minutes; a place was scheduled where privacy was possible. The interviewer informed the potential interviewee that the conversation would be taped when she was first contacted. Tape recorded interviews were transcribed verbatim except for five interviews in the Navajo language that were translated into English before transcription.

The semi-structured or interview guide approach allowed interviewers the freedom to probe and to ask questions in whatever order seemed appropriate. In the general interview guide, a set of issues were outlined and explored with each respondent. The questions were prepared to make sure information was obtained from a number of people by covering the same material. The issues were not necessarily covered in a particular order and the actual wording of each question was not determined ahead of time. The questions were designed to encourage women to talk about their lives and how they perceived and described the importance or irrelevancy of physical activity on a day to day basis. Elements of time and space were inherent in the responses. For this paper, we used primarily data from two questions asked about typical weekdays and typical weekends. These questions, however were examined in light of the entire interview to ascertain how the women viewed their everyday lives. This qualitative approach also facilitated understanding and identifying patterns through an exploration of specific cases.

A total of 30 African American women from South Carolina cities and 26 American Indian women from New Mexico participated in the interviews. Data analyses were conducted using the constant comparison technique, a systematic method for recording, coding, and analyzing qualitative data. The goal of this technique was to maximize credibility through comparison of groups and data. Three stages comprised the data analysis process. First, "pieces" of data were organized by identifying, reducing, coding, and displaying categories of data using the NUD*IST program. The second stage included integrating the categories and their properties by comparing them to one another and checking them back to the data. In addition, the entire interview was examined to ascertain what other comments were made to help understand more about everyday life. In the third stage, categories were delimited and refined, if necessary, to further focus a "story" related to the data and how it fit together with a priori or emerging criteria. The goal of this technique was to maximize credibility through comparison of groups and data. Through this qualitative aspect, we were not necessarily concerned with a singular conclusions, but with perspectives.

Table 1 gives a demographic breakdown of the sample. For purposes of this paper we described annual household incomes lower than $16,000 per year as lower income, $16–35,000 as mid income, and above $35,000 as higher income. In light of these women being "older", many were still responsible for their own children or grandchildren (37% of the African American had grandchildren as did 50% of the American Indian women).

Although it is not within the scope of this paper to delve deeply into cultural differences, we wanted to recognize the significance of some of these inherent differences that may be reflected in the everyday lives of the women of color we studied. We speak of women of color to denote the racial groups we examined. Further, we approached this study with the idea that these groups are not alike in their difference from white people. Each distinct group can be characterized by differences in history, family

Table 1   Demographics of Women Interviewed by Race

	African American (N=30)	American Indian (N=26)
Age in Years	57(SD=11)	56 (SD=12)
	40s=30%	40s=33%
	50s=27%	50s=33%
	60s=27%	60s=20%
	70s=17%	70s=3%
	80s=10%	
Marital Status	Married=50%	Married=47%
	Widowed=27%	Widowed=20%
	Sing/Div=20%	Sing/Div=33%
Raising Grandchildren	yes=37%	yes=50%
Number of People in Household	2.5 (SD=1.3)	4 (SD=2.3)
Number of Bedrooms	3.2 (SD=.9)	2.7 (SD=1.1)
Years of Education	15.5 (SD=3.8)	14.5 (SD=4.4)
Ave Hours Worked for Pay	46 (SD=26.7)	51 (SD=34)
Income	<$11999=30%	<$11999=30%
	$12000-15999=7%	$12000-15999=10%
	$16000-24999=10%	$16000-24999=27%
	$25000-34999=17%	$25000-34999=10%
	>$35000=27%	>$35000=23%

structure, social and political developments, traditions, values, and other constructs. We do not assume that describing people of color or even African American or American Indian captures any precise essence of culture. As a limitation of this research, we acknowledge the great diversity that exists that cannot be fully articulated in this type of study.

In light of the recent discussion by Henderson (1998), we would also like to clarify issues we encountered in researching diverse populations. First, neither of us are women of color. We tried to get the input of women of color in several ways. First, an advisory committee for the project was formed in both South Carolina and New Mexico consisting primarily of individuals who were like the sample. We used these individuals as a sounding board in developing the study and the study questions. Second, for the interviewers, we chose individuals who were of the same racial background as those being interviewed. Finally, we consulted with graduate students and colleagues who also had first hand information about women of color. We acknowledge certain limitations of this study, but we are confident that our data and analysis are trustworthy. Hopefully our work can contribute to the ongoing development of information about a diversity of individuals.

Typical Days

"Typical" days were not always easy for women in this study to define. Many of their activities were dependent upon what significant others did in their lives. Further, a typical day (week day or weekend) generally did not include regularly scheduled physical activity unless it was a routine part of what people usually did. In other words, except for a handful of women who walked consistently or attended an aerobics class, most women did not describe a regular plan for physical activity. Therefore, when any structured physical activity occurred, for most women it was atypical rather than typical. In this analysis, we sought to understand why this dearth of physical activity might be the case. In addition, most women in this study noted a clear differentiation between the weekend and the weekday in terms of their routine.

Weekdays

The women in this study could be divided into two typologies when they described their typical weekdays. Some women saw their weekdays as usually "routine". They had no problem indicating how their time was structured and where this activity took place. The second type were the "it depends" group. These women suggested that every day was different and their activities depended on what the particular day held. Almost all the women described a variety of household work tasks (i.e., fixing meals) that had to be done regardless of whether they organized their days by "routine" or "it depends".

Most of the women in this study rose early and went to bed relatively early. They indicated that they were tired at the end of the day. Most rose about 6: 00 in the morning to begin their days with such activities as taking a family member to work, preparing breakfast and lunch for children in the household, or getting ready for work. Most of the women described the value of a regular morning routine especially as it related to dealing with the "others" in their lives.

"Others" were a major influence regarding what happened each day. If a woman was needed by her spouse or a child, that took precedence over anything that the individual might have planned. The idea that "it depends" was not based on what the individual wanted as much as the schedule of others. Several women described specifically how their schedules revolved around children. This result was not surprising, but it did indicate how little control some women felt they had over their time. Even if they planned any type of regular leisure activity, it was frequently precluded by the needs of others. The ethic of care was clearly an organizing framework for the lives of most of these women.

Seasonal differences existed regarding typical days as these women of color described their lives. Some of these perceptions of seasonal change related to what the children or grandchildren were doing and whether they were in school or involved with other activities. Evenings were often reserved for children and obligations such as "going to their ballgames, carrying them around".

Many of the women in this study felt their weekdays were much too busy (see Nashanta above). A lower income African American woman who was divorced with no family stated similarly: "I mean, there's just not enough hours in the day". Structured physical activity or leisure (other than reading the newspaper or watching TV) was seldom mentioned as a regular part of the weekdays of most women. One married African American woman, however, stated that "Exercise seems to get done if it's scheduled in". For most women in this study, leisure time physical activity was infrequently mentioned as a part of their typical day. We might conclude that even if it was occurring, it was either taken for granted or it was not a significant part of everyday life. Further, for the most part this physical activity occurred close to home.

Several of the women in this study, primarily American Indian women, described walking as an activity that they did every day either for the pure exercise, to visit family or friends, or to feed animals. In these cases, it was clear that during the weekdays this routine was important, and sometimes necessary. For example, one married American Indian woman said, "And after he [husband] leaves for work then I go out and do my exercises. It's five days out of the week that I go do my walking in the morning".

Although women were involved in outside activities from time to time during weekdays, their primary contexts were paid work and the home. It seemed that as long as women were at home, unpaid work needed to be done. These women of color associated space at home with work rather than with leisure. Other than obvious aspects such as watching TV or reading, home appeared to be a gendered space where the expectations of being a caregiver to spouse, children, or grandchildren was omnipresent. These findings were not new but they underline the amount of time spent at home in an environment where leisure time physical activity was often not available.

In general, because weekdays were fairly unpredictable except for obligations such as paid work, structured physical activity was not easy to schedule. Further, the perception existed that time was already full for many of these women. A designated space in terms of time or place for physical activity was not evident in the majority of the interviews.

Weekends

Typical weekends were more complex for many of the women to describe. Although some routines were evident on the weekends such as doing laundry, fixing family meals, and going to church, the weekends provided more perceived variety. Because of the potential that weekends were perceived to have, describing them as typical was difficult. Generally, fewer leisure time physical activities were described on weekends than during the weekdays. The weekends, however, also seemed to be less stressful in terms of perceived demands on these women's lives. The weekend was often perceived as a "time to rest" although that was not always the reality for these women of color that we interviewed. A typical weekend did not usually include any kind of planned physical activity unless it related to shopping at malls where walking occurred.

Two primary undertakings emerged in the data regarding the weekend: getting "caught up" and "relaxing". A number of women saw these occurring in tandem. Some sense existed that the former was a prerequisite for the latter. One American Indian parent stated:

> On most of the weekends I clean house mostly, well maybe about five hours, or five hours that takes up most of my time. I cook and then I wash dishes, that's part of cleaning, and I go to the movies in the evenings.

Another widowed American Indian said, "My weekends are like picking up, cleaning up, and then, sit a lot". She went on to say "It's mostly I do more sitting on weekends unless it varies; every weekend is something different, especially at the times of the Indian dances".

Several of the women described how the weekend was the time to get "caught up", although many saw flexibility and less pressure in having two days available. One single American Indian woman said, "It depends on what I'm in the mood for...just doing the things that I have to do[referring to housework]". A married American Indian woman with children did laundry at the Laundromat at 6: 00 am on Saturday morning "when no one else is there". Another divorced African American parent remarked about the weekend:

> Well, that's the time I usually catch up on my housework. You know, clean my house, do my laundry. And I usually cook for the week and freeze things so it's not too hard, you know, during the week.

Just relaxing was also evident, although it often occurred in relation to having done other work. One divorced American Indian parent said:

> Only once in a while we get a chance to travel. But most of the time we clean house until noon time and then after noon we get to go out to see the relatives and visit.

Others saw the weekend as a respite from paid or unpaid work. One American Indian said:

Saturday I always like to take it easy. I don't want to do any housework, I like to sleep late, get up late....just be together with my family and just go eat out and that's it.

A 63-year old professional African American woman saw church as a primary activity of the weekend but she also described the weekend as a "calm down time". An African American woman noted, "But then usually on Saturday, I'm so tired I need something. I need a change, so I might do something". Another married African American woman who had no children in the household stated:

On the weekends, I get up when I feel like it. If I don't want to, I don't. If I feel like just eating and just taking a shower and whatever, that's what I do.

For these women of color, the weekend was a time when they could be involved in usual activities like church, meal preparation, shopping, visiting, and also have a chance to do something different.

Several woman mentioned going shopping on the weekend. Some of the shopping was for food, but other times it was an event that got the women out of the house. One married American Indian woman said about shopping, "We [family or friends] don't really always buy stuff, but we just walk around and look at things and spend the day together".

For a number of the African American women, Sunday was unquestionably a day for church. One woman simply made the statement, "Sundays we get to go to church, you know", and another said, "And then of course, I go to church on Sunday". A married African American woman said about the weekend:

And then it's usually going out and grocery shopping. Just the usual work — weekend clean-up work type things. Sunday starts all over with church.

The meaning of church for the African American women in particular was an area that was clearly important. The church was significant as a time and place central to their lives that involved a major commitment. Saturday was also seen as a day to prepare for Sunday. One older lower income single African American woman stated, "I cook Saturdays. I try to cook, get my church clothes ready, wash, get my clothes washed up for church. On Sunday I try not to have too much to do".

Overall, the weekend was a time for catching up, preparing for the week ahead, or a time to relax either with family or through church activities and worship. The women in this study seldom mentioned any major physical activity involvements as part of their leisure. Weekdays were more likely to be mentioned if any structured physical activity was to occur, although only a minority of women mentioned physical activity as a routine of the week. A sense seemed to exist that the weekend was a time to relax and physical activity was too much structure and perhaps too much like "work". Although the time seemed to exist on the weekend more than during the week, physical activity for the most part was not a planned aspect of the weekend for most of the women of color interviewed.

Leisure and space

As a result of this analysis of the descriptions of typical weekdays and typical weekends, a context for leisure and physical activity can be developed through grounded theory related to the growing body of knowledge about gender and space. The overall conclusion that can be drawn is that the older women of color in this study were physically sedentary as the statistics proclaim and as their stories confirmed, but they were generally busy. Lack of physical activity, however, could not be associated with laziness. Their lives, for the most part, were filled with activities. Some of these activities were more physical than others, but most women did not have any structured leisure time physical activities that they did, especially on weekends. Most of the women we interviewed knew that physical activity was "good for them", but it was a difficult aspect to fit into their busy lives.

The home was a focal point for the lives of most of the women interviewed. Mowl and Towner's (1995) observation that "places make leisure and leisure makes places" (p. 104) had implications for this home setting. Home was not much of a leisure setting during the week. The weekend held more likelihood for the home being a place of relaxation. One of the problems with the home, as other researchers have found (e.g., Deem, 1986) is that the home is perceived as an unpaid work place for women more than it is a leisure space. The power that the women of color held in this study related to how they defined that home place even though the influence of others had a major effect on how their days were structured. In the lives of these women of color, there was relative autonomy. The possibility of resistance existed in the private sphere of the home and their everyday lives. By resistance, Foucault meant the struggle against the forms of power that pervade everyday life and constitute individuals as subjects to anyone else (Wearing, 1996). Although busy, a sense existed that in everyday life, these women were in control of their home settings, and they allowed "others" because they were significant in their lives, to influence what was done. Within that control, however, leisure and particularly physical activity did not hold a high priority.

When structured physical activity occurred, it was likely to be in or near a home base, and not at a community center. For these women of color, the perceived opportunities that existed due to aspects of institutionalized racism for African Americans and geographical distances for the American Indian, may have resulted in a lack of community opportunities. Nevertheless, most examples of physical activity done on typical days were home-based. As Deem (1987) found, physical activities were more likely to occur when they could be flexible, done on short notice, and easily combined with other's activities in the household. If the women walked or even hoped to do more physical activity in the future, they saw the need for having equipment or opportunities at home or close to home. The gendered space of the home, however, with all the other obligations that existed there was not the best place to try to schedule regular physical activity. Those who went away from the home generally did so with a spouse or a friend. Lacking such a relationship made planning on a daily basis difficult at best.

Many of the women in this study perceived little metaphysical space for much of anything else in their already busy lives beyond what they were currently doing. Those that did indicate they took time to "relax" saw that as a necessary part of their lives. Although physical activity is often touted as a stress reliever, physical activity was generally not associated with relaxing for these women. Relieving stress did not involve physical participation as perceived by many of the women interviewed. They felt they did not always have that much control in their lives in going outside the home because of the impact of others who needed them on a regular, as well as unscheduled, basis.

The needs of others also resulted in a sense from many of these women of color that little time and space for leisure was possible in their lives, especially during the weekdays. Since a large percentage of the women either had children or were responsible for grandchildren, the impact of children was still significant even for those women who were getting beyond the "traditional" child rearing years. The home was the place shared with children and others, just as time was shared. Weekends offered the greatest potential for time and space for other activities but weekends were often taken with getting caught up and relaxing, and did not seem to include physical activity.

This research confirmed information that has already been uncovered about the settings of everyday life for other populations of women. Within the cultural context of these women of color, the influence of others was evident. Further, although physical activity was mentioned, sports were rarely an aspect of everyday life for these older women of color. The women in this study could identify a type of rhythm to their weekdays and weekends. Weekends offered the most freedom although this freedom was often contingent on "getting caught up". As Allen and Chin-Sang (1990) found, our interviews also indicated the strength that comes from family and social networks. Family was a sustaining focus that was directly reflected in the ways that women perceived their everyday lives. Further, the women of color in this study knew they needed to be more physically active for health reasons. Convincing them of the value of physical activity was not an issue. Finding ways to motivate them within their already perceived busy time and available space was the issue. Making activity a priority and getting it scheduled into the day was a challenge that became evident.

Further research is needed to address two issues. First, we need to continue to learn more about women of color and the context of their lives so that the education and intervention that is offered can provide meaningful results. Second, the home or areas close to the home offer the most potential for free time structured physical activity opportunities. Knowing more about how that space is used and the constraints that confine women in the home may also enable individuals to become more physically active. If the home is so gendered that it is impossible for any time of free time structured physical activity to occur, then we need to examine how that physical activity space can be expanded into the nearby community or set aside at home. Further, the places available for physical activity in the community must also be examined. Although time was a critical dimension described by the women of color in this study, the place and social setting relative to everyday life requires further examination.

*Acknowledgment: This research was supported by National Institute of Health Women's Health Initiative — SIP #22W-U48/CCU409664-03

References

Allen, K.R., and Chin-Sang, V. (1990) 'A lifetime of work: The context and meanings of leisure for aging black women', *The Gerontologist*, 30: pp. 734–740.

Baldwin, J.A., and Hopkins, R. (1990) 'African-American and European-American cultural differences as assessed by the worldviews paradigm: An empirical analysis', *The Western Journal of Black Studies*, 14: pp. 38–51.

Bloch, C. (1987) 'Everyday life, sensuality, and body culture', *Women's Studies International Forum*, 10: pp. 433–442.

Deem, R. (1986) *All work and no play? The sociology of women and leisure.* Milton Keynes, UK: Open University Press.

——— (1987) 'Unleisured lives: Sport in the context of women's leisure', *Women's Studies International Forum*, 10: pp. 423–432.

——— (1996) 'Women, the city, and holidays', *Leisure Studies*, 15, 105–119.

Henderson, K.A. (1998) 'Researching diverse populations', *Journal of Leisure Research*, 30(1): pp. 157–170.

Henderson, K.A., Ainsworth, B.A., Stolarzcyk, L.M., Hootman, J.M., and Levin, S. (1998) Linking qualitative and quantitative data to study the physical activity of minority women. Paper presented at the American College of Sports Medicine, June, Orlando, FL.

Henderson, K.A., and Bialeschki, M.D. (1991) 'A sense of entitlement to leisure as constraint and empowerment for women', *Leisure Sciences*, 12: pp. 51–65.

Henderson, K.A., Bialeschki, M.D., Shaw, S. M., Freysinger, V. J. (1996) *Both gains and gaps.* State College, PA: Venture Publishing.

Lenskyj, H. (1988) 'Measured time: Women, sport, and leisure', *Leisure Studies*, 7: pp. 233–240.

McDonald, D., and McAvoy, L. (1997) 'A literature review of Native Americans and Recreation: Cultural beliefs and outdoor recreation behavior', *Journal of Leisure Research*, 29.

Mowl, G., and Towner, J. (1995) 'Women, gender, leisure, and place: Towards a more 'humanistic' geography of women's leisure', *Leisure Studies*, 14, 102–116.

Robinson, J.P., and Godbey, G. (1993) 'Sport, fitness and the gender gap', *Leisure Sciences*, 15: pp. 291–307.

Rybczynski, W. (1991) *Waiting for the weekend.* New York: Viking Penquin.

Scraton, S. (1994) 'The changing world of women and leisure: Feminism, 'postfeminism' and leisure', *Leisure Studies*, 13: pp. 249–261.

Scraton, S., and Watson, B. (1998) 'Gendered cities: Women and public leisure space in the postmodern city', *Leisure Studies*, 17: pp. 123–137.

Shaw, S. (1985) The meaning of leisure in everyday life', *Leisure Sciences*, 7: pp. 1–24.

US Department of Health and Human Services. (1996) *Physical activity and health: A report of the Surgeon General.* Atlanta, GA: US Department of Health and Human Services Centers for Disease Control and Prevention, Center for Chronic Disease Prevention and Health Promotion.

Wearing, B. (1996) *Gender.* Melbourne, Australia: Longman.

Wells, C.L. (1996, March) 'Physical activity and women's health', *Physical Activity and Fitness Research Digest*, pp. 1–8.

Yeager, K.K., Macera, C.A., and Merritt, R.K. (1993) 'Socioeconomic influences on leisure-time sedentary behavior among women', *Health Values*, 17(6): pp. 50–53.

Zuzanek, J., and Mannell, R. (1993) 'Leisure behaviour and experiences as part of everyday life: The weekly rhythm', *Loisir et societe/Society and Leisure*, 16: pp. 31–57.

Leaky Bodies or Drying Husks?
Menopause, Health and
Embodied Experience

Eileen Green

**Centre for Social and Policy Research,
University of Teesside**

Introduction

The menopause is not a natural condition, it is a generalised label for competing discourses which centre around the physical, social and emotional changes which accompany women as they enter mid-life. Popular images of the menopause represent it as a turning point from which women decline into old age, a representation which is pivotal to the biomedical discourses which dominate the mass media. This decline is signified by bodily deterioration as the levels of particular hormones reduce, presenting a powerful set of embodied images of menopausal women 'leaking oestrogen', while their bodily parts re-arrange themselves outwards and downwards. This image of large, sweaty female bodies contrasts sharply with the equally popular picture of frail, white-haired old ladies suffering from osteoporosis or 'brittle bone' disease. Images which suggest that somewhere along the trajectory of menopause the fat and sweat drain away with declining hormones revealing the hobbling old crone, unless women heed the advice of the medical experts and arrest oestrogen deficiency through the panacea of hormone replacement therapy (HRT). The implicit message contained in such images is the necessity for (medicalised) self-surveillance on the part of menopausal women.

What is interesting about these images concerns both the contradictory nature of the corporeal images which they indicate and the uniform negativity of the messages which they transmit about the menopause. Western culture is saturated with embodied images of women and men, with women represented as soft, fluid, emotional bodies and men as hard, rational, dry bodies. The hormonal changes linked to the menopause can be associated with the uncontrolled 'leaking' of bodily fluids, transforming women into what Shildrick (1997) refers to as leaky, out of control bodies. Lupton (1998) has argued that the emotional body is often represented as grotesque and to be feared, due to the tendency for emotions to dissolve boundaries between inside and out or the public and private: "the body without boundaries, the permeable body, the liminal body, the leaking, fluid body has become a site of horror, dread and fear."(Lupton, 1998 p97). As well as rendering individuals open and vulnerable, emotions threaten social order and lead to a transgression between the public and private selves, resulting in unstable identities which have become linked to mid-life transitions. In western culture, women in mid-life are represented primarily as menopausal bodies: emotional, unstable and 'out of control', which has major implications for how they and others perceive them. A representation which reveals the obsession with control over biological change reflected in dominant western discourses which link health maintenance and medical surveillance.

The numerous references in biomedical discourse to hormones, mood swings and irritability are grounded in an essentialist view of women as primarily defined by their 'natural' bodies. Such views also reinforce the dominant cultural representations of women as sexed bodies which are a key site of medical intervention and surveillance. Medical messages that menopause is a disease needing treatment appears to justify expert intervention in the form of prescriptions for HRT and a barrage of health promotion literature. Literature which exhorts women to engage in what Harding (1997) has termed self-surveillance practices, practices which include body maintenance in the cause of preserving more youthful, 'feminine' (hetero)sexual bodies. Dominant debates about the merits and risks of HRT secure the menopause as the cross-roads between youth and old age for women and constitute it as primarily a bodily experience. Despite this, there is an absence of both theory and narratives about bodily experience (Nettleton and Watson, 1998). Although there is now an expanding corpus of sociological research on the body, the bodies in question are implicitly white and male and without voices. Women's accounts of bodily experience which might for example assist us in understanding the experience of menopause, are noticeably absent. Interestingly, many of what began as feminist alternatives to the medicalisation of menopause i.e. women's health discourses also focus around the HRT or not debate (Kaufert, 1982), reinforcing and reproducing menopause, albeit unintentionally, as a set of physical symptoms, rather than a life stage. However, as Locke (1998) comments: "women have not been willing consumers of each and every new technology and medication designed for their continued good health" (p. 36). Instead women's bodies are the site of contentious debate in terms of both their representation and medical interventions, debates which women themselves absorb and intervene in.

This paper provides a critical review of concepts of the menopause, arguing that dominant discourses (both popular and biomedical) construct it as a hormone deficiency disease which marks the boundary between youth and mid-life for women. Interrogating literature on the sociology of the body and feminist research on the menopause, the paper argues for the centrality of bodily experience to an understanding of the menopause as both a physical and socio-cultural process. Drawing upon data from women's narratives of menopausal experience, the paper concludes by stressing the need for more qualitative studies which explore the impact of 'difference'. In particular, we need to know more about the significance of the 'local', whether it be socio-cultural context or local biologies, upon perceptions and experience of the menopause.

Menopause as boundary marker

What is clear is that the menopause can be defined as both a boundary marker and a site of struggle or personal agency. It is also a forum around which sex and gender relations are reproduced (Butler, 1993). Theoretical analysis of the menopause has been dominated by biomedical models which conceptualise women's bodies as machines designed to deliver products related to fertility (Martin, 1997), with menopause signalling the end of this process via the cessation of menstruation. Recent sociological critiques of this model (Harding, 1997; Davis, 1997), have begun to problematise this view, including the concept of individualised risk which accompanies health promotion messages to women entering mid-life. This paper argues for the inclusion of women's lived experiences of the menopause, and the situating of those experiences within social and cultural context. An understanding of the significance of menopausal experiences across different cultures can contribute to the ways in which the female body is seen and interpreted both by women themselves and by professionals with an investment in the medical management of women's bodies (Oudshoorn, 1994). Popular discourses about the bodies and behaviour of women at mid-life suggest a uniformity which masks the impact of difference; not least in recognition and interpretation of menopausal symptoms. Bodies are historical and social constructions as well as biological entities which are mutable through time and space (Harraway, 1991). What is theoretically interesting about the menopause in this context is its socio-cultural significance as a boundary marker for bodies in transition from young to old, a change signalled by the cessation of menstruation which heralds loss of reproductive function.

However, as Locke's (1998) research on contrasting accounts of the menopause in North America and Japan confirms, women's embodied experience of this transition is subject to cultural difference and informed by what she terms 'local biologies'(p. 39). Locke argues that women's subjective experience of the menopause is culturally informed in such a way as to impact upon: expectations, knowledge and physical sensations and changes in the body. Such differences affect the production of both professional and popular discourses about the menopause, which underlines the importance of local biologies and the diversity of menopausal experiences. The menopause defies definition because it includes the recognition and interpretation of physical changes which are closely interwoven with women's accounts of wider processes of life changes in the middle years. Pivotal to our understanding of women's experiences of the menopause, are the ways in which they are represented as bodies which need to be carefully managed, whether it be by medical experts or by themselves through a mixture of personal care and 'self surveillance'.

The concept of self surveillance stems from Foucault's work which has been widely adopted by both sociologists and feminists alike, in particular his concept of the individual self created by surveillance (Foucault, 1986). Such surveillance practices, it is argued, constitute the body and invite individuals to govern themselves, observing and monitoring their own behaviour through the operation of disciplinary power (Nettleton, 1997). However, as Howson, (1998) observes, this work fails to address the gendered nature of both power and the bodies concerned. Reviewing theorisations of bodily surveillance, it seems that apart from Bordo's work (1989), none have addressed either the ways in which regulation creates specific identities or the processes through which these identities e.g. menopausal woman, are negotiated and internalised. It is the latter process which is the most interesting for my purpose. Howson's (1998) study of women's accounts of cervical screening is helpful here. She suggests that although the women interviewed about their experiences of gynaecological screening articulated a sense of embodiment and subjecting themselves to medical surveillance, they also developed a critical response to their experiences. Parallel accounts of women's embodied sense of the menopause, reveal a similar level of critical reflexivity towards the process, which constitutes them as active agents, rather than as passive victims of bio-medical discourse. Also important to notice, as we know from cultural geographers' accounts of the significance of place (Massey, 1994), are local, embodied knowledges (Howson,

1998) of the menopause. Interrogating these enables us to construct an analysis of the ways in which women think or reflect 'through the body' as a process for understanding and coping with menopause and mid-life. The next section of the paper attempts to de-construct generalist concepts of the menopause by analysing the different discourses which construct women as embodied subjects: ageing bodies at risk from leaking hormones.

De-constructing menopause: contradictory images

Competing discourses

The most popular discourses on the menopause are couched within a bio-medical model which describes it in terms of hormonal changes and their accompanying effects. An underlying discourse here concerns the centrality of hormones to (traditional) femininity. Oestrogen deficit it is implied, is linked to declining and therefore 'unstable' femininity. Hormone replacement therapy can remedy the defects attributable to oestrogen deficiency thereby securing femininity for a longer period, in addition to arresting associated physical risks (Harding, 1993). Feminist analyses of menopause provide an important challenge to such deficiency models of mid-life women, arguing that medical experts have both contributed to the litanies of risk and fear which surround debates about the use of HRT and obscured the health risks associated with it as a proposed 'cure' (Klein, 1992; Greer, 1991). Klein and Dumble (1994) argue that menopause experts who present HRT as safe, reliable and effective treatment for hot flushes, insomnia, and as a preventative measure in warding off osteoporosis, fail to reveal the inconclusive and as yet underdeveloped nature of the research needed to provide evidence to support such claims. Challenges to the discourse for HRT orthodoxy and medicalised health maintenance include individual women, organisations such as the National Women's Health Network in Washington (1989, 1995) and an increasing number of professionals (Locke, 1998).

In both bio-medical and feminist discourses which focus upon the physical symptoms of menopause, menopausal women are represented as a generic category rather than as individuals and groups who are positioned differently in relation for example to social class, ethnicity and degrees of able-bodiedness. Both discourses imply the existence of 'natural' womanhood and with it natural menopause, focusing upon an essentialised post menopausal body. In fact, as Harding (1997) argues, such differences between women contribute towards the degrees of risk (health and otherwise) which they may anticipate at this stage in their lives. Whilst it is clearly imperative that feminist accounts challenge prevailing biomedical models of the menopause, the suggested alternative discourses must adequately theorise the complexities of difference and commonality of representation and experience (Komesaroff et al, 1997).What we need to know, as Nettleton and Watson (1998) argue, is the extent to which the biological processes associated with bodies, impact upon their everyday life, including how they think about themselves. A number of writers have commented upon the convergence between biomedical and what can be termed 'wise-women' discourses, (Kaufert, 1982; Komesaroff et al 1997; Harding, 1997) both of which imply the 'truth' of the natural body, seeking to preserve it in different forms. As suggested above, more promising, but currently in its infancy is empirical research which includes women's differential accounts of the process of menopause and ageing Richards, 1997; Locke and Kaufert, 1998). Such accounts make a valuable contribution to the debate by revealing the diversity of experiences and the complexity of issues that women face in mid-life. A common feature of such research includes the finding that women's experiences of menopause are enmeshed in socio-cultural images of ageing and femininity, images which are constructed as part of the interaction between experience and social context. Richards et al's (1997) study of Australian women in mid-life and pilot data from a UK study (1) of women, well-being and the menopause provide us with crucial insights into the continuity of women's experience, particularly their reflections on and response to ageing. Unlike the messages contained in health promotion discourses which offer HRT as the 'cure' to out of control, menopausal bodies, qualitative research reminds us that women's relationship with their bodies has always been mediated by social expectations and cultural discourse. Since individuals are subject to embodied experience, as Davis argues we need to 'tackle the relationship between the symbolic and the material, between representations of the body and embodiment as experience or social practice in concrete social, cultural and historical contexts' (1997 p15). Crucial insights are provided by Locke's study of the Japanese discourse of 'konenki'(change of life), which has until recently been used to refer to all life cycle transitions in Japan, both male and female (Locke, 1998 p48). Locke argues that the dominant discourse around konenki has only recently become medicalised, which underlines the important impact of 'local biologies' and tells us more about the changing practices of Japanese medics and pharmaceutical companies than about the menopause. In contemporary Japan current debates about women's unpaid care of the three generation family eclipse those around the menopause in terms of political priority for activist women and elderly groups (Locke, 1998 p55).

Experiencing the menopausal body, re-constructing identity and 'self'

At the level of theory, the reassessment and re-interpretation of menopause has a broader significance than providing a much needed understanding of this juncture in women's lives, it also tells us about the ongoing process of identity construction. Although the menopause has been conceptualised as the pivotal point of transition between young and old, it is also possible to view the ways in which there is a continuity about the embodiment of women in discourses which construct them as subjects who are differently positioned. However, some theorists have argued in support of women's power to re-construct their identities at mid-life (Richards, 1997). Drawing upon post structuralist perspectives which stress the importance of gender as process, we can see that identity is linked to the continual and at times contradictory re-working of individual subjectivities via a complex interaction between personal agency and social context. This enables an understanding of how mid-life women can both re-make their identities around the time of the menopause (Green, 1998) and yet continue to be constrained by dominant bio-medical discourses which represent them as declining bodies. The theoretical tensions between feminist theorists and others who have drawn upon post structuralist (Nettleton 1998, Lupton, 1998) theories underpinned by Foucault's writings on power and agency are of interest here. The power of personal agents to 'choose' their identities, are hotly debated around the question of the limits of personal agency versus structure, for example in the work of Bordo (1993) and Davis (1997) on the body. The nuances of this debate are beyond my purpose here, suffice it to say that one axis of the debate centres around identity as the site of struggle between normalising structures of conformity and personal agency as resistance.

Arguably the most dominant discourse of femininity is that which links youthfulness, sexuality and thin bodies. As Davis (1997) comments, "Feminist research in cultural studies has provided a wealth of studies on representations of the female body in film and television, showing how cultural images in the media normalise women by presenting images of the female body as glamorously affluent, impossibly thin and invariably white (Bordo, 1993)". Feminist studies of women's accounts of the menopause demonstrate their acute awareness of the link between bodily transformations and sexual identities, often expressed through dry humour. Which leads me to pose the following question: can menopausal women's reflections on the ways in which (hetero)sexualised images of 'the ideal woman' marginalise older women, constitute a form of resistance to such stereotypes? Especially when in the same breath or space such accounts also mirror contradictory discourses of desire for traditional femininity. Engagement with such images is reflected in the comments of one of the women in the UK study (Green and Wadsworth, 1998), who humorously describes her experience of bodily changes:

> ....seem to put on weight and it's harder to get rid of. It seems to pile on in lumps … It always reminds me of when you buy a chicken and it's an old boiler. And inside … underneath the skin you come across these lumps of yellow fat … well … that's it! [laughing] I'm just an old hen!! Yes there are all these images of women you know a bird and a chick … spring chicken … well now women turn into old boilers!! [much laughing]

Critical reflexivity about her embodied self is clear in this comment, providing evidence of the meshing of body image and social relations. How we see our bodies is mediated by our social and cultural context; and the construction of body-image involves both the experience of bodily changes and our social perception of them (Nettleton and Watson, 1998). Later in the interview the same woman rather wistfully refers to becoming invisible, especially to men:

> … when you get older you become invisible anyway … it's hard isn't it? … I used to walk into a room and every man would turn around … I used to create an impression. And I don't anymore … you just think people look through you and you're not there...

— a comment which expresses contradictory emotions about sexuality and ageing. Her reflections demonstrate both resistance to the tyranny of 'feminine slenderness' and nostalgia for its passing.

Bordo (1993) acknowledges the debt of the 'new scholarship' on the body, including that of feminism, to Foucault; especially his concepts of 'docile bodies', 'biopower and micropractices' but reminds us that it was second wave feminism that 'discovered' the definition and shaping of the body in connection with personal politics of the women's movement. She comments as follows:

What after all is more personal than the life of the body? And for women, associated with the body and largely confined to a life centred *on* the body (both beautification of one's own body and the reproduction, care and maintenance of the bodies of others), culture's grip on the body is a constant, intimate fact of everyday life. (p. 17, original emphasis)

At a theoretical level, it would seem that the themes of risk and body management are crucial concepts to explore in relation to providing a framework though which to understand women's experiences of the menopause and ageing. Feminist perspectives on the sociology of the body (Bordo, 1993) and embodiment (Howson, 1998) appear to provide the most promising framework here, given the focus upon personal experience and the centrality of concepts such as agency and subversion. The next section of the paper will explore discourses of individualised risk, gendered bodies and self surveillance, as the background against which women manage their mid-life bodies.

Risky bodies: taking control

Concepts of risk, fear and control seem to permeate both public discourses on the menopause and women's health movement discourses. As Harding (1997) argues, this constructs a generic postmenopausal woman hungry for information through which to assess the nature of the potential risks and choose a health management strategy. This of course assumes a clear and identifiable start to the menopause and a uniform set of symptoms. Whereas the epidemiological evidence cites both a wide age span and an extremely broad and confusing set of physical and emotional 'symptoms', the use of HRT appears as a uniform preventative medical strategy which also reduces uncertainty. Despite the controversial nature of HRT, medical experts have claimed that the prescription of HRT should be both routine and long term to protect women against the risks of developing progressive, long term illnesses connected with oestrogen deficiency (Maclennan, 1992). Health promotion and popular literature extol its virtues, although as Coney (1991) and Vines (1993) point out the risks of taking HRT may exceed the risks of not taking it, e.g. the suggested link between HRT and increased risk of breast cancer. Such medical discourses assume that the risks associated with the menopause are both predictable and avoidable and imply that it is therefore individual women's responsibility to guard against such risks. Despite heavy promotion from the pharmaceutical industry, the safety of HRT remains unproven which leaves women in the position of having to calculate the risk factor themselves in relation to their own biographies, which as Klein and Dumble(1994) argue, in itself induces fear and uncertainty. Also as Lupton (1995) suggests, the 'healthy lifestyle' approach to health implies that women who do not manage their health and bodies are failing to help themselves and are therefore culpable. This ignores the point that healthy lifestyles are cultural constructions and that women are differently positioned to both interpret or take advantage of such strategies. Having the money, time and access to facilities which enable the specific diet and exercise strategies indicated will be heavily affected by factors such as social class, ethnicity and able-bodiedness. More importantly, the incorporation of the construct risk into medical discourses encourages women to make themselves objects of self-surveillance (Harding, 1997).

Evidence to support the impact of biomedical models is presented in the data from feminist studies of women's experiences of the menopause (Daly, 1997), which also confirm that women rely upon their own assessment of the risks, using both medical and informal knowledges (Green and Wadsworth, 1998). Richards et al (1997) argue that health risks associated with the menopause are distinguished through three main discourses: those generated by mothers and friends, another by the mass media on the importance of diet, exercise and HRT and the last, (also reflected through the media) by medical experts on the significance of family history. Most women had absorbed these messages by translating them into narratives of bodily self discipline. Narratives which come through most clearly in the accounts of a group of single women interviewed for the project who's responses can be grouped around a common theme of 'working the body'(2). This reflects discourses on the importance of 'managing the body' as an individual responsibility and resonates with the stereotypical embodied images of menopausal women which is described at the beginning of the paper: 'flushed and sweaty' bodies, in need of containment and concealment.

Women's perceptions of the need to work and control the body are accompanied by references to fear of ageing and developing their mothers bodies. Although mothers' experiences and advice were sometimes re-assuring and becoming like their mothers provided women with a sense of continuity; developing family 'lumps and bumps' reminded them very vividly of the physical effects of ageing. One of the participants in Richards et al's study sums it up by remembering "looking down one day and seeing my mothers feet"(1997: p. 72) — a comment replicated in one made by a woman in the UK study in describing her changed shape as she ages:

> ... and now I am like that ... (makes rounded shape with her hands) ... and now when I look in the mirror, I often say 'that's me mum's shape ... you become like your mum ....you do ... it's surprising. (Green and Wadsworth, 1998b)

Although many of the women interviewed described changes associated with the menopause positively, such descriptions were often accompanied by negative comments about their bodies:

> I think my attitude to life is probably more positive because I know I have got less of it. But my attitude towards this decaying heap which is my body ... well no, I'm not very impressed with it ... (Green and Wadsworth, 1998b)

Here we have powerful glimpses of menopause as embodied experience. A sense of what Howson (1998) refers to as 'vulnerable embodiment' is being drawn upon, often expressed in relation to connections with other significant women. The majority of women in Richards' study and our own pilot data felt that the physical symptoms associated with the menopause needed to be carefully managed, and might require medical intervention in the form of HRT, which involved assessing the associated risk factors. What emerges from these findings are strong messages about women's need to take control of their bodies during menopause, not least, so that they can get on with 'the rest of their lives'. Available evidence suggests that women may be choosing to take HRT, often along side of alternative therapies, to mask the debilitating symptoms of menopause, rather than as a long term preventative strategy (Richards et al, 1997; Green and Wadsworth, 1998). Of cause for concern here, is the lack of large-scale, longitudinal data on the pattern and level of HRT usage and its longer term effects. We can see women anxious to be in control in social situations i.e. at work or in public places, where to be overwhelmingly defined by their bodies would be undermining, but available research fails to inform us about the health risks attached to long term use of HRT.

Managing the mid-life body: the reflexive project of self

There is also a body of evidence to support the suggestion that women's mid-life reflections upon self and identity involve close emotional work as part of the reflexive project of self. Coming to terms with ageing involves emotional adjustments to change, which was most often reported as women experiencing a 'loss of balance', or being 'out of kilter'. Unsurprisingly, references to such emotional and social adjustments were often contained in broader narratives about life changes, where considerations of the centrality of their bodies were centre stage. This discussion leads us to ask some key questions. What is the relationship between the menopause as a set of physical changes or symptoms and its beginning as a signal of major life changes? Are menopausal women managing their bodies in the process of reclaiming their lives, which ultimately includes re-claiming their bodies for themselves? Cross cultural evidence, although limited, would suggest that both the inception and success of such a project is highly dependent upon both cultural factors and available socio-economic and time resources.

It would seem that women's re-assessment of their self identities, the balance of time available to them and their relationship with their menopausal bodies, constitutes what Giddens (1991) and Beck (1992) refer to as the 'reflexive project of the self characteristic of late modernity'. However, although this concept might usefully be elaborated to theorise the identity re-creation process which mid-life women are engaged in, as Turner (1995) argues, "one criticism of the Beck-Giddens approach to the self and intimacy is that it has very little or nothing to say about the ageing body, the image of the body and the tension between the inside/outside body and the reflexive self" (pp. 256–7). Their approach denies the importance of class, gender and locality as indicators of identity in what they refer to as 'late modernity'; they argue instead that ageing intensifies reflexivity which is forced upon individuals. The body becomes a project which requires managing via e.g. sport and exercise to achieve fitness.

Whilst women's accounts of the ageing process reveal numerous references to managing the body as it becomes socially and physically more vulnerable, those accounts are strewn with references to the perceptions of self and others around body image, youthfulness and sexuality. Although personal fitness appears as a consistent theme, how women feel about age-related changes to their bodies also emerges as a key issue. Discourses of managing the body are closely entertwined with narratives of emotion work for others; caring and relationships which limit the time available to work on the self. As Crompton (1996) argues despite the substantial changes which have occurred in women's employment patterns in Europe in the last decade, studies continue to provide evidence of women's lives being bounded by work and family obligations which limit their quest for autonomous identities. A finding replicated by Japanese data (Locke, 1993). The nature and level of paid work may alter as women enter mid-life but the juggling act appears to continue into old age although the players and elements are different, with grandchildren and very elderly relatives moving into the caring frame.

The European self project has to be fitted into available spaces in the changing matrix of work and caring roles, but can be morally justified. In Japan the individualism associated with the West co-exists uneasily with the legacy of ancestral values which privilege the discourse of the 'good wife and wise mother' in the home. Locke argues that any distressing symptoms experienced by Japanese women are likely to be suppressed in favour of "a display of self-control and discipline so that their social duties may continue uninterrupted" (Locke, 1998: p. 57), which underlines the point about the localisation of biology.

Listening to women's narratives about mid-life may shed more light on the impact of the local, be it place, space or culture, on identity construction and selfhood. Networks of support and friendship are central to women's accounts of their lives. Such networks are 'local' to family, households, and workplaces, and involve reciprocities of support and obligation which provide the shape and rhythm of daily life. Strategies for managing menopause and ageing are also interwoven with narratives about caring for the health and well being of others, whilst attempting to protect time for themselves.

The study of difference

Not withstanding the importance of comparative data in an international context, we also need more 'local' studies in order to assess the impact of difference upon the menopausal experience. The data from mainly small scale qualitative studies about women's accounts of the menopause is extremely valuable in terms of the glimpses it offers about the complexity of the physical, social and emotional changes experienced. Disappointingly however, the majority of published empirical studies involve white, heterosexual women from middle class backgrounds. We know little about the effects of culture, ethnicity and degrees of able bodiedness upon menopause as a social process. Similarly, although some studies of lesbian women in mid-life are emerging (Kirkpatrick, 1989; Jacobson and Samdahl, 1998) more studies which explore women's 'local' narratives of ageing, would enable us to explore the impact of sexual orientation upon identity and lifestyle. This emphasis upon the study of difference is clearly a priority for contemporary feminist analysis, however, it is also important not to lose sight of what Bradley (1996) refers to as 'the risk of remorseless fragmentation' (p. 102), whilst exploring the local narratives of particular groups. Localised knowledges can inform our understanding of the ways in which women are differently positioned or represented in discourses of gender, but we need to guard against becoming theoretically lost within discourses of individualism which can obscure the commonalities of gendered experience.

Recent writings on women's leisure (Wearing, 1994, 1995; Green, 1998) re-affirm the importance of 'time for oneself' and personal space as key components of women's leisure across differences of age, class and ethnicity. Also beginning to emerge, are more studies of the lives of older women (Freysinger, 1995; Cutler-Riddick and Stewart, 1994) which reinforce what is known about the centrality of female friendships for networking and support, both economic and social. In parallel, women's accounts of the menopause and mid-life (Richards et al, 1997; Komesaroff et al, 1997; Green and Wadsworth, 1998) contain numerous references to other women (friends and relatives), as important sources of health information and support. Close discussions and review of bodily changes, asking questions about what is 'normal' and/or expected at this point in their lives, what are the risks and how limiting bodily changes might become? form an important part of women's narratives. Although necessarily informal, such localised narratives can constitute key collective strategies. They represent an important component of women's own diverse accounts of the menopause and ageing which may challenge dominant biomedical discourses.

Conclusion

Although feminist studies of women's experiences of the menopause have begun to de-construct dominant biomedical discourses of menopausal women as leaky, decaying bodies in need of treatment, more research is needed on the impact of difference. Funding more localised qualitative studies of women in mid-life, which give voice to their experiences, would enhance our understanding of both the process of ageing and the ways in which gendered discourses construct women as primarily reproductive machines, in need of regulation and health surveillance. Having critically reviewed existing theoretical approaches to the study of the menopause and ageing, I have argued for the inclusion of an approach which draws upon the sociology of the body and embodiment. Feminist poststructuralist perspectives which address the importance of embodiment to the ongoing process of identity construction, can conceptualise women 'thinking through their bodies'. At a theoretical level this achieves three things, firstly it allows us to ground theoreticist discourses which construct women as fragmented subjectivities, by drawing upon their own accounts and secondly it addresses the commonalities of gendered bodily experience. Finally and perhaps most importantly, an approach which incorporates women's critical reflections upon their experience, constructs them as embodied agents who interact with and challenge dominant biomedical discourses. sÉ short they become active agents rather than passive subjects. Studies of the 'local' (both biological and social) can tell us more about the ways in which women reflect upon and challenge received messages about an 'old woman's place' in society.

Notes

1. A small pilot study conducted by Green and Wadsworth in the NE of England between 1997–2000 began in 1997 forming the basis of a larger ESRC/MRC funded project (www.york.ac.uk/res/iht). Focus groups and individual interviews were conducted with women between the ages of 38 and 70 who self-defined as post or currently menopausal. The focus of the study was upon women's narratives of menopausal experience, exploring the impact of differences of age, social class, able-bodiedness, ethnicity and sexual orientation. The empirical data has been collected by Gill Wadsworth as part of a related project.
2. Suprisingly given such a large sample, the women in this study were uniformly white, the majority were middle class and heterosexual by implication, which will of course have implications for the level and range of economic and social resources available to them

References

Beck, U. (1992) *The risk society*. London: Sage.

Bordo, S. (1989) 'The body and the reproduction of femininity: A feminist appropriation of Foucault', in A. Jagger and S. Bordo (eds) *Gender/body/knowledge*. New Brunswick: Rutgers University Press.

Bordo, S. (1993) *Unbearable weight: Feminism, western culture and the body*. Berkeley: University of California Press.

Bradley, H. (1996) *Fractured identities; Changing patterns of inequality*. Cambridge: Polity Press.

Butler, J. (1993) *Bodies that matter: On the discursive limits of 'sex'*. New York, Routledge.

Coney, S. (1991) *The menopause industry: A guide to medicine's discovery of the mid-life woman*. Auckland: Penguin Books.

Crompton, R. (1996) 'Paid employment and the changing system of gender relations', *British Journal of Sociology* Vol. 30, No. 3: pp. 427–445.

Cutler-Riddick, C. and Stewart, D. G. (1994) 'An examination of the life satisfaction on leisure in the lives of older female retirees; a comparison of blacks to whites', *Journal of Leisure Research* Vol. 26, No. 1: pp. 7587.

Davis, K. (ed) (1997) *Embodied practices: Feminist perspectives on the body*. London: Sage.

Foucault, M. (1986) *The history of sexuality: The care of the self* (vol. 3). New York: Pantheon.

Freysinger, V. (1995) 'The dialectics of leisure and development for women and men in mid-life: an interpretative study', *Journal of Leisure Research* Vol. 27, No. 1: pp. 61–84.

Giddens, A. (1991) *Modernity and self-identity: Self and society in the late modern age*. Cambridge, Polity Press.

Green, E. (1998) 'Women doing friendship: An analysis of women's leisure as a site of identity construction, empowerment and resistance', *Leisure Studies* No. 17, No. 3: pp. 171–185.

Green, E. and Wadsworth, G. (1998a) Disintegrating bodies: An analysis of women's experiences of the menopausal body. Paper to The British Sociological Association Annual Conference, Making Sense of the Body: Theory Research and Practice, 6–9 April, University of Edinburgh.

——— (1998b) Women, health and well-being project. Unpublished interview data.

Harding, J. (1997)' Bodies at risk: Sex, surveillance and hormone replacement therapy', in A. Peterson and R. Bunton (eds) *Foucault, health and medicine*. London: Routledge.

Haraway, D. (1991) *Simians, cyborgs, and women: The reinvention of nature*. New York: Routledge.

Howson, A. (1998) 'Embodied obligation: The female body and health surveillance', in S. Nettleton and J. Watson (eds) *The body in everyday life*. London: Routledge.

Jacobson, S. and Samdahl, D. (1998) 'Leisure in the lives of old lesbians: experiences with and responses to Discrimination', *Journal of Leisure Research* Vol. 30, No. 2: pp. 233–255.

Kaufert, P.A. (1982) 'Myth and the menopause', *Sociology of Health and Illness* Vol. 4, No. 2: pp. 141–166.

Kirkpatrick, M. (1989) 'Middle age and the lesbian experience', *Women's Studies Quarterly* 1 and 2: pp. not known.

Klein, R. (1992) 'The unethics of hormone replacement therapy', *Bioethics News* Vol. 11, No. 3: pp. 24–37.

Klein, R. and Dumble, L. (1994) 'Disempowering mid-life women: The science and politics of hormone replacement therapy (HRT)', *Women's Studies International Forum* Vol. 17, No. 4: pp. 327–43.

Komesaroff, P., Rothfield, P. and Daly, J. (1997) *Reinterpreting menopause: Cultural and philosophical issues.* New York and London: Routledge.

Locke, M. (1993) *Encounters with aging: Midlife and menopause in Japan and North America.* Berkeley: University of California Press.

Locke, M. (1998) 'Anomalous ageing: Managing the postmenopausal body', *Body and Society* Vol. 4, No. 1: pp. 35–61.

Lupton, D. (1995) *The imperative of health.* London: Sage.

Lupton, D. (1998) 'Going with the flow: Some central discourses in conceptualising and articulating the embodiment of emotional states', in S. Nettleton and J. Watson (eds) *The body in everyday life.* London: Routledge.

Maclennan, A. (1992) 'Menopause and preventative medicine', editorial, *Australian Family Physician* Vol. 21, No. 3: pp. 205.

Martin, E. (1997) 'The woman in the menopausal body', in P. Komesaroff, P. Rothfield and J. Daly (eds) *Reinterpreting menopause: Cultural and philosophical issues.* New York and London: Routledge.

National Women's Health Network (1995) *Taking hormones and women's health: Choices, risks and benefits.* Washington DC: National Women's Health Network.

Massey, D. (1994) *Space, place and gender.* Oxford: Blackwell.

Nettleton, S. (1997) 'Governing the risky self: how to become healthy, wealthy and wise', in A. Peterson and R. Bunton *(eds) Foucault, health and medicine.* London: Routledge.

Oudshoorn, N. (1994) *Beyond the natural body: An archeology of sex hormones.* London: Routledge.

Richards, L., Seibold, C. and Davis N. (eds) (1997) *Intermission: Women's experiences of menopause and mid-life.* Melbourne: Oxford University Press Australia.

Shildrick, M. (1997) *Leaky bodies and boundaries: Feminism, postmodernism and (bio)ethics.* London: Routledge

Turner, B. (1995) 'Aging and identity: Some reflections on the somatization of the self', in M. Featherstone and A. Wernick (eds) *Images of aging: Cultural representations of later life.* London: Routledge.

Vines, G. (1993) *Raging hormones, do they rule our lives?.* London: Virago Press.

Wearing, B. (1994) Rewriting the script: Postmodern women and leisure. Paper to the Australian Sociological Association Annual conference, Deakin University, Geelong, Victoria, 6–10 December.

Wearing, B (1995) 'Leisure and resistance in an ageing society', *Leisure Studies*: pp. 263–79.

The Absent Spaces of Lone Mothers' Leisure

Kay Standing

School of Social Science, Liverpool John Moores University

Introduction

> Not only do fewer women than men participate in leisure activities but women also participate in a narrower range of activities ... there emerges a picture of home-based, domestic leisure for women, especially for those from the lower socio-economic groups. (Talbot, 1981: p. 35)

> I'm always in a rush, always on the go, or having to do something you know. I don't have five minutes to myself ... It's not fair. (Karen, 31, white, divorced, 3 children, income support)

Leisure studies and the sociology of leisure (along with the related sociology of sport) have traditionally been an area where a patriarchal viewpoint was dominant — the study of men, by men — often from a Marxist perspective studying white, male working class culture (Williams, 1962: Clarke and Critcher, 1985). Theorists have only recently begun to recognise the significance of gender and race to definitions of leisure, informed by feminist perspectives (Deem, 1986; Green et al., 1990; Wimbush and Talbot, 1988).

In a late capitalist society, leisure remains defined in relation to paid work. Shifting relations of global capitalism in the 1980's led to high rates of male unemployment in traditional working class areas (such as mining and docks) and the proposed 'leisure society' failed to emerge (except perhaps for a privileged minority) for both economic and ideological reasons. For women, however, the work/leisure dichotomy with its assumption of 'free time' never encompassed their definitions of 'leisure'. The cultural construction of women as carers within the home and family leaves little space for traditional malestream definitions of leisure. Women's leisure is afforded a low priority both within the family and wider society (Green, et al., 1990).

Leisure, however, is a social process which changes over time, and is both historically and culturally constructed, and changing definitions of leisure have led theorists to debate the usefulness of the concept 'leisure' itself. Certainly in relation to low income lone mothers, as I discuss in this paper, 'leisure' is a problematic concept. However, to deny women leisure, and to deny that women have leisure, as is frequently asserted, is to deny women agency. For the lone mothers in my study, 'leisure' was not defined in traditional malestream ways, but rather in terms of 'space' and 'place' — of having time (and physical space) to oneself, and in terms of social relations, relaxation and sociability.

Leisure, no more than women themselves, is not a homogenous category. Women experience and define leisure in a myriad of ways, mediated by class, race/ethnicity, age, family situation and so forth. Feminist perspectives begin to deconstruct the work/play, public/private dichotomies to develop conceptualisations of women's leisure based in an understanding of women's differential positioning within a racially structured patriarchal capitalism:

> [f]or feminists, the everyday routines traced by women are never unimportant, because the seemingly banal and trivial events of the everyday are bound into the power structures which limit and confine women. The limits on women's everyday activities are structured by what society expects women to be, and therefore to do. (Rose, 1993: 17)

In the remainder of this paper I begin to explore concepts and meaning of 'leisure' in terms of 'space' and 'place' for a group of low income lone mothers.

Lone motherhood in the UK

Lone mother families now account for 19% of all families with dependent children, between 1.8 and 2 million children live in lone-mother households (Duncan and Edwards, 1997). 52% of lone mothers are divorced or separated, 35% single never married mothers (although these may have been in stable, cohabiting relationships), 6% from widowhood (Haskey, 1994). Within the category 'single' mother 54% were over 25 and only 8.6% teenagers (Bradshaw and Millar, 1991). Lone mothers remain economically disadvantaged (McIntosh, 1996) 70% of lone mothers receive their income from income support, and over 60% of lone mothers have incomes less than the national average. The 1992 General Household Survey found 42% of lone mothers had an income of below £100 per week. Only 24% of average income is provided by paid work, and over half of lone mothers in paid work part-time, with 31% working less than 21 hours a week (Duncan and Edwards, 1997). For the majority of lone mothers then, the paid work/leisure dichotomy does not exist[1] , and the economic status of most lone mothers means access to leisure facilities is limited.

Lone mothers however, are also discursively disadvantaged by popular stereotyping and deficit discourses propagated through both policy, government, academia and popular media (in itself a form of leisure). Leisure activities such as reading tabloid newspapers and watching television help to contribute to discourses on lone motherhood which both blame 'leisure' activities (sex, drinking etc.) for lone motherhood, and also construct an image of women without leisure time.

Drawing on the work of right wing American sociologist Charles Murray (1990: 1994) and the 'underclass' theory (e.g. Dennis and Erdos, 1992), New Right policy and rhetoric in the early 1990's depicted a stereotype of the reckless single teenage mother, pregnant because of her relentless pursuit of leisure/pleasure. Again this is linked to cultural and historical notions of working class women's 'respectability' (Smart, 1989) and gendered, raced and classed concepts of leisure.

Current UK government policy and discourses position lone mothers as a social problem[2], concerned both about state welfare expenditure, and the so called collapse of the (white nuclear) family. Lone mothers become positioned as 'victims' of economic circumstances. Under New Labour government initiatives lone mothers are encouraged into paid employment, without which they constructed as undeserving of leisure time.

The study

The data for this paper is drawn from my doctoral research based in-depth interviews with 28 lone mothers on low incomes, living on a large council estate in an inner city North London borough. The estate has a high rate of unemployment, a high percentage of lone mother families, and a large ethnic minority population. The research was not concerned with leisure, but with their involvement in their children's schooling. However, on reflection, discussion of leisure was explicitly absent from the interviews, yet implicitly always present. The absences of time/space for leisure were revealed throughout the interviews, as was the importance of social contacts.

The women were contacted through snowballing methods, a slow process, but one which allowed me access to a wide range of women defining themselves as lone, or single, mothers. The women were interviewed in their own homes (with the exception of five women, who were interviewed in my home[3]). The interviews were unstructured and lasted from an hour to four hours. The women are from a wide range of black and white ethnic backgrounds, and range in age from 22 to 48 years. They have varying degrees of family and kinship support, few have contact with the absent father, although several have new partners and continue to define themselves as lone mothers, as they feel their partners have no parenting responsibilities. All of the women have one or more child in primary school, some have older, and/or younger children, and/or other caring responsibilities (for elderly parents for example) all of which impact on both their opportunities for leisure.

For the majority of the women in the study (20), income support was their main source of income. Several of the women worked part-time in low paid domestic work in the unofficial economy. This was not an issue of 'fiddling the system', but one of survival; it was the only way they could afford any kind of a decent standard of living for themselves, and particularly, their children. Five of the women worked full-time, although one of these lost her job during the field work. The women who worked full-time had either an elder child in secondary schooling who took responsibility for younger children out of school hours, or extensive family support in terms of childcare. All earned below the limit for entitlement of family credit. Three women worked (officially) part-time. Several of the lone mothers received other forms of support from family, friends, absent fathers and new partners. This was not necessarily financial help but often help with child-care that gave the lone mother some 'leisure' time.

Lone mothers' leisure: the absences

Issues of relaxation and sociability have been defined as central to definitions of women's leisure (Green *et al.*, 1990: Deem, 1986). The overwhelming impression from all the interviews was one of a lack of time, little relaxation and an absence of 'leisure'. Whether in paid employment or not, women's days were filled with time for other people, housework, taking and collecting children to and from school, childcare, and other caring responsibilities (e.g., two women cared for disabled relatives). Many women emphasised the sheer monotony of daily routines, and an overwhelming sense of physical tiredness:

> ... up at quarter to seven ... get the children up, give them breakfast, get them ready, take them to school ... get home, tidy up, go shopping, them there's the washing, ironing cleaning, all the boring things ... then I go and pick Sky up, go and get Kylie ... walk down to station, pick Conor up ... do the dinner ... they watch telly or play a game, have a bath, get their 'jama's on, bed ... and it's the same thing every day, day in, day out. (Karen, 33, white, separated, 3 children, income support)

> ... we're out the door by 10 to 9 to get to school ... then I go back home, do a few things, maybe ironing ... some domestic boring thing, and the I go to work from noon til 3, then I race up to the flat ... race down and get the kids ... so its pretty hectic ... being a single mother that's one of the drawbacks, you're really pressed for time and energy ... I'm in bed at 10 most nights, I am so tired ... I was trying to watch this new show the other night and I was like, forget it! (Susan, 35, black, divorced, two children, part-time work)

The women frequently stressed the sheer hard work of parenting alone, and the lack of time and space for themselves:

> ... you are with the children constantly except when they are at school, and it can drive you crazy. I mean if they're fighting day and night, you know sometimes you just think 'oh please, I've had enough'. You got to try and distance yourself. I remember I used to lock myself in the toilet for 10 minutes just to get away from them, but now Jason knows how to pick the lock ... (Michelle, 28, white, single never married, 2 children, income support)

This concept of 'time for oneself' is one which is central to women's understandings of leisure. It is also expressed in terms of space, of not just having time to/for oneself, but of having physical space away from the children (expressed here by Michelle locking herself in the toilet).

Creating leisure space

However, this did not mean that the women had no leisure time. Leisure in terms of relaxation can be defined as an activity which constitutes a 'change' from the 'normal' routine[4]. Having a cup of tea and a chat with a friend or neighbour was conceptualised as leisure activity, and friends played a major role in defining leisure (see below). Reading books and magazines and watching television, in particular soap operas and 'chat' shows (such as Kilroy and Oprah), were also major sources of leisure, both in terms of times spent 'doing', and also as a common ground for conversation with others.

Leisure often continued to revolve around children. Few of the women had contact with absent fathers, and only 3 fathers were involved with their children on a regular basis, thus evenings, weekends and holidays tended to still be time spent with children, unless the women had family support nearby.

Lone mothers' leisure activities were often extensions of those of their children, for example going to parent and toddler groups, swimming, going to the cinema or to museums. These activities however are costly, and leisure time with children was often spent creating cheap or free activities (such as visits to the park or the library, watching videos). Whether however, activities with children can be defined as 'leisure' is problematic, they certainly gave the women enjoyment, but illustrate the difficulties of definitions of leisure and the public/private dichotomy. In a similar way, weekends and holidays, because of the change of routine, less pressured pace, and opportunities to meet other mothers, were conceptualised as leisure times:

> Oh that's lovely [holidays]. We don't have to get up ... we don't have to get dressed, just do what we want to do ... I take them out, normally in the holidays, during the 6 weeks especially, there's something going on everyday at a library or a park ... and I have lots of friends round, we go to their house, they come to here ... I think it goes really quick you know, and we all seem to enjoy having the time off, getting out of the routine, you know, being able to do what we want to do, and at your own pace. Normally I'm always in a rush, or having to do something you know. (Karen, 33, white, separated, 3 children, income support)

Women also spent leisure time on activities which could be defined as 'work', knitting, making bread dough, sewing, gardening, walking the dog. Many of these activities were also done to generate income from sales of finished articles:

> I sit and knit all the time, while I'm watching telly, or talking to the kids ... he won't wear the stuff, so I make baby clothes and sell them at attic sales and stuff. (Desmie)

Work and education could also be seen as providing time and space for some of the women, turning on its head the work/leisure dichotomy, and demonstrating its irrelevance for the lives of many women. Paid work was seen not only as a means to a better income and more resources, but often as a 'break from the kids'. Several of the women held various home sales parties (selling books, Tupperware, Ann Summers). These 'parties' were viewed by the hosts and the women invited, not solely as sales and money making opportunities, but as a 'good laugh' and a night or afternoon out. The Ann Summers parties in particular were viewed as a social occasion, with drinks, jokes and a general 'hen party' atmosphere. For many women, not just lone mothers, the boundaries of work and leisure are blurred:

> I do book parties and Ann Summers ... it's great 'cos I get some money and have a laugh ... I mean it's hard work 'cos sometimes you have to work hard

to get them to buy stuff, 'cos no ones any money round here you know, but its a bit of fun as well, specially if you have a few drinks and start trying the gear on ... it can be a good night out you know. (Grainne, white, Irish, 32, two daughters, separated, income support)

Education in particular was often conceptualised in terms of 'leisure', again stressing the importance of sociability:

I can't go out at night, 'cos you can't drag the children 'round at night, so you are very isolated a lot of the time. I find that difficult, that a lot of the time I don't hold adult conversation you know. That's why I'm going back to college ... 'cos I need to mix with adults again. (Michelle)

Five of the women were involved in a job retraining scheme run (with a crèche) on the estate, and three were involved in some form of day time adult education programmes (basic literacy, ESOL, and jewelry-making)

For many of the lone mothers the absence of a partner had mixed effects on leisure time. In many ways it was a constraint on leisure, an absence of income and someone else to show childcare in order to 'go out', yet it also created opportunities for leisure. Several women remarked they had less housework to do so more time to themselves, and no one to criticise their chosen activities or choice of friends:

... the best things are coming home and not having to cook for somebody, wash for somebody, no dirty socks stinking out my washing basket, not having to worry if they're going to start arguing, no-one telling you that you can't have your friends round ... (Christine, 27, white, divorced, 2 children, income support)

For nights out, most of the women relied on relatives or older children to baby-sit.

Sociability is important in women's definition of leisure, contact with family, friends and neighbours. Some women, especially those without family support, found lone mothering an isolating experience. However, many of the lone mothers in my study were members of a supportive network of lone mothers, meeting regularly, sharing childcare, information and advice, toys and clothes:

My friends you know, I'd go mad without them ... we meet up nearly every day at each others house, or in the park ... the kids play and we have a coffee and a good gossip. There's always people round here, it's like a mad house (laughs). (Christine)

Again, many mothers had met, or continued to meet, at toddler and mother and baby groups, where children could play and they could socialise.

Friendship is also important for the sense of identity it provides (Allan, 1989; Ribbens, 1994). Friendship ties can serve to both reaffirm and challenge women's formal role positions, for example as lone mothers, depending on the social networks in which they move.

'Place' in lone mothers' leisure

Other researchers have stressed the importance of neighbourhood and location for the friendship and leisure of mothers (Green *et al.*, 1990). Allan (1989) has examined the role of friendship within social life, pointing not only to its emotional, but also its social and economic uses. Other writers (e.g. Ribbens, 1994) have pointed to the importance of informal reciprocal arrangements regarding childcare amongst mothers. This was one of the main forms of support that friends provided for the lone mothers in my study.

For most of the women, network support from other lone mothers served to both reinforce their identity as lone mothers, and also to challenge the deficit discourses on lone motherhood by placing their own, and their friends, experiences outside of these discourses. For others, however, the mere presence and awareness of a significant number of lone mother families in the locality provided psychological support for their mothering practices. In this way, the constructed commonality of the locality, with a high number of non-traditional family forms, served to provide a 'normalising discourse' on lone motherhood (Phoenix, 1996):

> I mean I am a single parent, but you know, I live in an area where there's lots of different sorts of family groupings. So it's not uncommon that people are dealing with children who live with their grandparents, or who are with one parent or living with aunties, or what have you. So they're [the teachers] quite used to dealing with lots of different family relationships. (Fiona, 42, white, divorced, one daughter, full-time work)

In this way, despite the negative dominant discourses on lone motherhood nationally, localised discourses provided a context in which lone mothering was seen, by the women themselves as 'normal' and inside discourses on 'good mothering'.

However, locality can also be a constraint — women's fear of violence and the appropriation of public spaces by men (Stanko, 1985) The Manor estate where the research was based is case in point. The estate was discursively constructed as a 'problem inner city estate'. It is a large estate housing approximately 2, 500 people in low to medium rise blocks of flats linked by low level and overhead walkways. It was designed with a small open space in the centre housing a community centre and a line of shops, of which only a newsagents remains. There is also a nursery and job retraining scheme which provides some employment, childcare and training for the residents. The nursery, however, is also a source of resentment, as it is underfunded, and the limited number of places allocated throughout the ward, rather than giving priority to residents of the estate. The community centre was also not used by the women in the research, open primarily in the evenings as a youth club. Many of the women were reluctant to go out at night, feeling their leisure outside the home constrained by the locality. The sense of enclosure, combined with dark alleyways and gardenless homes, makes for a woman-and-child-unfriendly environment The benefits of the traffic free pedestrianisation of the estate, which allows children to play safely and provide areas where the women could meet and talk, were perceived by many mothers to be outweighed by the appropriation of physical space by 'gangs' of teenage boys and young men:

A lot of their friends from school live on the estate, so they can play, and it's safe in that there's no traffic or roads, you just have to watch who they play with. There's a certain element I wouldn't want them hanging around with, mixing with ... It's mostly teenagers, one teenage gang of boys who are little shits ... By the same token I don't go out late at night ... its not safe. (Susan, 33, black, divorced, 2 children, part-time work)

This perception of criminality is echoed by the local police in a crime prevention report to the council detailing police call-outs to incidents on the estate. The police report is ungendered however, unlike the experiences of the women on the estate, whose 'fear' is not of an ungendered 'youth', but of 'young men':

There is a general grouping [of calls] in the centre of the estate around, inside and under the high rise housing units which surround the square with its shops and community hall. A significant proportion of calls belong to the 'disorder' category, which includes disturbances, drunks, and rowdy youths [...] often calls do not directly result to crime but rather anti-social behaviour and youths with nothing to do. The call pattern is symptomatic of an area where youths [in the broad sense of under 25s] are bored and rowdy. Residents have surrendered certain areas to street gangs [...] Extensive home made or commercially fitted security grilles on properties throughout the estate show a disproportionately high fear of crime amongst residents. (Police Crime Prevention Report, January, 1996)

The problem is exacerbated both by the lack of facilities on the estate, either for youth or for mothers, and the general poverty of the area. Outside the estate there are plenty of leisure facilities, clubs, sports facilities, gyms and so on, but all are expensive and few of the women used the sports facilities in the area

Conclusion: making leisure part of life

Research on women's leisure from women's perspectives is growing, mainly from feminist writers and researchers. However, the differential situation of different groups of women still needs to be integrated into work on women's 'leisure'. Definitions of leisure which are based on the work/leisure, public/private dichotomies are inadequate to conceptualise lone mothers understandings of their lives. Leisure is not a concrete entity which can be studied autonomously from the 'rest' of lone mothers' lives, but is bound up in everyday activities, routines, and notions of place and space. Notions of leisure need to extend beyond pursuits of sport, recreation and activity to include the social. Leisure for many of the women in my research was the chats, coffees and cigarettes, the time and space for themselves. Research needs to begin to explore the 'absent spaces' to reveal to myriad of ways time is used within the lives of lone mothers to create 'leisure'.

Notes

1   Despite New Labour's attempts to 'encourage' lone mothers into paid employment through initiatives such as 'New Deal for lone Parents' and 'Welfare to Work'.
2   For further discussion of the various discourses around lone motherhood see Duncan and Edwards, 1997.
3   I also lived on the estate. The women who chose not to be interviewed in their own home either lived with extended family, or in bed and breakfast accommodation. In all cases, privacy was an issue in the location of the interviews.
4   See Graham (1990) on smoking and 'tea and fag breaks' amongst women.

Bibliography

Allan, G. (1989) *Friendship: Developing a sociological perspective*. London: Harvester Wheatsheaf.

Bradshaw, J. and Millar, J. (1991) *Lone parents: Policy in the doldrums*. London: Family Policy Studies Centre.

Clarke, J. and Critcher, C. (1985) *The devil makes work: Leisure in capitalist Britain*. London: Macmillan.

Deem, R. (1986) *All work and no play? The sociology of women and leisure*. Milton Keynes: Open University Press.

Duncan, S. and Edwards, R. (eds) (1997) *Lone mothers in an international context: mothers or workers*. London: UCL.

Graham, H. (1993) *Hardship and health in women's lives*. London: Harvester Wheatsheaf.

Green, E., Hebron, S. and Woodward, D. (1990) *Women's leisure, what leisure?*. London: Macmillan.

Haskey, J. (1994) 'Estimated numbers of one parent families and their prevalence in Britain in 1991', *Population Trends* , 78: 5–19.

McIntosh, M. (1996) 'Social anxieties about lone motherhood and ideologies of the family', in Bortolaia Silva, E. (ed) *Good enough mothering? Feminist perspectives in lone motherhood*. London: Routledge.

Murray, C. (1990) *The emerging British underclass*. London: IEA.

——— (1994) *Underclass: The crisis deepens*. London: IEA.

Phoenix, A. (1996) 'Social constructions of lone motherhood: A case of competing discourses' in Bortolaia Silva, E. (ed) *Good enough mothering? Feminist perspectives in lone motherhood*. London: Routledge.

Ribbens, J. (1994) *Mothers and their children: Feminist sociology of childrearing*. London: Sage.

Rose, G. (1993) *Feminism and geography: The limits of geographical knowledge*. London: Polity.

Smart, C (1989) *Regulating womenhood*. London: Routledge.

Stanko, E. (1985) *Intimate intrusions. London: Routledge and Kegan Paul.*

Talbot, M. (1981) 'Women and sport — social aspects', *Journal of BioSocial Science* 7: pp. 33–47.

Williams, R. (1962) *Culture and society*. Harmondsworth: Penguin.

Wimbush, E. and Talbot, M. (1988) *Relative freedoms: Women and leisure*. Milton Keynes: Open University Press.

The Everyday Lives of Sportswomen: Playing Sport and Being a Mother

Gertrud Pfister

University of Copenhagen

Introduction

The combination of paid employment and unpaid housework is the basis and the precondition of the functioning of modern industrial societies. In the western world, women's lives have been determined, traditionally, by the gender specific segregation of work which has meant that women have had the primary responsibility for domestic work and childcare (among others Beck, 1986). However, the reality for many women today, and in the past, (particularly working-class women) has been a dual role combining both paid and unpaid work in the public and private spheres. As we approach the millennium, the notion of individual choice and the equalising of gender relations appears to be making little difference for many women as they face the 'double burden' of career and family.

The following contribution is based on theoretical considerations about the gender order which takes into account the gender specific division of work and the meaning of house work as well as the social construction of gender on both levels — the society and the individual. I am following Judith Lorber's suggestion that one should fit different approaches together "in a coherent picture of gender as a process of social construction, a system of social stratification, and an institution that structures every aspect of our lives because of its embeddedness in the family, the workplace and the state as well as in sexuality, language and culture" (Lorber, 1994: p. 5).

Many empirical studies confirm that housework and domestic labour remains women's work not only in Germany but everywhere in the Western world. In 1998 a German survey showed again that house work is done mainly by women. According to the Federal Office for Statistics, young women between 20 and 25 years of age were engaged on average two hours and 40 minutes per day in housework and child care, whereas men of the same age spent for this kind of work only one hour. Women in the age group of 25 to 30 years worked four and a half hours for home and family, men only one and a half hours. Huge differences could be found regarding the time spent for child care: Women care for their children one hour 20 minutes per day whereas men did this for only 15 minutes (quoted in *Tagesspiegel* 22. July 1998: p. 32; see also Blanke *et al.*, 1996).

It can be seen that it is becoming a mother that creates a great demand on women's lives. There is now a considerable body of literature and research that suggests that 'mothering' is socially constructed by dominant ideologies that identify what it is to be a 'good' mother. This places powerful emotional, social and physical responsibilities on women that potentially have profound repercussions on other aspects of their lives. Although it cannot discussed in detail in this article, the complexities of 'being a mother' or indeed how women negotiate around house work/child care, paid work and leisure, it is focused on how women combine their identities as 'mothers' and as 'sportswomen', how mothers deal with the constraints of their leisure and how they use sport for empowering. Recognising that combining paid work and mothering can result in contradictions, negotiations and pleasures for different women, or indeed for the same women over a period of time, it is interesting to explore the experiences of women who have attempted to combine two other potentially important aspects of life — motherhood and sport.

It should be mentioned that being a mother and being an athlete is also discussed in another context. If it is a question whether mothers have the right to leave their children for playing sport, then mothers taking risks and participating in dangerous sports is a still more contested terrain. High risk sports have been and are looked upon as a demonstration of masculinity, even as machismo. What have women and even mothers to seek in sports like car racing or mountaineering? The deaths of the famous "mountaineering mum" Alison Hargreaves on K2 in 1995 and the Austrian downhill ski racer Ulrike Maier led to a heated debate in the mass media whether women should have the right to 'play with their lives'. Alison Hargreaves herself felt, as she confessed in her diary, to be pulled in two, wanting her children and wanting K2. Whereas the media described the death of Hargreaves as tragic and emphasised her being a mother, the fatal accidents of male climbers were depicted as heroic deeds even if they left a pregnant wife.

Leisure and motherhood

Although there has been little research in Germany that has focused specifically on leisure and motherhood, English studies of women and leisure in the 1980s provided some data relevant to this group of women. And Shaw (1994) discussed the empirical findings about the "constraints on women's leisure" in her endeavor towards constructing a framework for the analysis of women's leisure.

One of the key issues raised relates to the significance of 'time' as a concept for understanding women's experiences of leisure. Among others Jurczyk (1997) emphasised the social construction and the gendered nature of time. In her view "doing gender" and "doing time" are closely intertwined. Both the Sheffield Study (Green *et al.*, 1987) and Rosemary Deem's study of leisure in Milton Keynes, England (1986) reported the significance of the fragmentation of women's time in relation to their opportunities to take part in leisure activities. Women's time is not neatly compartmentalised into 'time for work' and 'time for leisure'. Indeed for women with children their time becomes dependent on children's sleep patterns, feeding times, school structures, partner's work demands, illnesses, children's leisure activities and so on. The very notion of a separate sphere defined as leisure has little meaning for many women with children. As Stanley (1980) argues, we need to look holistically at women's lives if we are to understand how they experience and define leisure. Leisure for many women is not an activity or something that they 'do' but rather a moment snatched for quiet thought between meals, relaxing in a warm bath or meeting and making friends with other mothers (Green, 1998).

The responsibility for children and the necessity to be always available do not mean that there is no free time, but that the planning of the leisure in advance is difficult, if not impossible. Often this leisure occurs whilst working as some women explained in Deem's (1986) research. She records how some women define watching television whilst ironing as leisure or having coffee while their children play. What is clear is that leisure for mothers has to be negotiated around the many and varied demands of their fragmented lives. Therefore Wimbush and Talbot (1988) used the term "relative freedom", and Opaschowski invented the term "in-between-leisure" (1989: p. 21). One of the mothers who was interviewed by Wimbush and Talbot (1988) described her situation in the following way: "Before you have your baby you never would believe that it is like it is, that you have to think about the baby every single minute".

For many women the leisure of their children and/or their partners take up much of their time. Women service other people's leisure often at the expense of the production or consumption of their own leisure. Thompson (1999), in her study of women's leisure in Australia, discusses how women take their children to sporting activities or leisure pursuits, wash and iron sports clothes and prepare and serve meals for their partner and guests. Although some of these things can also give pleasure and enjoyment, they do not provide freedom of choice so often described as an essential feature of 'leisure'.

Other factors which affect the leisure of many women, particularly those who are young mothers or single mothers, are their lack of mobility and financial resources (Wimbush, 1988). Many women do not have access to the 'family car' and for those who do not have their own income from paid work, there is often little access to money to spend on their own enjoyment. These issues become even more pertinent when considering lone mothers who are often existing on state benefits or have very low incomes (Klein, 1992).

Clearly a crucial problem mothers are confronted with concerning leisure activities is child care. Often the expenditure of time and financial resources to organise child care is so great that it seems to be easier to forget about the leisure activity. Many women rely on partners and family for childcare and it remains a fact that provision of childcare is by no means a norm for leisure opportunities.

However, it is important to recognise that mothers' leisure lives are not totally determined by the restrictions imposed by time, finance, partners and so on. Rather we have to ask how women do use their leisure time and how they negotiate time and space in spite of the many restrictions imposed on them. Women create their own positive experiences and gain 'relative freedom' in their leisure lives (Wimbush and Talbot, 1988).

There are some studies which show that women can use and do use leisure and physical activities as resistance and as empowerment. "The argument for resistance is based on two important theoretical notions: first, the idea of agency and second, the idea of leisure as freely chosen or as self determined" (Shaw, 1994: p. 15). Learning new skills, gaining strength and endurance, feeling competent, getting to like their own bodies, developing a positive physicality, challenging gender ideology, all this can lead to an increase of self confidence and self efficacy and can thus contribute to an empowerment of women (Henderson and Bialeschki, 1994; Shaw, 1994; Deem, 1996;

Deem and Gilroy, 1998). But we should not overestimate the empowering effect of physical activities. There is no question that sport can also have negative effects on women's bodies and lives. Deem (1996) points out that empowerment through leisure and sport does not necessarily "have a huge influence on women's lives; though it may affect their bodies and their identities it is unlikely to make their work less monotonous, give them more money or transform their relationship".

Furthermore just as 'women' cannot be used as a universal concept to describe the lives and experiences of all women, neither can 'mother' be used without recognising the importance of difference and diversity between mothers (see especially Deem, 1998)

Sport participation of mothers

The leisure and sport activities of women are as our research project has shown the result of life long processes of socialisation, but also of the concrete conditions of life. Being a mother would appear to have the potential to powerfully influence women's opportunities to take part in sport. There is little quantitative or qualitative research that considers sportswomen who combine motherhood with a physically active lifestyle.

In Germany, no research about the physical activities of mothers is available. A representative survey which was conducted in the 1970s showed that people who were married, in comparison to unmarried people of the same age, were decisively underrepresented in the sport active population. The drop-out-effect after marriage was much higher with women than with men (Schlagenhauf, 1977: p. 143). Regional studies and surveys which are not specifically differentiated according to marital status, sex and age provide enough data to suggest that women reduce their engagement in sport after having children (Meyer, 1992). For example, in a survey conducted by Lange, 38% of women involved in sport activities were married in comparison with 54% of women not active in sport (Lange, 1994: p. 46)[1].

The research sample

In the following part of this paper I share with you the result of a research project about the "Experience and Meaning of Sport in the Lives of European Women" which has been conducted in Norway, England, Spain and Germany (Fasting *et al.*, 1997). In each of these countries we interviewed 60 women active in tennis, soccer or gymnastics/aerobics both on a recreational and at a high performance level. Here I want to focus on the German project. Whereas 17 of the 60 Norwegian women interviewed were mothers, in the German sample of 60 women there were only 7 mothers. Therefore, we decided to interview additionally 10 mothers who were actively engaged in sport on the recreational level. Therefore, we could analyse 17 interviews with mothers who were between 24 and 36 years of age. Of these, six were engaged in gymnastics/aerobics, 8 played tennis and 3 played soccer. One of the soccer players and one of the tennis players were top level athletes, the others did sport as leisure activity. Two of the mothers lived apart, while the others lived with a partner. Six of the mothers participating in our project had one child, eleven had two children. The children were aged between 5 months and 6 years. At the time of the interview, 10 mothers did not work outside the home, and seven were in full time or part time employment.

We asked these mothers who were actively engaged in sport about the meaning and function of sport in their lives. We were interested in how mothers organised their everyday lives and how they found time and the opportunity to participate in sport.

Our qualitative semi-structured interviews followed interview guidelines, especially because of the international comparison; but we also encouraged the women involved to express their own ideas and interpretations.

The interpretation is based on a qualitative content analysis, in which we categorized the texts on a more and more abstract level, but also used the full text for correction and explanation (for more details see Fasting *et al.*, 1997).

The meaning of physical activities in the lives of mothers

The interviews showed clearly how important sport was in the lives of the mothers involved in our study. However, we have to take into consideration that our interview partners are a group of women who have developed a very strong commitment to sport. They are women who have continued to be active in sport despite the responsibilities and burdens of family life. None of the mothers we interviewed could imagine a life without sport. Some of them said that they would only stop being active in sport if they were forced to by illness or disability: "But even then, I would always be active in sport, some way or another". When she had another child, said another woman, "I would put my activity on the back burner for a time ... and after one year I would try to get back to sport again".

On the one hand, mothers reported the same motives for their engagement in sport that are mentioned in broader participation surveys: fun, enjoyment, relaxation, social life, slimness, fitness and health. On the other hand, women with small children appeared to have some specific reasons for their sporting activity. For example, they put special emphasis on relaxation and compensation because of the isolation and the burden of their family responsibilities.

"I like being a mother", said a tennis player, who described later in the interview how she used her tennis in order to "release emotions, as a means to compensate for problems that have banked up, just to play and not having to use your head". Sport was also used to channel aggression. Another mother confessed that: "After one year of baby care I really longed to kick and to push ... I just wanted to release everything ... ". The following comment is typical of the positive way sport was viewed by so many of the mothers: "I love to be a mother, but there has to be some compensation, this is very important for me", said a tennis player who describes, in another part of the inter-view, how she uses tennis to deal with emotions and aggressions. "To escape the every day work and to meet somebody else than just children", this was the motivation for another mother for her engagement in sport. To provide much needed social contacts, "to come out of the daily routine", "to see and to meet other people", or "to achieve, to win and to be accepted for this", were all the benefits of sport identified as important by the women interviewed. One tennis player, for example, told us: "I am very ambitious, that means I have to have certain goals which I want to reach. And I can do this in sport, whereas I cannot do it in my job at this period of my life". Sport offers the opportunity to get positive feed back in a time, when mothers are staying at home or working part time. For the majority of mothers we interviewed, competition had lost its importance". I am not angry any more if I play tennis. In former times I would have thrown my racket ... really it was terrible. But now I think there is something which is more important than sport. And I play even better because I am not so tense".

Many women were convinced that doing sport meant doing something for health and wellbeing. In addition, several mothers identified the importance of sport in helping them regain fitness after child birth, to get back their "old body" as some of the mothers interviewed emphasised. They mentioned the importance "to regain the figure" or "to lose weight". In spite of the responsibility for children and housework mothers also wanted to maintain fitness and develop and keep a positive feeling towards their bodies. In a very similar way, the women interviewed by Henderson and Bialeschki (1994) discussed the reasons for being active in sport: "For these women, feelings of well-being connected with the bodily experience seemed to be the major reason for their commitment to physical recreation" (p. 28).

Most of the women interviewed reported that physical activity helped them to develop a positive body concept. Most of our interview partners, as well as the mothers, were convinced that sport activities improved their self confidence. We can therefore assume that physical activities contributed to an empowerment of mothers. However, we should not forget that this is the subjective impression of the women interviewed and that it is not established whether these women could transfer the positive effects of physical recreation and sport to other areas of their lives (see Pfister, 1998).

Negotiating the constraints

Lack of time

These positive values attached to sporting participation can only be achieved through the negotiation of the many constraints women have to face as mothers responsible for children and the home. One of the key problems mothers have to negotiate is, as has been mentioned above, lack of time. One of the interviewed tennis player complained: "I nearly cannot manage any more, I do not know where to take the time. I am really ready for the holidays".

The pressure of lack of time means that these women are forced to set priorities and organise their work efficiently. "The easiest thing is to reduce house work. I do not cook, I just do not have enough time. So my child gets ready made food, I cannot help it. And I cannot clean the windows every day or clean the floor".

When mothers take the time for sport they have the problem that "something else has to play second fiddle". Lack of time is often connected with a feeling of guilt as the mothers perceive that they do not have enough time for all their responsibilities. Some of our interview partners doubt if they have the right to take time for themselves to play and enjoy sport: "You always have such a bad conscience. You are gainfully employed and then you take your leisure time, and you do not spend all your energy on your child. This cannot be OK". "This is the consequence if you have children" said a tennis player, "you have responsibilities which take a lot of time and you cannot just leave and play sports".

Whereas some of the women talked about 'developing a guilty conscience' because their physical activities take the time which should be "invested in their partners or in their families", other women we interviewed decided deliberately to prioritize their own interests and not to yield to expectations from others. This was also a point of the women participating in the study of Henderson and Bialeschki (1994: p. 21). One mother of three kids said: "I would rather let the house go and know that I am taking care of myself by going to aerobics and stuff than find a way to have the perfect house and feel like crap all the time. So I have to do my thing and if someone has to wear dirty jeans for a couple of days, then they will just to have to do that ...".

The mothers we interviewed found ways and means to deal with their restricted time budget. They not only reduced the house work, some of them also changed their type of sport, or reduced the intensity of sport engagement. Several of our interview partners participated for example in aerobic lessons, because this was the most effective way to exercise without wasting time. Another mother described how she hurries to her fitness course and how she leaves without showering in order to save time. For all the mothers, efficient organisation of their day and an effective use of time was the precondition for their engagement in sport.

But the women participating in our study not only mentioned difficulties, most of them also talked about the positive sides to live with children. One woman put it like this: "It is right I reduced my sport activity quite a lot because of my family. I go much much less often to the tennis court. But, on the other hand, it is wonderful when my family comes with me. I play tennis and I can see my partner and my daughter, this is great". Mothers have only a very restricted time for leisure, but they seem, as many interview passages showed, to enjoy these few hours very much.

Who cares for the child?

A major issue for mothers, who want to be active in sport, is the question of childcare. Who cares for the children if the mother wants to play tennis or go to aerobics? Many of the women interviewed were convinced that it was their responsibility to organise child care during their physical activities. This was also an expectation imposed on them by others which some of them identified as a major pressure. Around a third of the women had organised regular care for their children during the time they took to participate in sport. Although it was a relief once the time and care was negotiated it involved considerable organisation. A German teacher told us how her father looked after her child during her working hours. After work she drove to the home of her parents, fetched her child and took it with her to the tennis court where the other grandfather waited in order to play with her child while she was playing tennis.

Another third of the interviewed women had sometimes a fixed appointment for child care but they had to change this arrangement very often, for example, because of the shift work of the partner. The other women had no fixed routine and so had to find new arrangements each time they wanted to play or take part in sport. For mothers with small children it is extremely difficult to meet spontaneously for jogging or playing tennis: "You are not free any more and if somebody calls and asks, lets play tennis, then you have to look if there is a baby sitter or no, how you can handle the situation, who are not very flexible".

The women we interviewed most frequently used members of the family as baby sitters which had advantages and disadvantages. Partners played the most important role for looking after the children and most of the women commented on the support they received from their partners. Many described their partners as actively involved in sport or at least interested in sport. This had some positive advantages, as one of the German tennis players noted: "He is the whole day on the tennis tournament and the child is with him ... and I like it very much to have them with me when I play"

There can also be a conflict of interest when both partners like to play sport. Some of the fathers seemed to take it for granted that their interests and activities should have priority and that the child care "always sticks to the wives". So several women commented that "he goes always to his sport and leaves me here alone", or "he forgets about agreements and does not keep appointments" Generally, however, the mothers we interviewed were supported by their partners emotionally and — to a high degree — also in practice.

It became apparent that many of the women who were involved in tennis or football often took their children to the sports ground with them, especially if the children were of school age. One soccer player described how her team mates loved to play with her daughter on the touchline. Often, other children are playing around in the tennis club or on the soccer field and this helps to keep them all busy.

Few of the women had access to, or made use of institutional childcare. Nurseries or Kindergarten tended not to be open when the women wanted to participate in their sport and the women who are involved in team sports have fixed training hours which are mostly in the early evenings. It is unsurprising, therefore, that there was little mention in the interviews of institutional child care. Some fitness studios offered child care as a special service which was mentioned by some of the interviewed women. They welcomed this service in principle but pointed out, also, that this does not solve all their problems. Only in a few of the studios is child care included in the fee; in other studios it has to be paid for in addition which many women cannot afford. Often child care is offered only at certain hours which may not be suitable for an individual's specific needs. Some of the women we talked to were also sceptical of the quality of the child care offered.

Most importantly many of the mothers commented on how time and energy consuming it is to transport a baby either to the studio or to grandparents. The baby has to be satisfied, fed, dressed in new diapers; you have to take fresh diapers, food, fresh clothes and playing things, a cart or a carrying bag with you and so on. It is totally understandable that some mothers prefer to stay at home even if there is child care offered.

A key issue in relation to this is the responsibility and 'duty' that many women feel towards their children. Many women still seem convinced that they should care for their children themselves. Often there is a classic case of the 'triple bind' of paid work, childcare and sport/leisure. Many women feel that they are already leaving their children in order to have paid work and thus feel pressurized to not take time for themselves which takes them away from their children again.

Conclusion and perspectives

Our project shows that sport can play and continues to play an important role in the lives of women even after they have children.

As mentioned in the introduction we can assume that the level of sport activity decreases after the foundation of a family. However, the statements of our interview partners suggest that women with a close commitment to sport try to be physically active after having children.

Also I focused here on the German data, a comparison between the statements of the mothers from England, Norway and Germany showed that, in principle, there were no fundamental differences in the interviews of mothers from the three countries involved. All the women stressed the general importance of sport and, also, the difficulties in combining family, physical activity and paid work. Women appear to use the same strategies of negotiation independent of their nationality. Therefore we can assume that the structural conditions of the lives of the mothers in our sample are more important than cultural differences.

Physical activities have similar meanings for the mothers and they appear to be especially important as a compensation for the strain of every day work. Mothers have to organise child care in order to participate in sport and it was apparent in our interviews in all countries involved that it remains the woman's responsibility and is a complex and time-consuming task.

Therefore the provision of efficient childcare would seem to be still a priority if we want to improve the access to leisure and sport for women with children. However, not only mothers, but fathers as well have to demand child care facilities in clubs, studios and other sport settings.

One solution to the dilemma of child care could be to organise sport activities for families. In a survey of the German Gymnastic Federation 61% of the women asked and 48% of the men reported that they prefer to do sport with their families. But there is a huge discrepancy between supply and demand. Less than 10% of all sport clubs offer courses or groups for parents and children. In addition, training studios and leisure centres have developed which take care of the children while their parents are exercising. These have become popular and are opening up opportunities for some mothers at least for those who can afford to pay for this opportunity.

However, "family sport" can be played independently of clubs and organisations in swimming baths, skating rinks, parks, lakes and so on. In a German survey around 40% of the sport active married women reported that they do sport with someone from their family[2]. Many mothers do enjoy to do sport with their children and see this as a positive aspect of family life. For some mothers, parent-children courses/activities are the incentive to start or to renew a regular physical activity. However, these courses or family activities also have disadvantages as they do not meet the needs of many mothers who desire "time for themselves" away from responsibilities of the home and children. Family activities and sports such as swimming, bicycling or hiking may satisfy the need to be physically active, and can be pleasurable and fun. However, they remain constrained by the need to care for and be responsible for others. They do not give the freedom that many women desire to 'be themselves' and to have the time and space to engage with sport on their own terms.[3]

Notes

1   Anja Lange (1994) conducted a representative survey. Unfortunately her results are not differentiated according to marital status, number and age of the children. In spite of this problems, some of her results support the theses that married women and women with children are less physically active than single women. Other studies support this assumption as well; see Meyer 1992: p. 38.

2   Lange (1994: p. 58): 51% of the married women who had not been involved in sport would like to do sport together with their families (Lange 1994: p. 188).

3   I want to thank Sheila Scraton for translating the article and for many ideas.

References

Beck, U. (1986) Risikogesellschaft. Auf dem Weg in eine andere Moderne. *Frankfurt/M.: Suhrkamp.*

Blanke, K., Ehling, M. and Schwarz, N. (1996) Zeit im Blickfeld Ergebnisse einer repräsentativen Zeitbudgeterhebung. *Stuttgart; Berlin: Kohlhammer*

Bundesministerium für Frauen und Jugend (1992) Frauen in der Bundesrepublik Deutschland. *Bonn: Bundesministerium für Frauen und Jugend.*

Bung, P. (1996) 'Körperliche Aktivitäten und Sport in der Schwangerschaft', TW Sport + Medizin *8, H.1, S., pp. 19–38.*

Deem, R. (1986) All work and no play. The sociology of women and leisure. *Milton Keynes/Philadelphia: Open University Press.*

——— (1996) 'Sport and physical activities — how important are they to women's leisure?', paper to the European Women and Sport Conference, Stockholm.

Deem, R., Gilroy, S. (1988) 'Physical activity, life-long learning and empowerment — situating sport in women's leisure', Sport, Education and Society *Vol. 3, No.1: pp. 89–105.*

Fasting, K., Pfister, G., Scraton, S., and Bunuel, A. (1997) 'Cross-national research on women and sport: Some theoretical, methodological and practical challenges', Women in Sport and Physical Activity Journal *Vol. 6, No. 1, pp. 85–109.*

Green, E. (1998) Women doing friendship: an analysis of women's leisure as a site of identity construction, empowerment and resistance, in: Leisure Studies *Vol 17, No. 3, pp 171-187*

Green, E., Hebron, S. and Woodward, D (1987) Gender and leisure: A study of Sheffield women's leisure. *London: The Sports Council.*

Green, E., Hebron, S. et al. (1988) 'Leisure and male partners', in E. Wimbush and M. Talbot (eds) Relative freedoms. *Milton Keynes/Philadelphia: Open University Press, pp. 37–48.*

——— (1990) Women's leisure, what leisure?. *London: Macmillan.*

Henderson, K. and Bialeschki, D. (1994) 'Women and the meanings of physical recreation', Women in Sport and Physical Activity Journal *3, No. 2: pp. 21–37.*

Jurczyk, K. (1997) 'Zeit als Machtfaktor. Stabilität und Erosion der unterschiedlichen Zeitmuster von Frauen und Männern im Alltag', Teil 2, in: K. Weis (ed) Was ist Zeit?. *München: Akademischer Verlag, pp. 117–151.*

Klein, M.-L. (1990) Familiensport in der Bundesrepublik — zwischen Wunsch und Wirklichkeit. Unveröffentlichtes Manuskript. Bochum.

—— *(1992) 'Sozialräumliche Bedingungen des Frauensports — Das Beispiel Ruhrgebiet' in Kröner, S. und Pfister, G. (Hrsg.) Frauen* — Räume, Körper, Sport. *Pfaffenweiler: Centaurus, pp. 146–160.*

Lange, A. *(1994)* Sozialisation zum und durch Sporttreiben: eine Querschnittsuntersuchung an erwachsenen Frauen. *Bochum: Brockmeyer.*

Lorber, J. *(1994)* Paradoxes of Gender. *New Haven/London: Yale University Press*

Meyer, M. *(1992)* Zur Entwicklung der Sportbedürfnisse. Eine Analyse der Sportnachfrage im kommunalen Kontext. *Diss. Köln.*

Ochel, A. *(1989)* Hausfrauenarbeit. Eine qualitative Studie über Alltagsbelastungen und Bewältigungsstrategien von Hausfrauen. *München: Profil.*

Opaschowski, H.W. *(1989)* Freizeitalltag von Frauen. Zwischen Klischee und Wirklichkeit: Rollen, Rituale und Rücksichtnahmen. *Hamburg: BAT.*

Ostner, I. *(1978)* Beruf und Hausarbeit. Die Arbeit der Frau in unserer Gesellschaft. *Frankfurt/New York: Campus.*

Pfister, G. *(1998)* Sport im Lebenszusammenhang von Frauen. *Ausgewählte Themen. Schorndorf: Hofmann.*

Reichle, B. *(1994)* Die Geburt des ersten Kindes — eine Herausforderung für die Partnerschaft. Verarbeitung und Folgen einer einschneidenden Lebensveränderung. *Bielefeld: Kleine.*

Scarr, S. *(1987)* Wenn Mütter arbeiten: wie Kinder und Beruf sich verbinden lassen. *München: Beck.*

Schlagenhauf, K. *(1977)* Sportvereine in der Bundesrepublik Deutschland. *Schorndorf: Hofmann.*

Shaw, S. M. *(1994) 'Gender, leisure, and constraint: Towards a framework for the analysis of women's leisure',* Journal of Leisure Research Vol. 26, No. 1: pp. 8–21.

Stanley, L. *(1980)* The problem of women and leisure. *London: SSRC/Sports Council*

Thompson, S. M. *(1999)* Mother's taxi: Sport and women's labor. *New York: State University of New York.*

Wimbush, E. and Talbot, M. (eds) *(1988)* Relative freedoms. *Milton Keynes/Philadelphia: Open University Press.*

Using Eichler to Inform Family Leisure Research

Laurene A. Rehman

University of Waterloo

Intrroduction

The term 'family' may cause one to think of a variety of people (e.g., mothers, fathers, children, grandparents, aunts, uncles). These concepts spring to mind as a result of our societal and cultural backgrounds and have been constructed through a number of organizations including the media, and educational and religious institutions. From these forces, people have developed images of what an 'ideal' family constitutes. This 'ideal' tends to consist of a mother, a father, 2.5 children, a house, a pet, and a car and has continued to be reified through the institutions mentioned earlier. As a result, people are continuously bombarded by images of what constitutes a 'traditional' or 'nuclear' family. Yet, even though this 'ideal' no longer exists for the most part, due to the changes occurring within family types (e.g., single parents, lesbian couples, gay couples, remarried couples), these traditional images continue to remain a strong influence upon today's families (Eichler and Bullen, 1986).

The significance of this traditional influence can be seen in the predominance of research being conducted on the family which continues to focus upon 'white', middle to upper class, heterosexual, married, 'nuclear' couples. This research has maintained a traditional focus and has not recognized the increasing diversity of families or the variety of members' experiences. Therefore, the results obtained from this research have limited applicability to the majority of modern families.

In addition, Eichler and Bullen (1986) state that the results may even have had limited use in the past as the 'nuclear' family may never have constituted the majority of families. While examining journal accounts of families from the 1850s to 1870s in southwestern Ontario, Eichler and Bullen (1986) found that two generational family households were more likely the norm than a nuclear or single family household. This was because a newly married couple could rarely afford a separate household and, therefore, they tended to share accommodations with their relatives or unrelated families. These insights highlight the limited use for research which is solely focused upon nuclear families.

A nuclear family based approach has also been utilized by researchers to examine families' leisure activities. Much of the family leisure research has included similarly limited samples and, therefore, has also had limited applicability (Bialeschki and Pearce,

1997). However, feminist researchers have started to move beyond these narrowly-defined groups and have started to examine other families (e.g., lesbian mothers, couples with a child with a developmental disability) (Bialeschki and Pearce, 1997; Mactavish et al., 1997). This research has started to document a more accurate representation of the experiences of today's families.

By examining more diverse family types, these researchers have assisted in uncovering the gendered nature of the family and its leisure. Interactions occurring on a daily basis within the family both construct and deconstruct relations of power based on gender (Shaw, 1994). Relations of privilege and subordination become enacted through the negotiation of time, responsibilities, income, decisions, and relationships within the family (Shaw, 1994; Zvankovic et al. 1996). The family, therefore, serves as a gendered space. Eichler (1983) argued almost two decades ago that biases (e.g., monolithic, conservative, sexist, microstructural) have prevented researchers from recognizing the gendered nature of the family. These biases resulted in research which operated from the following assumptions: the nuclear family was the norm, there were 'natural' roles for different members of the family, there was a similarity of experience among members, changes did not occur, and only the 'household' unit was important (Eichler, 1983). Although Eichler outlined these biases several decades ago, many are still apparent in modern research. Within this paper, the family leisure research will be critically examined to determine: where these biases are still evident in present analyses, where these biases have been removed, and how researchers should advance in the future.

Evidence of biases in family leisure research

This section will explore some areas where problems remain within the family leisure literature, as well as some of the impacts they may be having upon families within society.

'The family that plays together, stays together?'

Eichler's (1983) concerns can still be seen today in much of the family leisure research utilizing a social psychological perspective. These studies have tended to paint a 'rosy' picture, emphasizing that 'the family who plays together, stays together' (Orthner and Mancini, 1990). It is believed that interacting together (as a family unit) will in some way strengthen the familial bonds (Orthner and Mancini, 1990). In other words, participating in leisure activities as a family is believed to have the following effects: a reduction in the possibility of parents becoming divorced, an increase in the likelihood that as children age they will continue to remain involved with their families, and an overall improvement in family interactions and communication (Crosby, 1991; Orthner, 1975; Orthner and Mancini, 1990). It is suggested that to obtain a 'long lasting' family, it is necessary to engage in family activities that involve parents and children interacting together on a regular basis. The idea of strengthening family bonds has become increasingly important to many people due to the increasing rate of divorce that is being portrayed in demographic statistics (Googins, 1991). Googins (1991) predicts that one half of all marriages begun in the early 1980's, in North America, will end in divorce. People are, therefore, being scared into finding ways to 'stay together' (Googins, 1991).

Yet, one of the largest problems with utilizing these statistics as evidence of the need for family leisure is that it ignores the social context of these families. There have been a variety of factors which have led to the increasing divorce rate, including: the development of a unified divorce law, the decrease in social disapproval surrounding divorce, and the unwillingness of people to accept emotional and/or physical abuse and marital difficulties (Eichler, 1986). By focusing solely upon the divorce statistics, the focus is taken away from the reasons behind the statistics.

In addition to focusing on increased family stability, social psychological leisure researchers (e.g., Orthner, 1980; Orthner and Mancini, 1990; Rosenblatt and Cunningham, 1976) have documented a number of other benefits of family leisure. These have included: increased marital interaction, increased parental satisfaction, and a buffering of stresses (Holman and Jacquart, 1988; Orthner and Mancini, 1990; Rosenblatt and Cunningham, 1976). Family leisure, therefore, has been portrayed in a relatively positive and beneficial manner by researchers operating from a social psychological paradigm.

By focusing primarily upon the benefits of family interaction, this approach to research has not recognized the dimensional and gendered nature of the family. Instead, a monolithic view has been adopted which has ignored the unenjoyable experiences. For example, conflicts and disagreements that may occur when the family is 'forced' into participating with one another are forgotten (Orthner and Mancini, 1990; Shaw, 1994; Shaw and Dawson, 1998). In a study of families from southwestern Ontario, Shaw and Dawson (1998) found that family leisure could produce not only a number of benefits (e.g., child development, 'fun', family interaction), but also a variety of constraints to the participants' enjoyment and satisfaction. The conflicts that resulted when people were encouraged to participate together, when they were less than enthusiastic about it, meant that participants did not always share an enjoyable experience (Shaw and Dawson, 1998). Shaw and Dawson (1998) found that family participation was especially problematic for adolescent children. These children wanted the chance to forge their own identities as separate from their families and were, therefore, interested in participating in leisure activities either alone or with their friends (Shaw and Dawson, 1998). Larson, Gillman, and Richards (1997) in a study of fathers, mothers, and young adolescents found a similar need by adolscents for time away from the family. They found that, for the adolescents, time away from parents with peers proved to be more enjoyable than time with their parents (Larson et al., 1997). As a result, family leisure may not be seen by all members of the family as an entirely beneficial experience (Larson et al., 1997; Shaw and Dawson, 1998).

Shaw and Dawson (1998) found a constraint to family leisure enjoyment for parents was related to an ideology of familism. Parents in the study commented that participating together as a family was a part of their 'duty of parenthood' or their obligation (Shaw and Dawson, 1998). In other words, family leisure could sometimes operate as something they were required to do, as opposed to something they were interested in, or wanted to do. Parents were concerned about serving as good role models for their children, about assisting in their child's development, and ensuring their children had adequate physical activity. In order to ensure these positive circumstances ensued for their children, the parents felt they were required to facilitate their families' leisure experiences. This issue seemed to be even more important for the single-parent households. Single parents were spending the same amount of time per week in family leisure activities as the double parent households, however, the single parents were performing these activities by themselves and without the assistance of another parent. In other words, the activities in the double parent households did not always involve both parents participating with their children but could include one parent or the other, while in the single parent households the sole parent was involved in all family activities. Therefore, the single parents were contributing a greater amount of their individual time to family leisure activities.

These unique insights into the multi-faceted experiences of family leisure, however, cannot be obtained without adopting a more critical and multi-dimensional approach to examining family leisure than has been used by many leisure researchers. Therefore, future research should recognize not only the 'rosy side' of family leisure, but also the less enjoyable (Shaw, 1997). As well, it is important to recognize the 'baggage' that researchers carry with them into their research. For example, one must question what the term 'family' means and what connotations are associated with it. The recognition of the socially and culturally constructed nature of the word 'family' will ensure that researchers are able to obtain a true representation of what constitutes a 'family's' leisure, rather than simply assuming that all family leisure is beneficial.

Gender roles: Mother and father as static entities?

Another area where evidence of biases continues to remain in family leisure research is in the examination of gender roles. Eichler (1983) explains that we have used gender roles as a means of examining the differences between men and women. For example, women may have several roles including mother, wife, sister, daughter, while men may also have a number of roles including father, husband, brother, son. Certain expectations are carried with each role in regard to what is considered appropriate behaviours, actions, and attitudes (Barnett and Baruch, 1985). As well, the simple knowledge of these expectations may constrain or shape how an individual acts in certain situations. As a result, women operating within the mothering role are expected to be nurturing, caring, and attentive to their children and/or partner(s) (Crosby, 1991). The problem with this approach is that it does not allow for change or negotiation of roles. The roles of mother or father (for example) are not static entities, but instead are fluid concepts that include a variety of life situations, challenges, and benefits.

Therefore, before one can move beyond 'biased' family research, it is necessary to recognize the fluidity of life roles. It is not possible to simply compartmentalize people's life roles (e.g., mother, father, son, daughter) and assume that these terms are universal and stable concepts. Instead, researchers must allow for individuals' or participants' subjective interpretations of these roles to ensure they are an accurate representation of their life situations.

Women and the ethic of care

A final area of family leisure research that is less apparent in its biases focuses upon women and the ethic of care. Gilligan (1982) was one of the first researchers to examine the ethic of care in relation to women. In an analysis of three different research projects she conducted, Gilligan (1982) found very different modes of thinking for men and women. She argued women tended to define themselves in the context of human relationships and to judge their self-worth on the basis of their ability to care (Gilligan, 1982). As a result, women valued caring, nurturing, and the development of relationships higher than other concepts (e.g., justice, objectivity, rationality) (Gilligan,

1982). These relationships produced a sense of interdependence for the women with the people around them (Gilligan, 1982). Therefore, paying attention to one's own needs became seen as selfish, while the protection of others was valued (Gilligan, 1982).

When Gilligan (1982) tried to match these findings with traditional theories and research, she realized the gender-neutral stance to the traditional approaches. For example, when Kohlberg's six stages of moral development were matched with her results, women were found to be deficient in their moral development and reasoning (Gilligan, 1982). This was because relationships were considered less important than 'objectively, fair, or just resolutions to moral dilemmas' (Gilligan, 1982, p. 20). In other words, if Kohlberg's stages of moral development were applied universally to men and women, women's more 'subjective' approaches to reasoning would be devalued, while men's more 'objective' approaches would be valued.

In order to counteract the gender-blind approach of these traditional theories, Gilligan (1982) concluded that one must recognize and address the confusion that has occurred throughout history because women and men have been speaking different languages while assuming they have been using the same. Once society's eyes have been opened to this fact, then they will be better equipped to address the existing inequities (Gilligan, 1982). Gilligan (1982) argued this will not only result in a better understanding 'of relations between the sexes but also [give] rise to a more comprehensive portrayal of adult work and family relationships' (p. 174).

Gilligan's (1982) research on the ethic of care has highlighted that women's greater concerns for social responsibility and social obligations places a constraint upon their lives and personal situations as 'others' are often placed before 'self' (Gilligan, 1982). This placement of others before self results in women performing duties and tasks for others before thinking of their own needs. Henderson (1990) has highlighted how this constraint may impact upon women's leisure by reducing their sense of entitlement to participation. Women may feel they are less entitled to their own leisure and must place the needs of others before their own due to the ethic of care. As a result, women may feel they have less of a 'right' to time for themselves (Henderson, 1990).

However, care must be taken when assuming women are inherently or biologically more caring than men. Bem (1993) identifies several major flaws with this emphasis on women's biological differences including: it ignores the role of social context, it ignores the effect of psychological gendering, and it ignores the fact that many of these supposedly 'inherent' differences could disappear in some social contexts. Further, focusing on 'caring' may lead to a devaluation of women's other capabilities. Labeling women as different from men and sustaining this process through the examination of the various characteristics existing between men and women may contribute to what Bem (1993) refers to as gender polarization. Labeling women as nurturing and men as objective or rational does not allow for the many finer differentiations occurring both between and within each gender. Instead, a two-tiered scale is created with women placed at one end and men at the other and a boundary is established between the two. This ignores the fact that many women may not value caring as their primary role and many men may ascribe to the nurturing caretaker position (e.g., a male nurse).

Tong (1989) has raised a similar concern about the concept of the ethic of care. She questions whether women's role as carers has truly been a proud celebration of womanhood, or whether it has instead been simply a strategy for survival (Tong, 1989). Have women acted as caregivers and nurturers solely as a means of surviving in a patriarchal world or have they freely chosen this role?

Care must, therefore, be taken not to assume the traditional association of women with domestic labour and the family has been a result of choice or preference (Tom, 1993). Further, assuming caring comes 'naturally' to women, neglects the significance of socialization and the whole process through which indoctrination of values occurs (Baines, Evans, and Neysmith, 1991). Women are taught to be caregivers right from a young age. For example, the Fisher Price toy company has a commercial on television which shows a little girl learning to cook just like her mother, but at her own 'baking centre'. At the same time, one must be careful when raising a debate about nurturing not to de-value its role and women's accomplishments in relation to it. Some of these advancements can be seen through the 'caring professions' of nursing, social work, and teaching. Within each of these professions women have made huge advancements into the realm of paid labour. Therefore, one should examine the concept of the ethic of care with an open and critical eye, rather than a patronizing one. This critical eye should recognize that the ethic of care may operate as a constraint to some women (and men), but does not necessarily exist for all.

Evidence of a removal of biases

Despite biases still remaining within family leisure research, there has also been increased recognition and removal of many. Just as families have been changing, so has the research conducted upon these families. Due in part to the advancements of feminist leisure researchers, there has been an increased recognition of the diversity in family experiences. As well, people have started to realize that this diversity carries over into a family's leisure activities. This realization has resulted in a greater inclusion and examination of 'what is family leisure?'. As a result, family leisure research has started to move away from a narrow focus and has instead begun to adopt a more dimensional approach. This section will examine areas where a more diverse approach can be seen in family leisure research, including: the topic of leisure as resistance, the recognition of a non-universal family existence, and uncovering the guilt of fathers.

Leisure as resistance to family leisure

By adopting a more critical and diverse approach to examining family leisure, it has been possible to recognize a new benefit of leisure—leisure as a form of resistance. That is, leisure has been found to serve as a means of resisting traditional socialized gender roles for some women (e.g., Freysinger and Flannery, 1992; Bialeschki and Michener, 1994). This is because leisure may provide a sense of empowerment for women and enable them to feel they have a right to a leisure of their own (separate from that of the family) (Freysinger and Flannery, 1992). These feelings of empowerment are developed as women gain a sense of competence from mastering new skills through personal leisure activities (Freysinger and Flannery, 1992). Further, these feelings of empowerment may offset some of the social obligations and social responsibilities (noted earlier in relation to the ethic of care) that may constrain women's personal leisure. For example, Freysinger and Flannery (1992) in a longitudinal study of women found that personal leisure provided women with freedom from some of their other life roles (e.g., wife, partner, mother) and also a freedom from the devaluation of these roles. It enabled the women to become aware of themselves and to challenge their definitions of self. As a result, these women felt they had a 'right' to pursue their own leisure outside of the family (Freysinger and Flannery, 1992).

Bialeschki and Michener (1994), while conducting interviews with fifty-three mothers reaching the end of their active role as mothers, found a similar benefit from personal leisure. Leisure provided the women with a chance to 'focus on self' and to, thereby, recognize the role for self as separate from responsibilities to others (Bialeschki and Michener, 1994). However, the chance to focus upon self had not always existed for these women, they commented that the focus upon self had not been possible during their active mothering stage. Rather, the ability to think of oneself had only returned to them (as it had existed before they had children) after their active mothering role was finished. Now that their social responsibilities were being reduced as their children 'left the nest', they were then able to bring a focus back to themselves. This movement back to recognizing the self was referred to as 'full circle mothering' (Bialeschki and Michener, 1994) and enabled the women to escape from the traditional gender roles associated with motherhood (e.g., nurturer, caretaker).

The awareness that leisure can operate as a form of resistance to traditional gender relations would not have been possible if a more critical examination had not been conducted of the family. If this group of feminist researchers had simply continued to assume that family leisure activities were beneficial to all, then the recognition of personal leisure as a form of resistance would not have been recognized. Instead, people would have continued to assume that all members of the family benefited equally from family leisure. As well, the importance of 'time away from family' for women to forge their own personal identities would not have been realized.

Recognition of a 'non-universal family' existence

There has been an increased recognition that much of the research conducted on family leisure has utilized privileged participants. By utilizing only 'white', middle to upper class, well-educated, heterosexual couples, the predominant number of families are being ignored. Yet, despite the fact that researchers are starting to recognize the limitations of their work and that a 'universal family' does not exist, few people have examined other groups.

Tirone (1997) is one researcher who has moved beyond some of these privileged groups. While conducting a study on the leisure of women of South Asian descent, she found that the women sustained alternative definitions and meanings of family from European and North American women (Tirone, 1997). For these women, family was 'central' to their definitions of self. As a result, they considered time spent with the family and family activities to be more important than time for self, 1997. In fact, time for self was considered to be 'selfish'.

The benefits that the alternative meanings of family that Tirone's (1997) study highlighted can be seen if one attempts to apply a North American or European translation to the South Asian women's definitions. A eurocentric analysis of the women's definitions of family may lead one to assume the women were constrained by an ethic of care. The women's concerns and emphasis upon family may have resulted in little time for themselves as separate from the family. Yet, Tirone (1997) found that the women did not feel constrained by their concerns for family, rather they felt people who had less of an attachment to their families would be more likely to be constrained as they would not have as many social connections or networks to draw upon.

Hunter and Whitson (1992), in a study of Canadian women who were living in a small town, provided confirmation that many North American women who do not have strong and/or close family connections do suffer from constraints to their personal leisure. They found that the majority of the women were isolated from their extended families and had to perform all of the household duties and care for their children on their own.

Bialeschki and Pearce (1997) conducted another study which has moved beyond traditional research populations. Their study focused upon lesbian mothers and their experiences with leisure. Leisure was recognized as time for self, time for the couple, and time for the family. Time for self enabled the women to achieve a sense of relaxation. This time was possible because the women had a mutually egalitarian sharing of household responsibilities. Leisure for the couple allowed them to have a chance to share time together; however, this time often took a lot of effort to negotiate. Finally, leisure for the family enabled the women to develop bonds with their children. This time also enabled the women to validate and legitimate their alternative kinship structures and served as a challenge to the norm of heterosexuality. Therefore, the lesbian mothers developed similar definitions of family leisure as previously examined, yet they were also able to move beyond these traditional definitions and provide some additional insights (e.g., the benefits of egalitarian relationships, the challenges associated with negotiating time for the couple).

Yet, despite the insights of Tirone (1997) and Bialeschki and Pearce (1997), the majority of research on family leisure has continued to assume there is some type of 'universal family' existence and that findings from privileged populations can easily be transferred to other groups. Therefore, unless further research is conducted with non-white and non-privileged populations, the definitions society has of family will continue to be Eurocentric and narrow. Future research should move beyond traditional research samples and should strive to examine families from a wide variety of life situations and contexts. The challenges, however, with conducting research into more diverse families will include: determining how to gain access to these families, ensuring the researcher does not impose their own views upon the families, and ensuring the families subjective interpretations are obtained.

Uncovering the guilt of fathers

A final area of research that has arisen from the adoption of a more critical approach to family leisure has uncovered the guilt of fathers in relation to their role within the family. LaRossa (1995) found that there is a difference between the culture of fatherhood and the conduct. The culture of fatherhood refers to fathers' desires to be a part of the family and its activities, while the conduct of fatherhood serves as a documentation of fathers' actual behaviours (LaRossa, 1995). Although LaRossa (1995) found that the majority of fathers wanted to be a functional part of their families, they tended to be functionally absent.

This discrepancy between desired and actual behaviour resulted in feelings of guilt for many of the fathers in the study (LaRossa, 1995). Fathers experienced guilt over their lack of participation and assistance within the family unit and their lack of assistance with the organization and facilitation of the family's leisure activities

(LaRossa, 1995). As well, White (1994), in a study of eleven fathers, found that the men were also concerned about their children's perception of their role within the family. In other words, the fathers experienced guilt over their children's recognition of their minor role within the family's daily routine (White, 1994). The fathers believed they were seen by their children more as 'friends' with the ability to grant privileges and the power to accommodate the desires of their children, while the mothers were believed to play a greater role in their children's lives. As a result, many of the fathers commented about feelings of dissatisfaction they had with fatherhood and their father-child relationships.

Yet, despite these feelings of dissatisfaction and their desire for greater involvement with their children, most of the men did not spend much time with their children (White, 1994). White found that most of the time fathers spent with children was on the weekends and usually involved sports activities. Work pressures were used to justify the fathers' low involvement with their children.

The pressures and guilt placed on fathers may be even greater for men who are single fathers (LaRossa, 1995). These individuals may not have the assistance of another care-giver in the household and may, therefore, face additional challenges to developing their father-child relationship. However, little is known about the challenges of single fathers, as the predominance of the literature has focused upon married men, and more specifically 'white' married men.

Therefore, further research is needed into this new area of research which has started to recognize the challenges associated with fatherhood. Questions to explore could include: What role do fathers play in their children's lives? Is this role changing with the changing nature of families? Does this role differ for single fathers? What impact does race/ethnicity have upon fatherhood?

How does research advance from here?

Much of the research on family leisure continues to maintain a biased approach as outlined by Eichler (1983), several decades ago, in reference to family research. This biased approach has resulted in the following assumptions: family leisure is always beneficial, gender roles are fixed or stable entities, and women are constrained by an ethic of care. Utilizing this type of approach when conducting family leisure research has resulted in a relatively static perception of the family with little room for fluidity or change. Yet, there has also been increasing evidence of the removal of these biases. For example, the benefits of leisure as a form of resistance have been recognized, there has become increasing realization that there is not a 'universal family' existence, and the guilt of fathers in relation to their role within the family unit has been examined.

To continue these advancement within family leisure research, it is necessary to recognize Eichler's (1983) original proposition that we adopt a 'multi-dimensional' approach to family research using a 'feminist science' approach. This alternative view point is very similar to one that Henderson (1994) elaborates upon in an examination of feminism. Henderson (1994) refers to her approach as 'feminist empiricism' and explains how it can be used to uncover problems within traditional science and research. This approach would involve recognizing the gendered nature of the family, recognizing the subjectivities involved in family roles, recognizing that caring is only one of the roles that women and men fulfill, and examining other ways that the family can be considered a gendered space which not only includes members, but may also exclude.

References

Baines, C., Evans, P., and Neysmith, S. (1991) *Women's caring: Feminist perspectives on social welfare.* Toronto: McClelland and Stewart, Inc.

Barnett, R.C., and Baruch, G.K. (1985) *Gender and stress.* New York: Free Press.

Bem, S.L. (1993) *The lenses of gender: Transforming the debate on sexual inequality.* New Haven and London: Yale University Press.

Bialeschki, M.D., and Michener, S. (1994) 'Re-entering leisure: Transition within the role of motherhood', *Journal of Leisure Research* Vol. 26: No. 1: pp. 57–74.

Bialeschki, M.D., and Pearce, K.D. (1997) "'I don't want a lifestyle — I want a life": The effect of role negotiations on the leisure of lesbian mothers', *Journal of Leisure Research* Vol. 29: No. 1: pp. 113–131.

Crosby, F.J. (1991) *Juggling: the unexpected advantages of balancing career and home for women and their families.* Toronto: Maxwell and Macmillan Canada.

Eichler, M. (1983) *Families in Canada today: Recent changes and their policy consequences.* Toronto: Gage.

Eichler, M., and Bullen, M. (1986) *Families in Canada: An introduction.* Toronto: The Ontario Institute for Studies in Education.

Freysinger, V.J., and Flannery, D. (1992) 'Women's leisure: Affiliation, self-determination, empowerment and resistance?', *Loisir et Societe/Society and Leisure* Vol. 14: No. 1: pp. 303–322.

Gilligan, C. (1982) In a different voice. Cambridge, MA: Harvard University Press.

Googins, B.K. (1991) *Work/family conflicts: Private lives-public responses.* Westport, CT: Greenwood Publishing Group, Inc.

Henderson, K.A. (1990) 'The meaning of leisure for women: An integrative review of the research', *Journal of Leisure Research* Vol. 22: No. 4: pp. 228–243.

——— (1994) 'Perspectives on analyzing gender, women, and leisure', *Journal of Leisure Research* Vol. 26: No. 2: pp. 119–137.

Holman, T.B., and Jacquart, M. (1988) 'Leisure activity patterns and marital satisfaction: A further test', *Journal of Marriage and the Family* Vol. 50: No. 1: pp. 69–78.

Hunter, P.L., and Whitson, D.J. (1992) 'Women, leisure and familism: Relationships and isolation in small town Canada'. *Leisure Studies* Vol. 10: No. 4: pp. 219–233.

LaRossa, R. (1995) 'Fatherhood and social change', in E.D. Nelson and B.W. Robinson (eds) *Gender in the 1990's: Images, realities, and issues.* Scarborough, ON: Nelson Canada, pp. 365–379.

Larson, R.W., Gillman, S.A., and Richards, M.H. (1997) 'Divergent experiences of family leisure: Fathers, mothers, and young adolescents', *Journal of Leisure Research* Vol. 29: No. 10: pp. 78–97.

Mactavish, J., Schleien, S., and Tabourne, C. (1997) 'Patterns of family recreation in families that include children with a developmental disability', *Journal of Leisure Research* Vol. 29: No. 1: pp. 21–46.

Orthner, D.K. (1975) 'Leisure activity patterns and marital satisfaction over the marital career'. *Journal of Marriage and the Family* Vol. 37: No. 1: pp. 91–102.

Orthner, D.K., and Mancini, J.A. (1990) 'Leisure impacts on family interaction and cohesion', *Journal of Leisure Research* Vol. 22: No. 2: pp. 125–137.

Rosenblatt, P.C., and Cunningham, M. (1976) 'Television watching a family tension', *Journal of Marriage and the Family* Vol. 38: No. 2: pp. 103–111.

Shaw, S.M. (1994) 'Gender, leisure, and constraint: Towards a framework for the analysis of women's leisure', *Journal of Leisure Research* Vol. 26: No. 1: pp. 8–22.

—— (1997) 'Controversies and contradictions in family leisure: An analysis of conflicting paradigms', *Journal of Leisure Research* Vol. 29: No. 1: pp. 98–112.

Shaw, S.M., and Dawson, D. (1998) *Active family lifestyles: Motivations, benefits, constraints, and participation.* A report to the Canadian Fitness and Lifestyle Research Association.

Tirone, S. (1997) *Leisure in the lives of youth of South–Asian descent.* Doctoral dissertation. University of Waterloo.

Tom, A. (1993) 'Women's lives complete: Methodological concerns', in B.C. Long and S.E. Kahn (eds) *Women, work, and coping: A multidisciplinary approach to workplace stress.* Quebec: McGill-Queen's University Press, pp. 32–50.

Tong, R. (1989) *Feminist thought: A comprehensive introduction.* Boulder, CA: Westview Press.

White, N.R. (1994) 'About fathers: Masculinity and the social construction of fatherhood'. *ANZJS* Vol. 30: No. 2: pp. 119–131.

Zvonkovic, A.M., K.M. Greaves, C.J. Schmiege, and L.D. Hall. (1996) 'The marital construction of gender through work and family decisions: A qualitative analysis'. *Journal of Marriage and the Family* Vol. 58, No. 1: pp. 91–100.

Mothers on Family Activity Holidays Overseas

Jenny Anderson

Head of Marketing and Leisure, Southampton Institute

Introduction

The aim of this paper is to examine motivation towards the family holiday from the perspective of mother and child where separate provision is offered for parent and child. A specialist overseas watersports tour operator supported this research. Over two hundred questionnaires were completed as a part of the welcome briefing in resorts in Greece, Spain and Turkey. There were separate questionnaires for parent and child. In addition in depth interviews were conducted with mothers, fathers and young people on a watersports holiday on a Spanish resort.

As today's parents and children become accustomed to separate leisure provision at home and on holiday they have become skilled consumers. As market opportunities expand to meet this demand it might be argued that families are losing some of the skills and experience to spend longer periods of leisure together. The separation of family leisure provision has become a marketing opportunity. The paper explores attitudes of mothers, fathers and children to this development.

There have been growing pressures in the negotiation of personal leisure time. This is particularly true for parents of young children who are also in paid employment. As part of the 'juggling generation', these working parents are striving to run homes efficiently, pursue personal leisure activities, as well as meeting the ever growing leisure aspirations of their children by ferrying them from one event to another. Many of these 'time jugglers' clearly fit into a 'cash rich-time poor' category. This is usually an intensive stage in the life cycle where a combination of work, family and home commitments all impact on parent lifestyles at the same time.

The structure of society is changing and life stages are harder to predict. Parenthood results in a shift from shared marital activities to child centred family recreational patterns (Horna, 1989). As today's young adults strive to maintain 'young' lifestyles, and build capital assets, parenthood is delayed. In the UK the average age of a woman having her first child is 28 years. Whilst there are growing numbers of single parent families, the focus in this paper is on two parent families who make up 80% of households with young children. There is an emphasis on high income, high leisure spending, dual earner families.

The aim of this paper is to examine motivation towards family activity holidays from the perspective of the parent, and of the child, where there is separate provision for parent and child. Where possible, the differing attitudes of mothers and fathers towards sport as a holiday activity will also be explored. In comparison to other women, the leisure of women in higher socioeconomic income groups is more varied, involves a greater degree of participation in out-of-home activities, takes place with a wider range of social contacts and is more geographically dispersed (Kay, 1996). Where women and men work within the family, family and leisure roles are becoming more symmetrical but this pattern is clearly not complete nor universal (Kay, 1996).

The parent chooses sporting activities on holiday to satisfy his/her personal needs and aspirations, and also as part of his/her role as a parent on holiday, to provide activities for children and meet their needs and aspirations. Because parents frequently make the initial decisions to encourage children to participate in sporting activity, an understanding of family leisure decision making is critical (Howard and Madrigal, 1990). In sailing and windsurfing, the role of parents has been highlighted as significant in getting children afloat (Anderson, 1994, Anderson, 1996). One third of young people are introduced to watersports on holiday, half of them in the UK and half abroad (Anderson, 1996)

To explore this further, a profile of changes in family leisure in the home and family sporting participation outside the home environment is developed. Again, sailing and windsurfing are used as examples. The negotiation of leisure time within the family unit with an emphasis on the role of the mother as an adult, and as a parent is discussed. As the women's role in the workplace evolves, are these changes reflected in the negotiation of leisure time within the family unit where both parents work?

In defining family leisure in the home environment, Larson and Gillman (1997) include activities which families perform together and all leisure activities in the home whether undertaken together or separately. Orthner (1975) describes family recreation activities as individual, parallel and joint. Individual recreation includes those activities which a family member performs alone or with non family members, either within the home or in the community. Parallel activities are those that occur within the family shared space or time, but do not include substantial amounts of interaction. Joint or shared leisure which involves the couple and is also assumed to include other family members, is found to have the greatest impact of family satisfaction, interaction and stability.

The notion of families spending happy periods of 'joint' leisure together is a persistent marketing image. Family togetherness has long been being part of the 'mythology of tourism' (Seaton and Tagg, 1995). However, it could be argued that there is a growing trend of separation of leisure within family groups. Changing pressures from the workplace with flexible hours, 24–hour working, short term temporary contracts, longer working hours, fewer quality jobs, mean parents are simply not around to provide child care at those times when they have traditionally been in the home.

Within the home environment, the development of central heating and of the 'electronic bedroom' has ensured the spread of the family through the home. Provision of customised leisure experiences for parent and child has become a market opportunity through the commodification of leisure. Commercial providers, understanding the time pressures on today's parents, have made available alternatives ways of occupying children's time in the home environment.

In the extended home environment safety fears have altered the nature of young people's daily leisure in many areas of Britain. Young people who were once allowed to play out on the streets and local neighbourhoods now spend time in 'safer' organised activities such as holiday play schemes, after-school clubs and crèches. Perhaps, it could be argued, as a result of this, families are losing some of the skills and experience to spend longer periods of joint leisure together, and are therefore more inclined to select commercial alternatives.

The argument being developed here is that, in families where both parents work, the 'programming' of young people's leisure time is becoming the 'normal' experience. As mothers have moved into the workplace, whether part or full time, alternative child care is sought for after school, and school holidays. Parents have become accustomed to paying for child care and for their children's leisure experiences. Parents, rather than children are deciding how their children's leisure is spent. Rather than just for play, relaxation and child care, this leisure time may be used for self improvement, learning new skills such as sport, art, drama or nature study.

Family leisure decision making

Literature on the role of family leisure and home life is multiplying. All social groups, families included, exert a powerful influence on their members to conform to particular values and norms which results in a negotiated compromise rather than an enactment of any one individual's desires (Crompton, 1981). The holiday activities of each member of the group will be affected by the preferences of the other members of the group. However in this context it should be noted that most previous research in related areas has been based on the purchase of leisure products rather than tourism products.

Early research indicated that the man, as head of the household, made all of the family's decisions unilaterally. From that, the notion that the wife was the purchasing agent was added. Sharp and Mott (1995) suggested decisions were shared with differing levels of responsibility depending on the nature of the project. Davis (1976) identified sub decisions such as when and where to purchase. This was taken further by Jenkins (1978) who explored the role of family members within each sub decision. Jenkins found wives had a lower input into these decisions. This work was taken further by looking at family groups of varying compositions.

Filiatrault and Ritchie (1980) found that husbands dominate decisions where there are children, and the relative influence varied more between husbands and wives across sub decisions, and varied more in families than in couples. One study (Sharp and Mott, 1956) found joint husband-wife decisions were more likely in high income families than low income families, whilst Wolgast (1958) indicated the reverse. Thornton *et al.* (1997), in reviewing literature to date, suggests that results are confusing.

In a study of decisions made by families visiting Alaska on holiday (Nichols and Snepenger, 1988), 66% families employed a joint decision making mode, 13% of households were wife dominant, and 21% were husband dominant decisions. Families with husband dominant decisions were more likely to be involved in outdoor pursuits such as ski or snow mobile, camping, hunting. As watersports are so male orientated, perhaps this is significant? This is a complex area and more work is needed into the overt and covert nature of gender roles in such decisions.

Mothers and leisure

For mothers taking part in leisure with children the experience is often seen as an extension to the parental responsibility rather than as leisure activities within their own right. Thus these experiences are still pleasurable but still more like work than leisure. It is this final point which is of greatest interest in this paper — the significance of personal leisure to mothers within the family — and the negotiation of that time for individual leisure within shared space and time. The personal satisfaction from extended family leisure time depends very much on individual needs and aspirations. Do fathers, mothers and children want the same type of fulfilment from family activity holidays or do they have different priorities?

In reviewing contemporary leisure research Kay (1998) notes it is the way in which family leisure time is available for women which has implications for their leisure activities. Deem (1982) in her research on women and leisure found that many women felt constrained about the time they had for leisure. Working women have less leisure time than men (Wimbush, 1987). Factors such as when periods of free time occur, whether they occur regularly, predictably and as blocks of time or whether they arise more spontaneously, in an irregular pattern of short time spells has implications for the way in which such time can be used for leisure (Deem, 1986).

Women may also have a reduced entitlement to their own leisure as a result of their commitment to creating successful leisure experiences for their families:

> There is a contradiction between the pleasure and satisfaction that women accrue in helping to create positive family leisure experiences and the organisational and emotional work that is needed to make these experiences successful. (Shaw, 1992 in Daly, 1996: p. 172)

Women are more likely to put aside their own leisure interests even if it is shared leisure (Freysinger, 1995). Time is consequently unequally allocated within households. Different entitlements for work and leisure has given rise to 'time collisions' in gender relations (Pasero, 1994, p. 186 in Daly, 1996). However, as Rapoport and Rapoport (in Critcher, 1995: p. 68) emphasise, the issue in families is not just about time:

> There are barriers and frustrations; sacrifices and trade offs, conflicts and struggles that occur in the process of evolving satisfying life styles. The construction of life styles involves dealing with remittances and constraints.

Mothers, the ethic of care and leisure

Men and women tend to share views about the value and importance of spending leisure together as a family, but women are more likely to define that part of it as work (Shaw, 1992). Fathers are more likely to perceive time alone with children as leisure and a source of satisfaction (Freysinger, 1994). Shaw (1992) feels that this is perhaps because fathers see this as a choice. As fathers are now more involved in day to day parenting, and as more mothers work, new patterns of support may be emerging.

Mothers' activities with children are often seen as an extension to the parental role responsibility rather than leisure activities in their own right, rendering those experiences as pleasurable but more like work than leisure. Women may sense a lack of entitlement to their own leisure, their self interest in this area being subsumed in an 'ethic of care' and their lives are structured in taking care of others (Kay, 1996). The ethic of care has received considerable attention in the literature. Mothers may get less enjoyment out of family leisure because they may put others before themselves (Henderson, 1991).

Henderson *et al.* (1996) assert that although an ethic of care can be a positive aspect of woman's development, and caring for others is a positive attribute for all to have, several research studies have documented how this 'ethic' constrains women's leisure. Kay (1996) also remarks that:

> Ethic of care is the continual and overriding responsibility which many women feel for servicing the needs of other people, so that their lives are structured around taking care of others. (p. 152)

Ethic of care is often linked with a woman's lack of sense of entitlement to leisure. A woman's leisure may be constrained by feeling guilty about pursuing her own pleasure instead of attending to family obligations (Harrington and Dawson, 1995). And Samuel (1996: p. 80) also notes that "The ideology of families, which reifies women's care-giving roles, [is] another way in which the ethic of care can be seen as a leisure constraint".

Kay (1996) also suggests that women's leisure is inextricably bound to and linked with their non leisure roles. Wimbush (1987) suggests that the motherhood role is socially construed as one where the 'good mother' is portrayed as someone who devotes her personal time, energy and resources to attending to the needs and welfare of her children, husband and home. She believes that the central ideology of motherhood is the notion of self denial (or lack of entitlement):

> For women, having children brings the expectation that they will give up or restrict their involvement for the sake of family needs. (Wimbush, 1987: p. 23)

Henderson *et al.* (1996) take this further by exploring the concept of a mothers' perception of her entitlement to leisure for her self.

Many questions remain unanswered about values, meanings and commitments of time as they are experienced on a daily basis. The politics of time is central to our understanding of current gender politics (Daly, 1996) and, in a sense, attitudes to the ethic of care. What is of interest in this paper is whether mothers' attitudes towards personal leisure, and caring for their children in the 'home' environment are similar to attitudes to their attitudes towards personal leisure on holiday. Again the focus is on the dual income working family.

Family holidays

There is anecdotal evidence that the concept of the programming of children's leisure may be transferred to the family holiday so that parent and child may go to the same place, yet have separate and different experiences. Orthner's classification (1975) of family leisure may therefore be applied to extended periods of leisure time such as family holidays.

For those who can afford them, organised family holidays have undergone evolutionary changes over the last twenty years. This is particularly true for higher income working parents coping with the longer working hours and increasing pressures of modern life. Parents feel 'they deserve a break'; essentially they have a choice — whether to select individual, parallel or joint holiday experiences. Parallel leisure activities are central to this paper i. e. family activities in the same space and time but without significant interaction on holiday. For nuclear, dual income families with children the shift from joint to parallel leisure in the home environment has been mirrored to family holidays. It is the attitude of parent and child to this provision which is of prime interest in this paper.

Overseas activity holidays

The main factors impacting on the growth of activity holidays in the UK and overseas are the economic climate and levels of confidence, consumer desires for more adventure and personal satisfaction from their leisure time and the increase in numbers of families looking for a holiday to suit a wide variety of family members (Mintel, 1995). Beioley (1996) recognises that the element of choice of activity is becoming increasingly important to families and has been developed by Centre Parcs. For those inclined, family holidays have moved on from 'sun, sea and sand' to the realms of learning new skills, getting fitter, and self improvement. In the acquisition and development of sporting skills' for both child and parent, the holiday is taking on a more prominent role. Activity holiday takers are more adventurous, more curious and out-going, place more weight on self improvement and would rather be busy than just relax (Leisure Consultants, 1992)

Prospects for the UK activity holiday sector are seen to be strong because of a fragmentation in leisure interest (Mintel, 1995). Activity holiday takers are more likely to be younger and from the AB social groups as a whole' Beioley notes this is particularly so in the cases of golf and sailing (Beioley, 1996). In addition the family market, as a part of the activity holiday market, is seen as being underdeveloped in the UK and having a particular potential for growth (Beioley, 1996).

There is little published information about activity holidays overseas; however there has been a growth in overseas inclusive tour operator provision of children's clubs. Mass market operators, such as Airtours and Thompsons, and niche operators, such as Club Med, Neilson, Sunsail and Mark Warner offer destinations with children's clubs, often with an element of instruction. There has also been an increase in the range of overseas activity holidays. It is estimated that watersports form 10 % of all activity holidays overseas (Beioley, 1996).

The context of this study into parent and child attitudes is family overseas sailing and windsurfing holidays where there is separate sporting provision. Traditionally the profile of watersports participants is male (80: 20), middle class and white (Anderson, 1994). As overseas watersports holidays at the height of the season are an expensive option, it is no surprise that the target group for this study are middle class, dual income, professional families — previously defined as the 'time jugglers'.

Children and family leisure decisions

The influence of children, originally ignored and later dismissed as having no influence, has attracted more attention. With the advent of sport tourism and growing interest in young people and sport, the roles of parents and children have come under greater scrutiny. Where a mother halts her career to care for children the father assumes a position of greater economic importance — with the potential for exerting more decision making power over holiday purchases. However, it is suggested mothers can harness the children in this decision (Filiatraut and Ritchie, 1980). However Thornton, having reviewed more general research on leisure related family decision making suggests children only possess a role in making small scale choices and none in major resources-binding infrequent purchases such as holidays. These pre-travel decisions remain firmly in the parents domain (Darley and Lim, 1986)

The main holiday is an expensive investment, emotionally, and financially. The interest is in whether the periods of extended leisure such as family holiday, reflect the every day patterns of leisure home environment, or whether they provide a contrast in terms of individual, parallel or joint leisure. Are the roles of mothers and fathers in the context of family leisure similar? There are many facets of this debate — the particular focus here is that of attitudes of parent and child towards sport on the holiday.

Research methodology

The methodology has two separate but related parts; research includes both qualitative and quantitative methods. Firstly, a self completion questionnaire was administered for parents and young people. Secondly, ethnographic in-depth interviews were carried out with parents and children at one sailing and windsurfing centre on the Mediterranean.

Self completion questionnaires were completed as a part of the welcome briefing in eight resorts in Greece, Spain and Turkey (n=145). In addition to an explanatory letter from the research team and tour operator to the centre managers, there were separate questionnaires for parent and child. Eighty child questionnaires and sixty five parent questionnaires were successfully completed over the summer of 1997. A specialist overseas watersports tour operator supported this research.

To complement the quantitative research, in depth interviews were conducted with mothers, fathers and young people at one watersports centre in mainland Spain. Sailing and windsurfing instruction were offered on the holiday with two hour sessions in the morning and afternoon. Royal Yacht Association (RYA) qualification assessments were available. There was a choice for family members — and the opportunity for young people to go into Surfbusters (5–12 years) or Sea Urchins (2–5) years. The 12 and overs joined adult classes. I spent a week at this centre on a family watersports holiday during which in-depth interviews were conducted. Every family group (n=15) with children was included in the interview schedule, with longer interviews of about an hour taking place with families with younger children. Notes taken in the interviews were written up every evening, and were word processed on return to the UK before being analysed qualitatively. In most instances young people were interviewed separately from their parents, (having previously gained permission from parents). It was more difficult to encourage younger people (the under 10s) to talk openly and it took longer to gain their confidence. Overall, interviews with this age group were less effective. The presentation of results includes both quantitative and qualitative data.

The families

As anticipated, two thirds of all families fell into the AB social classification. In terms of gross household income — half earned over £60,000 and one third earned over £70,000. Typical occupations were doctors, lecturers, teachers, managers and accountants. Two thirds of families (66%) had four family members on holiday, just under one fifth (17%) had five, and 14% had three members on holiday, while only 3% had two members, and 3% had not brought a member of family on holiday with them. The average age of children in the survey was 12, with young people of 14 years being the median, and 62% of the young people over 8 years were male.

Thirty of the 145 families completing the self completion questionnaires used child care facilities whilst on holiday. At home all parents had used relatives / friends for paid child care in the previous year. Half had used an after school club, and a third had employed a child minder or an au pair. These parents were skilled consumers of paid child care in the home environment and their children are used to being looked after by others. This pattern of child care was extended to the holiday situation.

Family watersports history

Dinghy sailing was the 'favourite' watersport for both young people (51%) and parents (61%). For young people, windsurfing (31%) was the next most popular watersport and, for parents, yachting (17%) and windsurfing (16%) were popular. One third (32%) of families owned a sailing boat, 29% owned a wind surfer, and 9% owned a yacht. A quarter of parents were members of the governing body (RYA).

In terms of experience a fifth of the young people had never participated in watersports, 17% had one years experience and 13% had two years. Only 9% had more than five years experience. Half of the young people (51%) had no watersports qualifications, and a third had Level Three Royal Yachting Association and above. Many of the fathers, in in-depth interviews, said they had done watersports when they were younger.

In terms of frequency of participation, half of parents were not committed serious watersport users in the home environment. Rather they were 'dabblers' who took watersports up seriously on holiday. This pattern was more marked for young people with over two thirds having participated in sailing or windsurfing only once or twice in the previous year. This was not anticipated at the outset of the survey.

When parents participate in watersports in the home environment they are more likely to participate with their children than without. In fact only 10% never participated with their children. There were differences between dinghy sailing, windsurfing and canoeing, dinghy sailers were more likely to participate as a family than with other watersports. This reflects the nature of the sport — many dinghies and yachts need at least two people to sail, but not many can accommodate four.

In exploring holiday booking, child and adult perceptions of understanding of the decisions were similar with half of the adults (53%) and almost half of the children (49%)

feeling that the whole family had contributed to the decision. Children saw mothers as being more dominant in decision making than the parents did themselves. Mothers processed 52% of all bookings. Similar research exploring the booking process on sporting courses for young people in the home environment indicated mothers process 80% of all bookings (Anderson, 1994). Again this was predictable. The following are summarised examples illustrating the point.

> Gillian made the initial holiday booking but her husband actually paid for the holiday. [Non sailing mother, husband, and teen age son]

> Sue does the hunting for the annual holiday and throws out suggestions to the family. She goes to Thomas Cooks for ideas but they book direct. Pete likes to make the holiday decision quite soon after the summer holiday so he can have something to look forward to. Pete always makes the final decision but Sue has a veto. Children, so far have always agreed with their choice. [Teacher, husband and three teenage children]

In terms of activities undertaken on holiday, motivations were similar. The activity that parents and young people most wanted to do on holiday was sailing, followed by windsurfing. Sailing was relatively more popular with parents and windsurfing was more popular with young people. For young people under 12, having fun (25%), followed by being with their family (22%) were aspects they most liked about family holidays. For older young people (over 12) the fact that their parents paid for all the extras was important.

There was less commonality between parents and children in deciding what was important to them about choosing this holiday. There was low correlation between factors that parents and children see as important. For parents the range of activities and courses on offer was the most important aspect of the choosing the holiday. For young people water quality, followed by range of equipment was the most important factor. Further qualitative research is needed to explore what the term 'water quality' means to young people (Table 1).

Table 1　　A comparison of factors seen to be very important by parent and child in choosing the holiday

	Child		Adult	
Range of activities	38%	(3)	65%	(1)
Range of courses	15%	(7)	59%	(2)
Water quality	46%	(1)	58%	(3)
Provision for children	38%	(3)	56%	(4)
Range of equipment	43%	(2)	54%	(5)
Wind strength	23%	(4)	37%	(6)
High performance equipment	20%	(6)	19%	(7)
Local culture	8%	(8)	19%	(8)

One of the features of these watersports holidays was that separate provision was made for children, including play and instruction in watersports. A key function of the questionnaire was to explore the motivation of parent and child towards this separate provision on holiday. There was a high level of correlation between the views of parents and young people when exploring the reasons for going into Surfbusters, i.e. separate child care (for 5–12 year olds). The joint identification of 'fun' and 'good competent instructors' is similar to surveys looking at young peoples' sports courses within the local community (Anderson, 1995). A further similarity is that young people value the opportunity to make new friends more highly than their parents. These results were not unexpected. Perhaps the fact that only half of parents claim that they put children into Surfbusters to give them time for their own sport is more surprising (Table 2).

Table 2:   A comparison of child and parent reasons for choosing to go to Surfbusters

	Parent		Child	
To have fun	80%	(1)	90%	(1)
To have good/competent instructors	53%	(2)	90%	(1)
To play safely (safe environment)	47%	(4)	83 %	(3)
To learn water skills	33%	(5)	53%	(4)
To gain on the water confidence	23%	(6)	41%	(5)
To make new friends	50%	(3)	33%	(6)
To make me like watersports*	7%	(8)	30%	(7)
To get fit	10%	(7)	7%	(8)
Because my parents want me to	7%	(9)	N/A	
Parent only				
Give you time for your own sport	53%			
Give you time for a rest	13%			

Contrast in motivation between mothers and fathers

Both mothers and fathers were asked what they most valued and enjoyed about their holiday. This was an open question. Without exception, women talked in terms of the safety and happiness of their families first. Many women then went on to talk about their progress in watersports, usually in terms overcoming adversity:

Teresa was very clear about her motivation for the holiday which was the sun, sea and being able to get out in a dinghy when she wanted to. "I want to be able to get away from the kids and know they are happy. In an ideal world I would get out in a boat with my husband and spend time with him". [Sailing mother of two active children]

Despite having to look after her 12 year old son more than she had originally planned Sue was happy because she was sailing to a high level. She felt it was important to her that the family did things together. Sue felt her family was unusual in that their teenage children actually enjoyed spending time with them. [Sailing mother, part time lecturer, three children]

Polly had appreciated the instructor because he was calm and never pushed, he was exactly what she needed to raise her confidence. Everything was taught in a logical manner. 'I do not want to be overstretched — I want to keep within my capability. I'm not fit and I am fifty — I do not do any sport at home. I want to keep within my limits. I have a tendonitis injury. I learned a skill, secure it, and then moved on. I could not believe I went out by myself I was surprised I could get the sail up. [Windsurfing mother, teacher, one teenage daughter on holiday, an older daughter at home]

In exploring the mother's role on holiday there were many examples where the holiday was seen as an extension of the mother's responsibilities:

In the second week there was a problem with the youngest son in a family of five — the age profile of participants in Surfbusters had become younger and their son had not wanted to join the much younger children. It meant that one of the parents had to sacrifice their own lessons to take him out in boats because he was not old enough to join the adult classes. This responsibility fell mainly to the mother.

Jill and her daughter were in the same beginners wind surf class. Most of the time Jill relinquished her parental responsibility to the instructor but at others she felt she had to take extra care. At one point Jill could hear herself nagging her daughter to keep head up or keep the sheet in. On the free sail day, when instructors were not responsible for the group she suddenly felt she was a mum again and realised that she had given up that responsibility before.

Holiday motivation and the father

In reviewing the most valued and enjoyable points of the holiday fathers were far more focused on the practical achievements on the water. They were more single minded about their performances in the sport:

John, a management consultant was very good wind surfer, his prime aim is to be out and about on the water when the wind blew. He was cross about the day before because he had been out with a woman in a two-person dinghy when the wind had really increased. He wanted to take the boat in and go out on a wind surfer but felt unable to let the woman down. *[Father of two young active children]*

Pete, a GP, was totally committed to sailing. At the first night welcome meal he searched for people with trapeze ability so he could sail at the level he wanted to. His highest point on the holiday was when he went out in the centre's largest most prestigious boat with the Centre manager — very few did this. *[Father of three teenagers]*

Jim, a bank manager, was a very competent wind surfer. There was some excellent windsurfing kit available and he wanted to try it all out in the right wind conditions before he went home. [Father of one teenager]

Conclusion

The aim of this paper was to examine motivations towards family activity holidays where separate provision was made for parents and children. At the start of the research it was the difference between parent and child motivation towards separate provision, or parallel leisure, that was of interest. This research has shown that in fact there is a strong correlation between parent and child motivation towards separate child provision in that both parents and children have similar aspirations towards this, and were satisfied by the holiday experience. The central theme of the research moved with the analysis of data.

The role of women in the workplace is changing, as well as in in many sectors of society and aspects of life. In this study women mothers were mostly high earning professionals. In the in-depth interviews they were assured, self-aware and confident. Their holiday motivations appeared to be clearly thought through. The main holiday, even for those on high incomes, was a major investment which had been rationally considered.

For the mothers in this study, the holiday experience was often seen as an extension to the parental responsibility rather than as a personal leisure activity in its own right. The significance of this is about the role of personal leisure to mothers within the family unit — and the negotiation of that time for individual leisure within shared space and time. Fathers had a much clearer focus on their individual sporting needs and aspirations. That is not to say mothers were any more or less satisfied with their holiday experiences; the evidence in this study is that their aspirations and therefore satisfactions were different. The main motivation for these mothers appeared to be first to ensure the happiness of their families. In doing so, it could be argued that their own individual holiday motivations are subordinated to that of partners and children. When the crunch came (e.g. a sick child on holiday), it was the women who forfeited their personal leisure time.

The future focus of this ongoing research will be to explore further the role of mother and father prior to going on holiday by identifying and exploring the sub decisions, and motivations involved in booking a family activity holiday overseas. Once again a specialist watersports tour operator is supporting this research.

References

Anderson, J. (1994) 'Watersports participation in Britain', *Insights* (November): pp. D13–D20.

―――― (1995) 'Safety at their leisure — a study of youth sport courses', in L. Lawrence, E. Murdoch and S. Parker (eds) *Professional and development issues in leisure, sport and education* (LSA Publication No. 56). Eastbourne: Leisure Studies Association.

Anderson, J., Andrews, R., Edwards, C., Harris, I. and Savill, T. (1996). British Marine Industry Federation and Southampton Institute.

Anderssen, N. and Wold, B. (1992) 'Parental and peer influences on leisure time physical activity in young adolescents', *Research Quarterly for Exercise and Sport*, 63: pp. 341–348.

Beioley, B. (1996) '"Going for it" — activity holidays in the UK', *Insights* (November): pp. B27–B40.

Crompton, J. (1981) 'Dimensions of the social group role in pleasure vacations', *Annals of Tourism Research*, VIII: pp. 550–568.

Deem, R. (1986) *All work and no play? The sociology of women's leisure*. Milton Keynes: Open University Press.

Darley, W. and Lim, J. (1986) 'Family decision making in leisure time activities', *Advances in Consumer Research*, Vol. 14 (Association for Consumer Research, Provo, UT): pp. 370–374.

Davis, H. (1976) 'Decision making within the household', *Journal of Consumer Research*, Vol. 2: pp. 241–260.

Daly, K. J. (1996) *Families and time*. California: Sage Publications.

Filiatrault, P. and Ritchie, J. (1980) 'Joint purchasing decisions: a comparison of influence structure in family and couple decision making units', *Journal of Consumer Research*, 7: pp. 131–140.

Freysinger, V. J. (1995) 'The dialectics of leisure and development for women and men in midlife: An interpretive study', *Journal of Leisure Research*, 27: pp. 61–84.

Harrington, M. and Dawson, D. (1995) 'Who has it best? Labour force participation, perceptions of leisure and constraints to enjoyment of leisure', *Journal of Leisure Research* Vol. 27, No. 1: pp. 4–24.

Henderson, K. A. (1991) 'The contribution of feminism to an understanding of leisure constraints', *Journal of Leisure Research*, 23: pp. 363–243.

Henderson, K. A., Bialeschki, M. D, Shaw, S. M. and Freysinger, V. J. (1996) *Both gains and gaps. Feminist perspectives on women's leisure*. State College, PA: Venture Publishing.

Howard, D. and Madrigal, R. (1990) 'Who makes the decisions parent or child?'. *Journal of Leisure Research* 22 (3): pp. 244–258.

HMSO (1996) *General Household Survey*.

Horna, J. (1982) 'The leisure component of the parental role', *Journal of Leisure Research* 21 (2) 228–241.

Jenkins, R. (1978) 'Family vacation decision making', *Journal of Travel Research*, 16 (4) 2–7.

Kay, T. (1996) 'Woman's leisure and the family in contemporary Britain', in Samuel (ed.) *Woman, leisure and the family in contemporary society, a multi national perspective.* Wallingford. CAB International.

Larson, R. W. and Gillman, S. A. (1997) 'Divergent experiences of family leisure: Fathers, mothers and young adolescents', *Journal of Leisure Research*, 29 (1): pp. 78–97.

Leisure Consultants. (1992) *Activity holidays — the growth market in tourism.* Sudbury: Leisure Consultants.

Mintel. (1995) *Activity Holidays.* Mintel.

Nichols, C. M. and Snepenger, D. J. (1988) 'Family decision making and tourism behaviour and attitudes', *Journal of Travel Research* (Spring): pp. 2–6.

Orthner, D. K. (1975) 'Patterns of leisure and marital satisfaction over the marital career', *Journal of Marriage and the Family*, 37: 91–102.

Rapoport, R. and Rapoport R. N. (1995) 'Leisure and the Family Life Cycle', in C. Critcher, P. Bramham, P. and A. Tomlinson (eds) *Sociology of Leisure: A reader.* London: E & FN Spon.

Samuel, N. (1996) Women, Leisure and the Family in Contemporary Society: A multi national perspective. CAB International: Wallingford.

Seaton, A. V. and Tagg, S. (1997) 'The family vacation in Europe: paedonomic aspects of choices and satisfactions', *Journal of Travel and Tourism Marketing*, 4 (1).

Shaw, S. M. (1992) 'Dereifying family leisure: an examination of women and men's everyday experiences land perceptions of family time', *Leisure Sciences*, 14: 271–286.

Sharp, H. and Mott, P. (1956) 'Consumer *decisions in the metropolitan family', Journal of Marketing*, 21: 149–156.

Thornton, P. R., Shaw, G. and Williams, A. M. (1997) 'Tourist group holiday decision-making and behaviour: the influence of children', *Tourism Management*, 18 (5): pp. 287–297.

Thompson, L. and Walker, A. J. (1989) 'Gender in families: women and men in marriage, work and parent hood', *Journal of Marriage and Family*, 51, pp. 845–871.

Wimbush, E. (1987) 'Mothers with young children — understanding their leisure needs', in I. Henry (ed) *Women's leisure: Constraints and opportunities.* (ESRC/Sports Council/LSA Seminar). Published as Newsletter Supplement. Eastbourne: Leisure Studies Association.

Wolgast, E. (1958) 'Do husbands or wives make the purchasing decisions?', *Journal of Marketing* 23 (October): pp. 151–158.

New Women, Same Old Leisure: The Upholding of Gender Stereotypes and Leisure Disadvantage in Contemporary Dual-earner Households

Tess Kay

Institute of Sport and Leisure Policy, Loughborough University

Introduction

In the last 15 years, while men's employment levels have fallen slightly, British women's labour market involvement has been increasing, particularly among women with family responsibilities. Britain now has the second highest female economic activity rate among the European Union countries, and the dual-earner family is the norm. Such changes have implications for family roles and forms of organisation, and for men and women's behaviour and expectations beyond the workplace. This paper examines the implications of changing patterns of individual and household labour market involvement for one of the groups of women in the UK who have experienced those changes most acutely — mothers of pre-school children, in full-time employment.

Diversity in UK women's labour market involvement

Changes taking place in the British labour market since the 1970s have led to increasing polarisation in the situations of working women. Overall, female employment in the UK rose from 62% to 73% between 1975 and 1995, but this was not experienced by all groups in the female population. During the 1980s, increases in mothers' work involvement were concentrated in the most affluent and well-educated social groups and regions (Harrop and Moss, 1994). In the increases between 1984 and 1994, too, the main increases in mothers' employment came from graduate women living with a partner (Brannen et al., 1997: p. 1).

By 1994, mothers were more likely to be employed if they were in a couple household, had older children, had fewer children, had higher qualifications, were white, had a partner who was employed and had a partner in a non-manual job. Almost all of these differences (with the exception of age and number of children) had increased over the decade (Brannen et al.: p. 3). In some instances, groups of women had demonstrated opposite trends: for example, between 1984 — 1994, employment rose much faster for mothers with qualifications (the higher the qualification the higher the rate of growth) compared with those without qualifications among whom employment rates actually fell' (ibid.). As a result, it was only among women with qualifications that the rate of Female Working Age Inactivity fell during the last decade (from 28% in 1984 to 23.1% in 1996) (Labour Market Trends, September 1997: p. 344).

British women in less favoured situations experienced rather different trends over the last two decades. There was little increase in economic activity among women in lower status labour market segments, and for women without qualifications, Female Working Age Inactivity increased by just over 5% between 1991–1996 (ibid.). During the 1980s employment rates increased very little for women with large families, women with few qualifications, black mothers, female partners of non-employed men, and lone mothers, and in some cases employment levels for these groups declined (Harrop and Moss, 1994). Mothers in lower status jobs were also extremely unlikely to be among the growing number of women employed full-time (see Table 1). In the lowest occupational categorisation, only 2% of mothers with a child under 5 worked full-time by 1995 (Office for National Statistics, 1997); in contrast, 36% of mothers in professional or managerial occupations with a child of this age did so (see Table 2). Although the proportions rise for both groups as children's ages increase, the differential remains very strong: even when children are in compulsory secondary schooling (at ages 10-15), only 8% of women in the lowest occupational categorisation are in full-time employment, while 62% of those in the highest categorisation are. Overall, about 60% of working mothers in professional/managerial occupations work full-time while they have dependent children (aged up to 16), but only 10% of working mothers in unskilled jobs do so.

This divergence in women's employment patterns has been a significant contributor to wealth polarisation in Britain, and to emerging differences in household circumstances. During the 1980s the divide grew between couple households where both partners worked and those where neither had a job. Between 1975 and 1990, the proportion of couples who both worked increased from 51% to 60%; while the proportion with no earner increased from 3% to 11% (Kempson, 1996). The highest proportionate increase was amongst households with two full-time earners — up from 15% of couple households in 1984, to 22% in 1994. The increase was concentrated among parents with relatively high qualifications, high status occupations and smaller families (Kempson, 1996: p. 89). Women with high work involvement (i.e. in full-time employment) were therefore most likely to be partnered by men in comparable situations.

The total burden of paid work hours borne by households has become particularly high amongst these households. Mothers and fathers in professional and managerial jobs are more likely to work 'long' full-time hours (>40/week) than those in low-status occupational groups (Brannen et al., 1997, p.3). Between 1984–1994, the average weekly working hours of parents in two-earner families increased from 71.3 to 74.5, but in families with both parents in professional or managerial jobs they averaged 90 hours a week. In these households, a higher proportion of household employed hours were contributed by mothers — 39% compared to the average of 34%. At the same time, British fathers with dependent children were working, on average, longer hours than childless men with full-time jobs (Pullinger and Summerfield, 1997) (Table 3).

The high burden of paid-work hours borne by such households has implications for household workloads, family activity patterns, and for the circumstances in which divisions of domestic labour may be negotiated. The household activity patterns of dual-earner households have been examined by many writers. Such work has typically focused on the relationship between paid employment and divisions of domestic labour, and has shown that gendered inequality is prevalent. Male partners of employed women contribute more hours of household work than those of non-employed women, but the

Table 1 Economic activity status of employed women with children, by socio-economic group.

	% of socio-economic group					
	PR	EM	ONM	SM	SSM	USM
Full-time employed*	59	72	39	45	28	9
Part-time employed*	42	28	61	56	72	91
All ('000s)	88	507	2095	333	748	283

Source: Office for National Statistics, Living in Britain: General Household Survey 1995; data for Great Britain 1993-95 combined

Table 2 Economic activity of working age women (16–59), by own socio-economic group and age of youngest dependent child

	socio-economic group				
	PR	EM	SM	SSM	USM
Full-time work					
child 0–4	36	17	17	8	2
child 5–9	52	21	26	12	3
child 10–15	62	33	39	22	8
All	49	23	27	13	4
Part-time work					
child 0–4	26	35	40	26	49
child 5–9	26	47	38	42	59
child 10–15	21	46	39	47	63
All	25	42	39	37	57
All economically active (employed and unemployed seeking work)					
child 0–4	66	59	61	42	56
child 5–9	85	75	71	63	71
child 10–15	89	82	84	73	76
All	78	71	71	57	67

Source: Office for National Statistics, Living in Britain: General Household Survey 1995; data for Great Britain 1993–95 combined

Table 3 Average hours worked per week, by parental status and gender, 1996

	Parents		Non-parents	
	males	females	males	females
working full-time	47.9	41.0	45.9	41.2
working part-time	19.8	18.1	16.0	17.7
all in employment	47.1	26.9	43.0	33.7

Source: Labour Force Survey, Office for National Statistics

additional amount tends to be relatively small. Demo and Alcock's (1993) comparison of dual-income and single-earner American couples found that in households in which the wife was employed, she still undertook nearly three-quarters (72%) of the time spent by the household on domestic chores, compared with 81% for non-employed wives. Hochschild (1989) has shown that even in households in which the woman is the higher earner or the only one, male partners still do relatively little domestic labour. The division of household labour has therefore been relatively insensitive to recent increases in women's labour force participation (Greenstein, 1996).

British studies from the 1990s parallel this picture. Considerable gaps still remain in the relative contributions of women and men to unpaid work even when both are in full-time work. Overall, although full-time employed women spend less time on paid work than men, this is more than compensated for by their unpaid work and caring responsibilities (Brannen et al., op cit.). The gap is largest in the group that has seen most labour market growth — couple households with young children, among whom women spend 77 hours per week and men 68 hours in paid and unpaid labour (ibid.). Analysis of the parental activity patterns data from the National Child Development Study portrays a similar picture, confirming the extent to which mothers bear the main burden for domestic tasks in all types of British households (Ferri and Smith, 1996). In dual full-time earner households, two-thirds of full-time working mothers are responsible for cooking and cleaning, and four out of five for laundry.

Responsibility for domestic matters appears to be only slightly more equally shared in households in which women, like their partners, are in full-time employment. For mothers, working full-time only results in a very limited transfer of domestic responsibilities to others, whether to fathers or to paid help. In consequence, men and women's lives in these household diverge on three planes; in the hours of paid work they undertake; in the hours of unpaid work they undertake; and in the residual hours, of 'free' time, that each can access.

The study

This paper reports findings from the first of a series of studies into contemporary British women's lifestyles. The studies focus on the interaction of employment, domestic labour and leisure in the lives of women who differ from each other in their socio-economic and household status. This first study is an exploratory investigation into the parameters of leisure in the lives of an emergent sector within the female population: full-time employed women in SEG1/2, with one or more pre-school children. Women in this group are distinctive in pursuing a pattern of employment which is predominant among men but relatively unusual for women — i.e. working full-time, and continuing to do so when they have a very young child in the house. In contrast, most British women work part-time for at least part of their working lives, and/or drop out of the labour market completely, with these reductions particularly likely to occur during their children's pre-school years. The woman who works full-time, continuously, is therefore still something of an anomaly in Britain. The question for leisure researchers is whether, in comparison to other women, her unusual employment situation gives her unusual access to equity in leisure? Does full-time employment serve to legitimate women's leisure entitlement to the same extent as it appears to do for men?

The research investigated the lifestyles of full-time employed mothers of pre-school children through the framework of the work-family-leisure triad. Data collection was conducted through in-depth semi-structured interviews with 11 women in full-time employment and with one or more pre-school child. The interviews addressed four dimensions of the interviewees' lives: work, home, leisure, and the interaction between these three. The analysis presented here concentrates on those elements of the findings that might be expected to distinguish the lifestyles of this group from those of women with lower employment involvement. Particular attention is paid to interviewees' perceptions of, and access to, individual leisure. Three main themes are addressed:

i.   The current sample is distinctive because it consists of women who are mothers of pre-school children and are also full-time employed. How do women accommodate this dual role? What are its impacts on their attitudes and behaviour?

ii. In Britain, employment status is a point of difference between the sexes in most heterosexual partnerships: most men work full-time continuously, while most women have fragmented employment pattern. In this sample, in contrast, women's employment status is a point of similarity with their male partners. Is this erosion of gender distinctions in a couple's labour market roles mirrored within the home, in the way in which responsibilities are shared between the two sexes in household and childcare tasks?

iii. Leisure researchers have postulated a link between women's employment status and their access to leisure. What role does leisure play in the lives of these women?

After establishing the characteristics of the sample, the reporting of the results addresses these issues in three phases. Firstly, the ways in which the areas of paid work, home and leisure are represented in working mothers' lifestyles are described. Secondly, the extent to which the women perceive these three areas as sites of gender division within the household is examined. Finally, the women's own explanations for how such divides emerge are considered.

Results

Interviewees' characteristics

The 11 interviewees' personal, employment and household/family characteristics are summarised in Table 4 (following page). The women varied in their current household situation. Eight were married and living with their husband, and one was unmarried and living with her male partner. Two women were divorced; of these, one lived as a single parent and one with her new partner.

Working mothers' lifestyles: Women at work, home and leisure

i. Women at work

All 11 women had been in full-time employment prior to the birth of their first child. Most (9) had worked full-time continuously since completing their qualifications/training 7–14 years previously.

The women had a long-standing expectation of being in full-time employment ('I don't think that I ever thought that I wouldn't') and derived a strong sense of individuality

Table 4 Interviewee characteristics

Career	Current employment	Age of child(ren)
Arts Administrator	3 years	1 pre-school; 2 school age
Company Manager	9 + 2 years	1 pre-school
Lecturer A	8 years	1 pre-school
Lecturer B	7 years	1 pre-school
Lecturer C	11 years	1 pre-school
Library Services Officer	12 years	1 pre-school
Marketing and Sales Manager	12 years	1 pre-school
Office Manager	13 years	1 pre-school
Research Director	14 years	1 pre-school
Research Officer	8 years	1 pre-school
Teacher	13 years	1 pre-school

from their employment. The workplace was an important as a source of identity for each woman as a person in her own right, both before and after motherhood:

> [At work] I think people are interested in me. I am me. I am not somebody's wife or somebody's mother. [Manager]

> I enjoy being a mum, but I also enjoy being at work, and at work they knew me before he was born so I'm not 'Jonathon's mum' there, I'm me. I work because I enjoy it. There are obviously other reasons like finance and things like that, but the main reason is I enjoy it. [Library Services Officer]

Work allowed the women to express themselves, and to develop individual skills and interests that gained external recognition. They worked...

> To find your own way up. I'm trained for my career so I've had to carry it on. I don't think personally I would be very happy if I wasn't working and therefore I think you became dependent on having a job. [Lecturer]

> So that I feel I'm a worthwhile human being, is probably the bottom line! Having a career, having something which defines me as a useful member of society, is important, and a full-time job does that. [Research Officer]

Most of the interviewees had therefore regarded full-time employment as a major strand of their lives, and one which would continue uninterrupted through the parenting years. With this expectation, most had returned to full-time employment immediately after their maternity leave, and had done so quite happily. There were, however, exceptions. Two of the women found themselves very reluctant to go back to working full-time, although they had originally had every intention of doing so. In practice, their financial circumstances had given them little option. In one case, the woman concerned was in the position to accept part-time work, but was unable to negotiate reduced work hours with her employer. The other needed to maintain her salary in full; she had always considered herself to be quite career-centred and was now shocked by how unhappy she was to be returning to work:

> Before I had Rachael I was very work orientated and I was adamant that there wasn't any way that I was ever going to give up my job. Then I had her and I didn't want to go back. Things changed completely. I was absolutely besotted and it completely took me by surprise — I just didn't think I would think like that. It was a real shock. [Teacher]

In contrast to the two reluctant returners, one of the interviewees had had almost the opposite experience. She had stopped work when her daughter was born, but had returned by the time of the interviews:

> We didn't think for a long time we'd be able to have children so when we had her it was like 'oh my God' and I was hoping, HOPING I'd be able to stay at home, and I have to say that looking back, giving up my full-time job was the worse thing I did — for me. And I really regret it to the extent where I say to friends now, don't. [Manager]

She was now a strong advocate of full-time work for women in similar situations:

> Knowing how I felt you would just wither and die being at home. And when you look at it in your life, I know children are only small for a very short time but why ditch everything out of however many years' career you could have just for that time. It's great if you can freeze-frame your career and pop back into the workplace and carry on as though there's no change — but I [still] don't see why you should. OK — everything comes at a price but why should you? I think you don't have to give up your job and you don't have to change your life.

Other interviewees had similar feelings about the continued importance of work in their lives. Most felt that their commitment to work was unaffected when they became mothers:

> I don't think that my attitude has changed towards employment — my commitment has stayed the same.

> I'm still ambitious to do as well as I possibly can at work — I'm determined my career will progress. [Lecturer]

Nonetheless, if work commitment had stayed as high as previously, an even greater responsibility had now supplanted it as the women's first priority. Although their jobs were as important as before as sources of self-identity and personal achievement, in the overall balance of their lives, the tasks and responsibilities of mothering came first:

> Work is one further down the pecking order in terms of what I think is important because obviously my son is at the top so everything comes after that...

> So, [my daughter] always comes first and I feel that I'm looking out for her all the time, more so than for myself really. [Marketing and Design Manager]

It appeared that even for the highly work-oriented, professional working mother,

> What comes first every time is the children. They are the absolute priority. [Arts Administrator]

ii. Women at home

The research sought information on the division of domestic labour within households, with particular emphasis on ascertaining whether or not women considered household tasks to be shared equally between the partners. Women's views on why the current arrangement existed, and how satisfactory they felt it to be, were also elicited.

Most women reported a degree of shared responsibility for domestic tasks. Activities undertaken by male partners included both traditional male tasks (e.g. care of cars; DIY; heavy gardening), and, in some households, activities which in heterosexual households are more commonly carried out by women, such as household shopping and cooking. Despite this, women did not perceive the division of domestic responsibility to be equal. In comparison to their partner, most women reported spending a greater amount of time on the running of the household. Their sense of inequality did not stem, however, solely from their unequal share of household activity, but from the extent to which they felt an overall responsibility for domestic matters. Women displayed what might be termed proactive domesticity: it was up to them to identify what needed to be done in the household, and to ensure that it was carried out:

> Although lots of jobs may be done by the other partner, [the woman] has got the responsibility of making sure they happen. It sort of happens that I have to do a lot more of the thinking. It's making sure all the little things get done that have to be done. [Marketing and Design Manager]

'Doing the thinking' about home and family could pervade other spheres of activity:

> ... even when I'm doing leisure activity, I'm always thinking 'so-and-so should be happening' or 'I ought to really have done X'... there's always reminders. It goes with this women 'multi-tasking' that men can't do. [Manager]

Part of the women's domestic burden came from their main responsibility for childcare. This represented a substantial demand and was clearly classified by them as a form of household work. While time spent with their children could be a source of great pleasure, such activities were nonetheless laborious. Taking care of young children was demanding and difficult:

> All this about women at home with kids having an easy time — it's not like that, it's hard work — you can't do anything easily.

They emphasised the sense of responsibility borne by the parent — even in outwardly playful activities. Mothers could enjoy playing with their children without experiencing that time as 'leisure':

> When you go somewhere for the day or you go swimming — things which I would consider leisure activities — if you go with a small child you don't relax. So, it's leisure for them and it's sort of work for you. [Arts Administrator]

iii. Women at leisure

Three themes emerged from the women's reports of their personal leisure. Firstly, all had a sense that they needed leisure, but most struggled to access it:

> I feel I'm entitled to leisure time but it just doesn't happen.

One of the main reasons for this was working mothers' sense of time-debt to their children:

> I feel that because I'm working full-time, that the time I'm not at work is the children's time, particularly Kate's [the pre-school child]. [Arts Administrator]

I'm going to give myself something to do in the evening but it'll be after Jessica is in bed because I'm too anxious that because I work full-time that the free time I do have should be with her so when she's in bed I'll sort of start my life then.

I don't want to waste any time we have together doing something for myself.

In consequence, if work encroached on home time, the guilt of the working mother was well in evidence:

It took me 11 hours to mark 4 sets of assessments last weekend and Rachael kept coming to the table and saying 'Sssh daddy, we're working'. The result was that I felt incredibly guilty all I week so I didn't bring any marking home with me, to try to give her a bit more time. It's very difficult. [Teacher]

Secondly, women defined the essential qualities of leisure as 'time for themselves'.

My leisure time now usually means without children, without husband. It's for me. My own leisure time is for me.

At best, this was time when they had choice over activities — but if nothing else, it was time in which choice might be virtually non-existent but at least they were free from external demands:

By the time I finish doing everything in evenings, everything that has got to be done, although I really ought to go to bed at 10 o'clock because she gets up at 5, I'm so desperate to get some time on my own that I often stay up later than I should. [Marketing and Design Manager]

I could never understand why women could go for 2 hours a week and have their hair set it's only since I've had Philip that I've begun to realise that just sitting there where nobody expects you to be doing anything, you don't have to be thinking. That was the only time then when women had time for them selves...The options for a couple of hours out are much wider now but it's still a bit like you how to buy that time whereas for men I think it's still more accepted that they do it.

Thirdly, almost all interviewees contrasted leisure only with domestic and (particularly) childcare responsibilities. Only one mention was made of a need for leisure as relief from the demands of paid work; in every other case leisure was primarily defined as relief from mothering:

I think [leisure] gives you a break from your kids... I think really you need time to get out and just let off steam, calm down and think about yourself for a bit.

In fact, the demands of children could be so all-consuming that any time away from them became a form of personal time for mothers. More than one woman described her paid work time as time for herself — because time at work was protected from the intrusions of children's' needs. One mother emphasised this when she spoke of having the option to take a day's holiday, not to escape the demands of work, but to give herself child-free time:

It's quite difficult to explain — when I had the boys and I was at home all day, it could be overwhelming and felt like it was never-ending. Partly I feel I have time now on my own because I go off to work and I'm enjoying what I'm doing there. Because of the nursery if I ever felt like it I could take a day's leave and

Kate could go to nursery so I would have that time on my own. Because I've got that let-out then that's fine. [Arts Administrator]

Although the women spoke of leisure in terms of its defining qualities rather than as specific activities, some had nonetheless made a commitment to a regular, usually out-of-home, activity. This was an acceptable and effective strategy for ensuring they obtained the personal time they needed.

I have an evening class. Since she was only a few weeks old I got myself an evening class, last year I did social science and this year I'm doing woodwork, just so that I've got a couple of hours to myself in the evening. [Office Manager]

The gender divides

i. The work divide

Women felt that the dual role of full-time employee and parent was experienced differently by men and women. Their own experience was of substantial adjustment to priorities. Most felt that maximum time should be devoted to their child outside essential work commitments, and several adopted new strategies to achieve this. These included leaving work early, reducing excess office hours, reducing the amount of work taken home in evenings and at weekends, and reducing certain types of time-consuming work activities, such as travel abroad and other trips requiring overnight stays away from home.

I've cut my hours by about 30 — 40% I'd say. It's only affected me in that I've got less time to spend at work, that's all. So I'm busy trying to fit everything I did before into a smaller amount of time — which is not possible, but...! [Lecturer]

Women did not report any such adjustments in their partners' working arrangements, despite being invited to do so. In general, women felt that the arrival of children in the household had caused very little disruption to men's work activities. Fathers were described as being much more able to continue their previous activity pattern than mothers were.

He goes out in the morning and comes home at night which is basically his day because it's quite a long day for him, whereas I'm trying to juggle tidying up and getting Grace to nursery etc. He hasn't got the role during the week of house and work, he just does work.

Within the apparent similarity of full-time employment for both partners, we thus see divergence occurring: mothers reduced their level of involvement in their jobs to accommodate the needs of their child while fathers did not. In this respect, the employment status of the mother and father became a site of gender differentiation rather than convergence.

ii. The home divide

There was a lot of dissatisfaction among the interviewees over the extent to which their partners took less responsibility for the needs of the household than they did themselves. Women felt they had overall responsibility for household matters; in some cases the man's share of household activities [in the example below, ironing his own clothes][author's cynicism] were in fact tasks that had been specifically allocated to him by his partner:

> He does his own ironing, I made him! The state of his ironing is appalling... but I had to sort of delegate some things. [Company Manager]

The differences were particularly marked in the way in which childcare responsibilities were met within the household, with interviewees again reporting themselves as undertaking a greater proportion of childcare tasks than male partners did. Some experienced a double frustration with this situation: not only did they carry out on unequal share of this aspect of domestic work, but what they did was not recognised as being work-like. Men who did not classify their own time spent with their children as leisure, did seem to consider that time to be leisure for their wives:

> My partner thinks I'm got more leisure time than I should have but he doesn't take into account the time spent with Amber as working as such. [Marketing and Design Manager]

The women themselves saw only part of their time with children as leisurely, indicating differences in the way in which men and women perceived the time that each spent with their child. Some women did comment, however, that partners might also experience such time differently. One contrasted her own experience in this respect with that of her husband:

> He certainly doesn't see time spent with the family as relaxed or enjoys it as much as I do. I can get pleasure out of taking Kate into Leicester and doing some shopping and sitting in a cafe and having a drink together but for him it would be absolute purgatory, a real chore. [Arts Administrator]

Overall, women were frustrated by their partners' apparent inability to contribute as effectively on the home front as they themselves did — and as their partners seemed to do in other areas of their lives:

> I look around and I see grown men, competent and perfectly capable at work, professional people holding down responsible jobs, when you put them with a child for a day, they can think about the child and they can maybe get them some tea but they don't do any washing etc. It's either one or the other which I think if women operated at the same level the system would collapse. [Company Manager]

iii. The leisure divide

Women felt that their partners' leisure was different from their own in a number of respects. While women were determined to spend non-work time on their children rather than on themselves, fathers preserved personal leisure. Men appeared to have an automatic sense of entitlement to prioritise their preferred activities, which was strong enough to withstand the greatly increased household demands brought about by parenthood:

> ...his leisure time hasn't really changed. He still goes out and rides his bike and he still feels the he should be able to fit that in whether I can do something or not. I think that Jessica [daughter] is definitely a priority in his life, but so is his life. [Office Manager]

The coping conundrum

All of the women interviewed experienced inequality in home, work and leisure. They were all conscious of this and they were all dissatisfied with it. Some had taken steps to redress the imbalance — e.g. the allocation of selected household tasks to their male partners by some interviewees. Sometimes, less deliberate action had been required: a number of women said that the practical demands of the households' collective activities had made it inevitable that some revision of responsibilities took place. But the outcomes of such changes were limited and several of the women explicitly recognised that their ability to negotiate more satisfactory arrangements was compromised by prevailing gender ideology:

> Sometimes I get frustrated that I don't have more help from my husband. We do have some disagreements over lack of involvement in some activities. I think we're constrained definitely by this role in society... I mean I've never faced any discrimination whatsoever at work in terms of being a woman, but in the home there is still a very traditional attitude even if your partner does not feel he thinks traditionally — there's still the expectation there for the woman, even if she's working full-time, to do the vast majority of the household activities as well as work... My husband thinks it's something I should do and not something that I'm doing for him as well. I don't actually mind doing more than 50% but my husband thinks that's what should be done, he's quite happy that I do 90% of everything. He doesn't see any problem with that at all. [Lecturer]

> I think [women] are all brought up with a guilt complex about it. I think it's something to do with up-bringing and general attitudes. I think there are different expectations that we grow up with. I don't know if this is continuing through the generations but I've still got it and as far as I can tell every woman I meet has it to some degree. My sister has experienced her husband telling her she shouldn't go out to the pub in the evening because she hadn't had his tea cooked and things like that. She told him where to go but the attitude was there. Sometimes you hear it and you just don't believe it! [Research Officer]

At the heart of the inequitable distribution of paid and unpaid work lay leisure. The women's analyses of their household situations showed that men felt entitled to a life of their own in a way that the women did not. Notwithstanding the claims of children, home and partner, men would access personal time. This was a fundamental distinction between the sexes:

> I think attitudes [towards leisure] differ between men and women. The more I think about it the more I think we are different species from the same planet! I think men are much better at prioritising and saying 'I want this for me, so I'll walk out of this home and go to this', than women are.

> I read a quote in a magazine which I found really true and interesting: women do all they have to do and then make time for themselves with what is left, men do what they want to do for themselves and then everything else has to fit in around that. I think that's true, women do everything they have to for other people and what is left, even if it's only 5 minutes, that's for them, but fellas will say, well sorry, I've been to work, I'm going to the gym now.

I suspect there are more men with hobbies that are time-consuming than there are women as a matter of course. I'm generalising but I've always found it odd that men choose to go fishing, watch football, whatever, and they are all things that take you out of a situation where things need to be done, for example, Sunday morning you can't be getting Sunday dinner because you're sitting on the canal bank...

The inevitable consequence of men's investment of time and energy in personal leisure, combined with their limited effectiveness within the home, was the disproportionate burden on the working mothers — and it was women's ability to sustain this burden, however reluctantly, that allowed household activity patterns to remain so inequitable:

Because women do everything and they cope, the expectation is that they will continue to cope, and so their expectation is that that is what their lot is — so they do it...For those that cope, because they do, they are expected to cope.

Discussion

The superficial similarity and equality of employment status that the women in this study held in relation to their partners, masked a pattern of substantial gendered differentiation. In relation to the work role of the full-time employed mother, the study found that although the women were highly work oriented, they had to make practical adjustments to their work activities to accommodate mothering. Work was contained within fewer hours and in a narrower range of activities than previously. For the most part, fathers did not make changes of this sort. With the onset of parenthood, employment thus became a site of gender differentiation in work behaviour, despite most women's continued high commitment to employment. Secondly, in the domestic sphere, women carried out more household tasks and more childcare tasks than their partners did, and felt that overall responsibility for the running of the home was theirs. It was their unequal share of childcare tasks that was particularly important in necessitating a reduction in work time. Women were conscious that domestic demands were unequally shared with their partners, but had difficulty in achieving more equitable divisions of labour within the home, and showed awareness of the influence of broader social expectations in affecting this. The home front, too, therefore became an arena of increased gender differentiation. Finally, the differentiation in work and home roles was repeated in leisure. Women recognised their own needs for leisure but this did not in itself give them a strong enough sense of entitlement to it to override other demands. Some adopted strategies to commit themselves to taking regular leisure time, thus avoiding the question of repeatedly legitimising doing so. The women were conscious of practical and attitudinal differences between themselves and their partners in respect of leisure, seeing men as much more able to preserve an automatic right to their preferred activities.

The situations described by the current sample of full-time employed mothers were thus universally inequitable. There was no evidence that their relatively high employment status posed a substantial challenge to traditional gendered distinctions in couples' lifestyles. The presence of young children in the household led to the re-introduction of stereotypical divisions of responsibility, mainly brought about by women reverting to a traditional mothering role in their non-working time. In contrast, men's behaviour underwent little change at work and in leisure, and their relative share of overall household responsibilities actually declined as a result of their limited involvement in childcare.

The consistency of such evidence suggests little change is taking place and is in accordance with Hochschild's (1990) description of a 'stalled revolution' — in which the women have gone to work, but the workplace, the culture, and most of all, the men, have not adjusted themselves to the new reality. But is this the only interpretation? Gershuny, Godwin and Jones (1994) argue that much analysis of contemporary divisions of domestic labour derives from cross-sectional data which are not equipped to detect underlyinq processes through which behaviour changes emerge. The predominance of such studies leads to frequent reporting of very limited change in traditional male and female activity patterns, with couples in heterosexual households usually displaying strongly gendered activity patterns despite expressing commitment to a more equal arrangement. Gershuny et al. propose that a concept of 'lagged adaptation' is helpful in explaining this discrepancy. 'Lagged adaptation' recognises that active processes of adjustment occur within such households, but that a considerable time lag is likely to occur before the changes are manifest clearly in behaviour. This discrepancy between attitude and actuality suggests that conventional gender stereotypes are particularly resistant to behavioural change and thus pose a central obstacle to individuals' desires for less gender-specific roles.

Ridgeway (1997) has suggested that the apparent inviolability of traditional gender roles is particularly strong because gendered assumptions are unique in the extent to which they underlie our expectations of, and contributions to, interactions with others. Individuals are nearly incapable of interacting with one another when they cannot guess the other's sex. Ridgeway stresses that this distinguishes 'gender' from other social structural characteristics: 'people can usually interact with others whom they can't place on other major dimensions of inequality, such as class or race, but seem to have difficulty completing even trivial, routine exchanges with someone they can't classify by sex'. We therefore bring our assumptions about gender into play in our every interaction, and in doing so repeatedly reinforce conventional gender ideology.

Prevailing gender ideologies are further upheld by life-course behavioural factors. A salient finding of the current study was the extent to which changes occurred in women's employment involvement in response to parenting demands, which aggregate labour market data conceal. The women were able to respond to new demands by manipulating their work patterns to accommodate motherhood, and the availability of such options may be an important factor in explaining the greater likelihood of women remaining in full-time employment in those labour market sectors. The women's adaptive strategies contrasted with their descriptions of the continuity in their partner's lifestyles. This suggests differences in the extent to which the two sexes expect to actively accommodate new phases in the household life cycle. This a key distinguishing feature in the life patterns of men and women: continuity in men's employment, and variety and fragmentation in women's, is a substantial difference in the life-time experiences of the sexes. Women's lifestyles are characterised by change and adaptation at a number of levels. In part this occurs through interaction between women's own changing employment role and domestic role at different stages in the lifecycle, and in part it results from their tradition of shaping their own activities to fit the situation of their partner. For men, in contrast, employment is usually a site of continuity that survives consistent, resistant to the demands of other altered circumstances in their lives.

It seems likely that men's narrower experience and lower expectation of having to be flexible in their activity patterns may become self-perpetuating obstacles to appropriate household adaptation in dual-earner households. Women's more adaptive behaviour both compensates for, and reinforces, this. Holt and Thaulow (1996) suggest these differences are played out in the workplace: in female-dominated jobs, women are likely to create more flexibility than would be expected from the formal organisation of the work, but in male-dominated jobs, men create less. To some extent the identification of this culture of inflexibility is helpful in explaining men's unresponsiveness to demands outside paid employment. Holt and Thaulow also show, however, that when men do create informal flexibility, 'it is primarily in relation to hobbies or personal errands rather than domestic tasks or childcare', whereas for women, as with the current sample, creativity in manipulating work time is driven by the need to meet household demands. Men will show flexibility to undertake personal needs, but retain their peculiar ability to resist domesticity.

Conclusion

Women in this study may share their formal work status with their male partners, but difference in the lifestyles of the sexes arise from the different individual hierarchies of need the sexes construct. The position of leisure is significant in this hierarchy for being a residual category for women yet a source of legitimate demand for men. This arrangement bears out the continuing currency of the oft-identified 'ethic of care' so often invoked to explain women's constrained leisure experience. For full-time working mothers, the necessary balancing act which working women with children perform produces an interesting conundrum: mothering comes first in their lives, but it is work that they find their strongest sense of self-identity. Here, then, is a situation in which we find that women automatically experience conflict in reconciling the components of their lifestyle. The boundaries between spheres of activities become blurred, and conceptualisations of leisure fit poorly with established debates. Women refer to work as 'almost leisure' because, in comparison to the demands of childcare, work bestows the greatest of their very relative freedoms.

References

Brannen, J., Moss, P., Owen, C. and Vale, C. (1997) *Mothers, fathers and employment: Parents and the labour market in Britain 1984–1994*. Research Report no. 10. London: Department for Education and Employment, HMSO.

Demo, D. H. and Alcock, A. C. (1993) 'Family diversity and the division of domestic labour: How much have things really changed?', *Family Relations*, 42: pp. 323–331.

Ferri, E. and Smith, K. (1996) *Parenting in the 1990s*. Family Policy Studies Centre and Joseph Rowntree Foundation.

Gershuny, J. Godwin, M. and Jones, S. (1994) 'The domestic labour revolution: A process of lagged adaptation', in M. Anderson, F. Bechhofer and J. Gershuny (eds), *The social and political economy of the household*. Oxford: Oxford University Press, pp. 151–197.

Greenstein, T. N. (1996) 'Husbands' participation in domestic labour: interactive effects of wives' and husbands' gender ideologies', *Journal of Family and Marriage* 58: pp. 585–595.

Harrop, A. and Moss, P. (1994) 'Working parents: Trends in the 1980s', *Employment Gazette*, 102 (10): pp. 343–352.

Hochschild, A. (1990) *The second shift*. London: Piatkus.

Kempson, E. (1996) *Life on a low income*. York: Joseph Rowntree Foundation.

Labour Market Trends (1997) 'Working households, unemployment and economic inactivity', September, pp. 339–345.

Office for National Statistics (1997) *Living in Britain. 1995 General Household Survey*. London: The Stationery Office.

Pullinger, J. and C. Summerfield (eds) (1997) *Social focus on families*. Office for National Statistics. London: The Stationery Office.

Ridgeway, C. L. (1997) 'Interaction and the conservation of gender inequality', *American Sociological Review* Vol. 1, No.62 (April): pp. 218–235.

A Juggling Act: Women Balancing Work, Family and Leisure

Sharon Clough

University of Edinburgh

Introduction

An increasing proportion of women in the United Kingdom are in full-time and part-time paid employment, in all areas of the labour market, which raises a number of important issues about the articulation of employment, family and leisure in contemporary women's lives. The question of how to achieve some 'quality of life' through finding time and space for leisure is increasingly important for a growing number of women in the UK. The current debate about 'work/life balance' suggests that there is a dislocation between the public debate and private experience of women and men as patterns of employment change and impact on traditional gender roles. The increase in male unemployment, in female employment, in dual income families, in lone parents and in the number of women financially supporting families raises a number of gender issues. Further, there is strong evidence that the UK has longer working hours compared to other European Union countries. It is argued that the difficulties arising from combining paid work and parenting, the so-called 'juggling' of career and family commitments, are most acute for people in professional occupations. This has rekindled media criticism of women, who allegedly want to 'have it all', that is, a successful career and a family life.

Women in professional and managerial occupations are more likely to stay in continuous full-time employment than women in other socio-economic groups with pre-school and school age children. This group of women are more likely to delay having children until they have established a career and are more able to afford child care to enable them to stay in employment. Kay (1996) suggests that professional women, with family responsibilities may be developing 'distinctive lifestyles', highly differentiated from women in other socio-economic groups. She concludes that in the absence of appropriate research "the significance of employment as an empowering or constraining influence requires re-examination" (Kay, 1996: p. 63).

This paper reports on the first phase of doctoral research that seeks to explore the ways in which professional women perceive their leisure and its relative importance in their lives. It is based on an analysis of interviews with women lecturers from a number of universities in Great Britain. The qualitative research locates women's leisure lifestyles in the context of their everyday lives and in relation to the people who are

129

the most important in shaping their experiences of leisure. The study looks at issues of control and autonomy and the importance of organisational cultures within academic departments, and power relations between women, their managers and colleagues. Using the principles of grounded theory, it develops the inter-related themes, or motifs, which emerged from the women's narratives about balancing paid employment, unpaid domestic work and family responsibilities with their own leisure needs.

The research perspective is influenced by Giddens's theory of structuration whereby "structures are constituted by the actions of agents, but action itself is organised within the parameters of existing structures" (Bradley, 1996: p. 5). Thus the women involved are not seen as powerless and immobilised by patriarchal structures but can be seen as active agents struggling to control and change their lives. While in this, "Action and meaning and identity are patterned through and in terms of a distinction between male and female" (Acker, 1990: p. 146).

Working women's leisure

Feminist studies of women's leisure in the 1980s offered important critiques of 'malestream' approaches to leisure that were mainly concerned with the work-leisure dichotomy which rendered women's unpaid work invisible. Feminist scholarship in all areas of social science at the time was a 'recuperative action' that challenged "the silencing, stereotyping and marginalisation and misrepresentation of women" (DeGroot and Maynard 1993: p. 2). Feminist theories drew attention to the significance of dominant patriarchal ideologies in oppressing various aspects of women's lives, including access to leisure. The study of women's everyday lives emphasises the interconnectedness of women's experiences. In claiming that the 'personal is political' and by rejecting a political separation between public and private spheres, feminists have highlighted the significance of personal relationships and home circumstances in controlling women's leisure (Scraton 1994). The problematising of women's relations to the domestic sphere has been critical in reconceptualising leisure in a way that challenges the polarisation of work and leisure. Feminists recognised "the complex interplay of cross-cutting influences between women's identities and obligations within the home and in the sphere of paid work" (Green et al. 1990: p. 110).

Although they have been subsequently criticised for over emphasising the shared experiences of women and for neglecting women's resistance to patriarchy through leisure, a number of important empirical studies, such as Deem (1986) and Green et al. (1990) drew attention to gender inequalities and the constraints on women's leisure. Deem (1996) has defended her earlier work against accusations of over generalisation and has emphasised the empirical evidence that demonstrates the continuation of women's shared material disadvantages. The studies demonstrated that, on the whole, women have less personal leisure time; they have fewer resources to spend on leisure for themselves and that their leisure needs are often subservient to the needs of their families. Green et al. (1990) concluded that the negotiations that women enter into over their access to leisure and the extent to which men acted as significant 'gatekeepers' can be seen as a continuum of social control.

Research on women's leisure has produced some apparently contradictory findings with regard to the impact of paid employment on women's leisure. The combined pressures of paid work and domestic obligations often mean that women are 'time-impoverished' compared to men and experience greater 'time fragmentation' (Green,

1998). Although there are indications that women in paid work may experience 'role strain' (Green et al. 1990) and 'time stress' (Shank, 1986; Shaw, 1991), their leisure appears to be enhanced in terms of entitlement to leisure and greater personal resources; and "Employment also seemed to provide a source of women friends, status and a degree of control of life" (Deem, 1986: p. 30). A study of women in Sheffield found that those in full-time employment were more likely to compartmentalise areas of their lives than women whose unpaid work in the home showing that the boundaries were "complex, blurred and shifting" (Green et al. 1990: p. 10).

Feminist studies recognised that there may be significant shared experiences and meanings as well as diversity between and within differently located groups of women. Contemporary post-structural feminist theory focuses attention on identity, diversity and fragmentation of social experience and deconstructs bi-polar opposites such as work/leisure. In emphasising gender as a relational quality, women can be seen as engaged in the construction of meaningful identities where leisure is seen as a means of resistance and empowerment. The dilemma of post structural analysis is that it "at the very least, endorses new forms of pluralism through its focus on the specific positions of different groups, and, at its most extreme can undermine all notions of collectivities" (Bradley 1996: p. 3).

Women academics

The incorporation of the new universities and the expansion of higher education in the UK throughout the 1980s and 1990s has resulted in an increased number of women academics, although they are found disproportionately in the lower ranks and in less secure posts. The casualisation of staff, through fixed term contracts, disproportionately affects women, particularly as there are more women than men on short term research-only contracts. In 1997/8 33% of the total number of 127,568 full time academic staff and 69% of part-time staff in higher education were women; only 18% of Senior and Principal Lecturers and only 9% of Professors are women (Higher Education Statistics Agency 1999). The lack of literature seeking to explain this relative disadvantage may, as Acker (1994) suggests, reflect "a tendency to consider themselves members of an elite rather then a disadvantaged group" (p. 137). Despite the adoption of equal opportunity policies there is no doubt that women remain in a minority at the highest levels. "The impact of the imbalance on British academic life is extreme, especially when combined with tendencies towards hierarchies and elitism" (Acker, 1994: p. 137).

There is an ongoing debate about how to address discrimination, transform academic cultures and set targets to improve equal opportunities. Campaigns by the women's committees of the Association of University Teachers (AUT) have raised a awareness about a range of gender issues, such as the pay gap, 'glass ceiling', childcare and 'family friendly' policies and practices. Cockburn (1990) notes a "an important factor in women's disadvantage in work and in public life more generally is their disproportionate responsibility for domestic work, including care of young, old and ill"(p. 12). Universities have been slow to adopt employment practices that can effectively recruit, retain and promote women. Cockburn argues that sex equality policies can secure women's services in an increasingly tightening labour market but can lead to the contradictory effect of confirming women's domestic role, even for the celibate and childless.

It can be argued that the 'glass escalator' will carry younger women joining the profession to positions of power in academic life. However women's careers are more likely to be characterised by late entry, changes of direction, career breaks and fragmented service. Without a change in organisational cultures, discriminatory practice will continue as it is based on a number of enduring stereotypes; women are not interested in career advancement, they prioritise their families to the detriment of their jobs, only single women progress (Adler et al., 1993). As Cockburn (1990: p. 77) observes, "The way women do or do not fit into the schema of organizational life is seen primarily as a correlate of their marital status and more importantly whether they do or do not they have children". The perception that parenting and career advancement are incompatible for women has been reinforced by studies showing that women academics are less likely to married or have children than male colleagues (Sutherland, 1985).

In recent years rapid expansion of student numbers has resulted in increased academic and administrative workloads on staff. The report of an Association of University Teachers (AUT) time-diary survey of its members in 1994, 'Long Hours Little Thanks', noted that there were some strong indications of gender differences in academic and administrative workloads (Davies and Holloway, 1995). Women employed on the same grade as their male colleagues worked longer hours and performed more of the unacknowledged administrative tasks. Court (1994), however, suggests that due to the lack of perceived promotional prospects women's work orientations may tend towards intrinsic rewards, such as personal relationships and job satisfaction rather than extrinsic rewards, such as pay and promotion.

In a study of women managers in education, Hall (1996: p. 104) notes that "their working days were fragmented, people centred and continuously demanding". Feminist research on women in education, as managers or academics has tended to focus on their career progression and management style with relatively little consideration of the impact that working longer and harder has on personal lives. Adkins (1995) suggests sexual and family relations have been regarded as either external, or at most peripheral, to contemporary employment issues. She argues that "accounts which invoke family — career role conflict as an explanation too often simply blame the victim for not achieving a successful resolution of competing commitments or suggest that women are powerless in the face of social expectations" (p. 138).

Research evidence from studies of women managers (Fagenson, 1993) shows that women make choices relating to family and career experiences which influence their success in both spheres. Parasuman and Greenhaus (1993) discuss two theoretical perspectives on the lifestyles of women managers that emerge from the existing research. The first perspective, 'role conflict', suggests that they experience and focuses on stress and costs of combining career and family on personal relationships and on their children. The emphasis is on the 'overload' on the time and energy of women in senior management positions and on the difficult choices that women have to make between their career and personal life. The second perspective is one of 'role accumulation'; it focuses on the benefits to self-esteem and financial security of the multiple roles. It emphasises increased power in personal relationships and enhanced energy in all areas of personal and professional life.

Parasuman and Greenhaus (1993) identified three types of career orientation; career primary orientation, family primary orientation and career and family orientation. Such typologies acknowledge the possibility of change over time depending on life-stage, personal relationships and career factors. The primary focus of the first group is on success in their career, often at the expense of their personal lives. They were most likely to be 'childless' or 'child free', to give up time with friends and to consider intimate relationships as secondary. For the second group, employment fits around family and partner which may involve part-time employment and being the primary carer in dual-income families, where they earn less than a partner. The third group had high expectations both in terms of their parenting role and their career prospects. They were most likely to have a supportive family and particularly a partner more willing to share childcare and domestic roles. They were most likely to experience role accumulation or conflict.

Despite alleged shifts in the expectations of gender roles and an acknowledgement that male and female employees may both have parental responsibilities, the real effort to combine work and family life is too often seen as a woman's problem. Hochschild (1989) argues that employed women work the so-called 'second shift' at home and accommodate their male partners reluctance to take on domestic duties by adjusting their job commitments. Similarly Apter (1993: p. 10) states that "the second shift is not an isolated remnant of previous family history but a continuing symptom of the divisions between the personal life of the home and the more public, institutional life of work".

The introduction of the European Union Working Time Directive has focused attention on long working hours in the UK compared to the rest of Europe. There is growing research evidence to suggest that there are social costs to long and irregular hours of work for those in relatively privileged labour market positions in Great Britain. Corporate cultures that lead to 'overwork' and 'presenteeism' are said to be having a negative impact on personal and family lives. Zuzanek et al. (1998) suggest that professional people, 'the harried classes', have less leisure time than other occupational groups, particularly as intensive career building often coincides with the life-stage when professional couples have young children. An analysis of the 'leisure gap' between professional men and women cannot ignore the division of domestic responsibilities, particularly when they become parents. Schor's (1991) study in the United States found that contrary to conventional wisdom leisure time is diminishing; and moreover that there are gender differences, 64% of working women 'always feel rushed' compared to 38% of men. Her work has been challenged by Robinson and Godbey (1998) who argue that time budget data shows a diminishing 'free time gap' between men and women. It is possible that gender relations in the homes are becoming more equal and men are sacrificing some of their time and career priorities to share domestic tasks with women (Dench 1996).

Gregson and Lowe (1994) identified a trend towards greater reliance on 'waged labour substitution' in order to reproduce full-time dual career patterns of working. This raises a number of questions about who is responsible for organising paid domestic help, what happens when there are problems with the arrangements and to what extent the paid domestic help facilitates professional women's leisure.

Results

The research for this paper is based on in-depth interviews with twelve women lecturing at a number of Universities in England and who taught a range of subjects. Two were employed on fixed term contracts, two of the lecturers and one of the Principal Lecturers were working part-time, two of the women were Senior Lecturers working full-time, the other women were full-time lecturers. The women ranged in age from twenty seven to fifty three and had entered lecturing from a variety of backgrounds; academic research, industry and teaching. Nine of the women had partners, of the three without partners one had no children and two were single parents. Ten of the women had children, ranging in age from three years to twenty one years old; four of the women had one child, five had two children and one had three; nine of the women had children of school age.

The interviewees were asked about their career paths and career orientation, about their family responsibilities, their domestic arrangements and what they considered to be their leisure. The women were asked about the extent of the flexibility that they felt they have within their jobs and the control that they have over their time. The interviewees talked about the contexts of their leisure; who they were with, what it meant to them as well as the types of activities, when and where they took place.

Four types of leisure pattern emerged from the analysis: p. family leisure, partner leisure, work related leisure and personal leisure. Family leisure included a variety of family activities, meals and celebrations such as birthdays, Christmas. It included servicing children's activities and family holidays. Partner leisure was time set aside to be with partners either in or out of the home; an evening, a lunch, a weekend or holiday, most often arranged and organised by the women rather than their partners. Work related leisure encompassed time spent on academic activities that they enjoyed including conferences, research and meetings with work colleagues, often during the working day for short breaks, lunches or at the end of the day, this often included eating and drinking, but also included some sport and physical activities. Personal leisure was the most highly sought after and the most precious. It was generally acknowledged as the most difficult to organise and preserve, particularly for women with children and partners to satisfy. Personal leisure plans were the first to be cancelled or postponed, demonstrating a lower priority than either work or family commitments. There was resentment about this but many felt an inevitability about their situations. Their acquiescence depended upon the time of year, with the women expressing less ability to resist the pressures at key points in the academic year, particularly at assessment points, due to their commitment to ensuring that they fulfilled their obligations to students and colleagues.

The women without children and two of those with older children said they were focusing on their careers through research and publications and taking on new roles in their departments or faculty. The others did not express a desire to advance in careers in terms of seeking promotion in the foreseeable future, but all felt that in order to advance they needed more time for research, something that would occupy evenings and weekends.

Women with younger school age children tended to perceive themselves either as on a career plateau, particularly if they were not geographically mobile, or if they had 'downshifted' to part-time hours. Two women who had specifically moved into higher education from industry felt that they had 'downshifted' in order to reduce their working hours to accommodate the needs of their children. Three of the women in this study had become part-time employees in response to caring responsibilities and were able to negotiate fractional contracts with their employers.

A number of the interviewees believed that they had become efficient time managers and thus more productive at work since having children. The women with children felt a strong sense of involvement in their jobs and were no less committed than those without, however they all said that their children came first, their work came second and their leisure last in their list of priorities:

J isn't happy with anyone else and I don't like to ask mum to baby-sit too often because she has him during the week and needs a break herself at the weekend. I enjoy my time with my child but end up with very little time for myself.

My own leisure is for me but usually get put on hold if there is a crisis either at work or at home.

All the women interviewed felt strongly about preserving their annual leave, but those that had been employed outside academia felt that the flexibility and the amount of leave was an important reason for leaving industry to work in higher education.

Having worked in industry where I was lucky to take my three weeks a year I have to say I find it very generous in the education system. I don't think I've ever filled in annual leave card. I take school holidays — full stop. I probably take way over what I'm supposed to have but that seems to be the norm.

A number of the interviewees felt that the flexibility and autonomy associated with academic life was being eroded and that this had a negative impact on their personal leisure.

Before I became Course Leader I used to spend more time in the week and at weekends going to exhibitions and working on my own design projects — especially my portfolio but now I'm swamped with time consuming admin.

Employment for these women was a site of 'relative freedom', that added rather than detracted from their self-esteem, in terms of social status and maintaining an identity outside of family life. They did however recognise that the competing demands on their time and energy had to be carefully managed.

I enjoy travelling to conferences and choose my venues very carefully.

Doing the MBA meant going on study weekends which were great fun- though I couldn't let T know I was enjoying myself — as he was stuck at home with our son.

They used a variety of different coping strategies, including negotiating alterations in their roles at work, deliberately avoiding certain kinds of tasks and often attempting to find time for themselves in the working day.

Our running group means a great deal to me, I need the exercise but it's a chance to let off steam rather and often helps me through the day. I know I would not do it on my own unless pushed so in fact I sometimes come in for the run when I could have worked at home for the day.

I feel entitled to some time to myself — but it just doesn't happen, unless I am really determined to get out of the house- the easiest way is to arrange to go out straight from work.

Those women with the highest levels of paid domestic labour, particularly live-in help, reported the least difficulty in satisfying their leisure needs. The women all expressed this as essential help for them personally:

The au pair does the school runs and I know that the children are safely at home having tea if I'm going to be late. She does a modest amount of light housework also baby-sits at least two evenings, which means I can keep fit and go out to dinner or have dinner parties. I pay an agency and choose carefully – they often become good friends.

I have a cleaner who comes in and also does ironing, in fact the best decision I ever made, so my weekends are not spent scrabbling around trying to make the house look half way decent. It actually gives me — buys me — leisure time.

The woman whose partner had responsibility for domestic work (the 'role reversal' couple), who commuted a long way to work by train, felt that she had little leisure. Her train journeys were used for paperwork and as she 'took over' in the evenings as soon as she returned home and at weekends in order to 'give her partner a break'.

If T didn't run a business from home and do the school run we wouldn't be able to cope especially with me leaving so early for the train and sometimes getting home really late.

The women with children reported spending considerable amounts of 'family leisure time', servicing their partner's and children's leisure. Several of the women reported on making an effort with varying degrees of success to find activities that satisfied all the family.

I'm really rather lazy but we do try to swim and we bought a car rack so we could go out to the park for family bike rides. My husband is inclined to race off and not even look behind to see where the children are so I get left bringing up the rear. He now knows that swimming with children takes twice as long as when he is on his own in the changing rooms.

I don't want my children to feel that they do less because I'm not there after school when lots of children have a very full social life, so quite often I dash home to take them to various clubs but then have to hang around waiting for them to finish. I sometimes read the newspaper but quite often take marking or other work with me.

The women with school age children stressed the importance of their relationships with close women friends, who they relied on to help out with childcare particularly in a crisis. They felt that the opportunities to build networks with other mothers were limited especially if they did not take and collect children from school.

I always finish early one day a week so that we can go out to tea or to the park. I don't want mine to miss out after school.

Of the two single parents, the one with a pre-school age child experienced the least personal leisure, particularly as the child rarely saw her former partner. Whilst the other, whose children were older had a fuller and more satisfying life, particularly as her children spent alternate weekends with their father and half the school holidays. Not having to negotiate with a current partner, she had made very positive efforts to have regular holidays abroad sailing with friends and had bought her own sailing boat that she used most weekends.

My boat is the best part of my life — it has been my lifeline. I moved to live near to the coast and commute two hours each way for work rather than stay in town. As a single person I can suit myself especially now that the children are older. My life is a lot better now than it has been, looking back I don't know how I did it — supporting myself financially, doing the house up and bringing up my children — I was going bananas.

Conclusions

All of the interviewees felt that they were entitled to leisure, but for the women in relationships this was not readily recognised by their partners and families. A number felt that their partners assumed their entitlement to leisure in the evenings and at weekends, but the women felt that they had to struggle to make their needs for rest and relaxation both understood and supported.

For the women with children their partners or ex-partners were often the 'gatekeepers' to their personal leisure, but they were also important facilitators. Gender inequalities in the home were most acute with the arrival of children for these women, even though they stayed employed they had to adjust their paid work involvement to accommodate the increased demands of the 'double shift'. Their leisure was increasingly 'family focused' and indeed those with children reported that their time spent on supporting their children's leisure decreased their personal leisure time. Some of the women deliberately chose and organised family activities that provided satisfaction for all family members. The paradox is that family oriented leisure time is both a source of satisfaction and frustration for women because they reported being the 'social secretary', that is primary facilitator and organiser of the family's leisure.

The women academics in this study do not present an homogenous group in terms of their lifestyles, they do however, share some similarities in the ways in leisure presents opportunities for resistance to paid and unpaid work and is something that is both valued and hard won. The women's career and family involvement's are interdependent and sometimes limiting. Paid work provides opportunities for challenging gender disadvantage in the home and opportunities for leisure during the working day, particularly for those who made a positive effort to make time for themselves. The narratives of the women in relationships include references to their experiences of leisure in relation to both their caring roles at home and their professional commitments. In trying to balance their needs with the needs of those whom they have relationships or for whom they have responsibilities they had to negotiate time and space for themselves. The greater their responsibilities at home and at work the more complex the negotiations. The 'trade-offs' that had to be agreed with colleagues, friends, partners and families in order to have some leisure were in many cases a testimony to their highly tuned negotiating skills. The women in this study were all highly organised and used to 'multi-tasking'. They believed in their abilities to manage both academic and family life, all expressed a desire for more personal leisure, but were aware that they would have to organise, instigate and negotiate time and space for themselves and resist the increasing pressures on them.

References

Acker, S. (1994) *Gendered education*. Milton Keynes: Open University Press.

Adler, S., Laney, J. and Packer, M. (1993) *Managing women*. Milton Keynes: Open University.

Adkins, L. (1995) *Gendered work*. Milton Keynes: Open University Press.

Bradley, H. 1996) *Fractured identities*. Cambridge: Polity Press.

Cockburn, C. (1991) *In the way of women: Men's resistance to sex equality in organizations*. Basingstoke: Macmillan.

Court, S. (1994) *Long hours, little thanks: A survey of the use of time by full-time academic and related staff in the traditional UK Universities*. London: Association of University Teachers.

Davies, C. and Holloway, P. (1995) 'Troubling transformations: Gender regimes and organisational culture in the Academy', in L. Morley and V. Walsh (eds) *Feminist academics: Creative agents for change*. London: Taylor and Francis.

De Groot, H. and Maynard, M. (1993) *Women's studies in the 1990s: Doing things differently*. Basingstoke: Macmillan.

Deem, R. (1986) *All work and no play? The sociology of women and leisure*. Milton Keynes: Open University press.

―――― (1996) 'Time for a change? Engendered work and leisure in the 1990s', *Leisure Studies* Vol. 16, No. 3: pp. 3–22.

Dench, G. (1996) *The place of men in changing family cultures*. London: Institute of Community Studies.

Gershuny, J. , Godwin, M. and Jones, S. (1994) 'The domestic labour revolution', in M. Anderson, F. Bechofer and J. Gershuny, J. (eds) *The social and political economy of the household*. Oxford: Oxford University Press: pp. 151–197.

Green, E., Hebron, S. and Woodward, D. (1990) *Women's leisure, what leisure?*. Basingstoke: Macmillan.

―――― (1998) 'Flexible work, disappearing leisure', in C. Aitchison C. and F. Jordan (eds) *Gender, space and identity* (LSA Publication No. 63). Eastbourne: Leisure Studies Association, pp. 111–126.

Gregson W. and Lowe M. (1994) *Servicing the middle classes*. London: Routledge.

Hochschild, A. (1989) *The second shift*. New York: Viking.

Hall, V. (1996) *Dancing on the ceiling*. London: Paul Chapman Publishing.

Karsten, L. (1995) 'Women's leisure divergence, reconceptualisation and change: The case of the Netherlands', *Leisure Studies* Vol. 14, No. 1: pp. 186–201.

Kay, T. (1996) 'Women's Leisure and the Family in Contemporary Britain', in N. Samuel (ed) *Women's leisure, and family in contemporary society: A multi-national perspective*. Oxon: CAB International, pp. 143–159.

Parasuman S., and Greenhaus, J. (1993) Personal Portrait: the Lifestyles of the Woman Manager', in E. Fagenson (ed) *Women and management*. London: Sage, pp.7–34.

Robinson and Godbey (1998) *Time for life: The surprising ways Americans use their time*. Pittsburgh: Pennsylvania State University Press.

Rubery, J. and Burchell, B. (1994) 'Divided women', in A. MacEwan Scott (ed) *Gender segregation and social change*. Oxford: Oxford University Press, pp. 80–120.

Schor, J. (1991) *The overworked American: The unexpected decline of leisure*. New York: Basic Books.

Scraton, S. (1994) 'The changing world of women and leisure: Feminism, post-feminism and leisure', *Leisure Studies* Vol. 13, No. 4: pp. 249–260.

Shank, J. (1986) 'An exploration of teisure time in the lives of dual care career women', *Journal of Leisure Research* 16: pp. 266–282.

Sutherland, M. (1985) *Women who teach in universities*. Stoke-on-Trent: Trentham.

Zuzanek J, Beckers, T. and Peters, P. (1998) 'The harried leisure class revisited', *Leisure Studies* Vol. 17, No. 1: pp. 1–20.

When Gender is Problematic: Leisure and Gender Negotiation for Marginalized Women

Diane M. Samdahl
University of Georgia

Sharon Jacobson
State University of New York, College at Brockport

Susan Hutchinson
The Pennsylvania State University

Introduction

We originally submitted this paper for the LSA 4th International Conference in response to a theme on 'Gendered Spaces'. In doing so, we argue that all contexts in which women experience life, including leisure, are inherently gendered spaces where people play out and confront the dominant ideologies associated with womanhood. We take leisure to be particularly revealing as a gendered space because it is a site where the ideology of personal freedom comes into direct confrontation with the constraints of gendered expectations.

As a hegemonic system that supports the status quo, gendered expectations are most effective when they are embedded so deeply that they become invisible. Thus, many women play out gender roles without ever understanding how cultural expectations have shaped and limited their choices and behavior. Those hidden ideologies of gender can be made most visible by studying marginalized women — that is, women who deviate in some fashion from what "proper" women should be. For us, the stories of old lesbians and women with acquired disabilities helped highlight the ideology of womanhood because these women were unable or unwilling to conform to the gendered ideal. Indeed, for these women gender was particularly problematic.

We believe that everyone — male and female — must negotiate gender in the context of their daily lives. We use "negotiation" as it is used in symbolic interaction (cf. Denzin, 1970; McCall & Simmons, 1966; Mead, 1934; Thomas, 1937), referring to the process of reaching a shared understanding of a situation, a shared meaning about attributes, behaviors, and expectations between interacting individuals. People negotiate in many subtle ways as they attempt to situate themselves comfortably in the social context of their lives. As we examined the stories of the women reported in this paper, we realized that not all women had the same ability or resources with which to negotiate gender. Likewise, we came to appreciate the situated nature of negotiation which requires a responsive Other who is willing to compromise if negotiation is to be successful.

In this paper we highlight the way that gender pervades our lives and show how different women responded to the gendered expectations that they were unable to meet.

We then discuss gender negotiation as a particularly salient framework for understanding women's leisure.

The Studies

This paper draws upon two distinct research projects. The first study was the masters research of Susan Hutchinson (1996) who interviewed eight adults (including five women) who had acquired brain injuries, in an attempt to understand how these people reconciled their disability with their prior sense of self. Our analysis here includes only the women from that study. A brain injury produces a range of physical and cognitive impairments in people who otherwise appear to be functioning normally. Problems include short-term memory loss; difficulty concentrating, organizing or problem-solving; and fatigue or chronic pain. Each of these women had been employed prior to her accident but none had been able to return to work after the head injury.

The second study was the doctoral research of Sharon Jacobson (1996) who interviewed eight lesbians over the age of 60 to understand how these women experienced and responded to discrimination due to gender, age, and sexual identity. Approximately half of these women had been in heterosexual marriages before coming out as lesbians and several had children and grandchildren. Each of these women self-identified as a lesbian and had been in at least one long-term relationship with another woman. We will refer to these women as "old lesbians" instead of using the more comfortable term "older" at the request of a national coalition of old lesbians. The term "older" implies that young is the normative state for comparison and these women wished that their age be a descriptive rather than a comparative feature.

The Women

After some deliberation, we decided the most effective way to present our ideas was to introduce several of these women and then discuss aspects of gender negotiation and leisure. This pattern parallels our own process of learning, for immersing ourselves in their stories led us to understand the salience of gender in these women's lives. We do not have time in this presentation to elaborate on the variety of gendered expectations that these women encountered so we encourage you to listen for gender ideology as you hear each woman's story. We introduce only four of the women here but our later discussion draws upon understandings which emerged from all thirteen women.

Mary. Mary is a middle aged married woman who had been the consummate wife, mother, and daughter before acquiring a brain injury in an automobile accident. She held a full-time job, did extensive volunteer work, and serviced her family in every conceivable way. She had been actively involved in her daughter's soccer activities and ran an immaculate, efficient household. Mary had had a supportive network of friends who often dropped by for coffee and conversation.

After her injury Mary suffered from exhaustion and weakness and had difficulty concentrating. She quit her job and struggled with familiar tasks like house cleaning, laundry, or cooking. Unable to be the wife and mother that she had been, Mary saw no role for herself in her family. She said, "Sometimes you do just feel like they're probably better off without me". Mary also withdrew from her friends because she had trouble organizing and serving coffee or maintaining a focused, coherent conversation.

Mary's family used to go camping and she took pride in having been the one to "do it all" — organizing the food and equipment, setting up and taking down the tent, and running the campsite as efficiently as she ran her home. After the accident Mary had difficulty with many daily household activities; however, she did not confront the extent of her disability until the family went on another camping trip and she was unable to take down the tent. As she related this story, it became clear that Mary's failure at camping was more significant and made her injuries seem more "real" than similar failures she had faced around the house.

Inez. Inez is a Chilean woman who acquired a head injury through a bicycle accident. Prior to the accident Inez had been busy all the time. She owned and managed a restaurant and also organized a dance program for Chilean children. Inez had ridden her bicycle everywhere, always had extra people around the house or at the dinner table, and had been the social hub for a large extended family.

After her accident Inez was unable to function in any of those roles. She believed she had gone crazy until her brain injury was diagnosed one year after her accident. She sold the restaurant and found it too painful to remain involved in the dance studio. Because Inez was unable to coordinate activities for her extended family, her sisters took over those responsibilities. In fact, Inez was so embarrassed by the extent of her disability that she no longer wanted to have extended family or friends around her home.

Barb. Barb is a 60 year old woman who has been divorced twice and has three children. At the time of the interviews Barb had been involved with another woman for several years. Her father and both of her husbands had been physically and verbally abusive, and Barb learned early to put the needs and comfort of others before her own. She described her role in family vacations as "slave labor" because she was responsible for absolutely everything. Even in her current relationship with a woman, Barb submitted to many of the wishes of her partner and felt irresponsible whenever she took time for herself.

Barb grew up in a mountain community where women were strong and competent — the women in her childhood used tools, took care of livestock, and often wore men's clothing. Once when she moved into a new apartment, Barb uncovered some books of lesbian fiction whose covers portrayed strong women wearing flannel shirts and heavy-soled shoes. Her first thought was "how marvelous!" and only later did she realize that the women in these books were portrayed as "other than a woman". Even though Barb did not identify as lesbian at the time, she felt invalidated by the suggestion that strong women were something less than good, decent, and moral.

During a recent vacation Barb and her partner were harassed on the highway. A male truck driver determined that these women were lesbians by signs and stickers on the bumper of Barb's car. He pulled up and drove alongside them for quite a distance, honking his horn and making obscene gestures with his hand and mouth. Needless to say, the women were quite frightened but this was not the first time they had faced open fear and discrimination. Barb and her partner had recently moved to a new home because of the "politics of hate" among their neighbors.

Anna. Anna is a 78 year old woman. Her husband died the year that she retired and she has had several long-term relationships with women in the twenty years since his death. Anna has two daughters and three grandchildren. She is a private person and though she has many friends she says she often feels out of place or different from the people around her.

When Anna's children were at home the family took precedent in her life; later, her ailing husband required much of her care and attention. After she was widowed Anna's life began to open up in new directions. She moved to a new town, quickly made new friends, and became involved in environmental issues. Several years later Anna met her first lesbian partner. She said, "[Up until then] I didn't realize there was any lesbian in me". After becoming involved in the lesbian relationship Anna put her energy into activities that supported feminism and the lesbian community. Her activist efforts are important to her; Anna said, "It feels good to know that you have done a little something".

While our study was underway Anna began dating a man whom she had known for a long time. She was reluctant to tell her lesbian friends about this and anticipated losing some of those friendships because of it. However, Anna's family and a few other friends had been openly supportive of this new relationship. Anna said, "When they learned that I found a man to love they were all delighted for me.... They were probably happier for me than when they learned about my relationship with a woman".

Confronting gender ideologies

Examining the above stories, it is clear that these women encountered gender ideology in many facets of their lives. Starting with the most obvious, these stories make a strong case that a "good" woman is a married heterosexual woman who is capable of being invested in the lives of her husband and children. She is responsible for housework and for managing a variety of social obligations; even her friendships are shaped by gendered expectations. It would be impossible to understand these women's lives — to comprehend what it meant to be an old lesbian or to have a brain injury — without understanding those characteristics in relation to the gender ideologies that surrounded them. The women in these studies were frequently and often painfully aware of how they differed from the normative expectations of what a woman should be.

Being different was a source of stress and frustration and some women never got beyond the stigma of being different. However, other women in these studies were more successful in negotiating an accepted place for themselves within their social environments. Whether or not a woman succeeded and felt accepted was related, in part, to her ability to negotiate gendered expectations. In this study, the women who had the most difficulty finding a comfortable place for themselves were those who held most tightly to the normative beliefs about what a woman should do and be.

We see this in Mary who had been the consummate wife and mother prior to her brain injury. Mary did not view this as a choice; for her, a woman was defined through her ability to manage her family and household. This belief was so strong, and the acceptable roles for a woman were so narrowly defined, that Mary was unable to accept the limitations imposed by her disability. She said, "I think I am afraid that if you do accept it, then what? What am I going to do?" Mary's position was made worse by the cognitive limitations imposed by her brain injury. She was literally unable to understand that responsibility for household chores could be re-negotiated in light of her disability, nor could she have accepted a new arrangement without feeling as if she were a failure. Likewise, her husband and daughter did little to help Mary adapt to her new limitations; Mary feared that her failures around the home would eventually drive her husband away. For Mary there was only one way to be a woman and that had been taken from her.

Inez, the Chilean woman with a head injury, and Barb, the lesbian woman who had divorced two abusive husbands, offer examples that are a bit more optimistic. Inez's brain injury forced her to give up responsibility for the large extended family. In her Chilean culture this was a significant loss. However, in retrospect Inez came to appreciate the freedom she obtained by relinquishing that role. She said, "Before, it seems like I was always pleasing everybody. ... Anything that anybody would ask me, I would do it. Right now, I just say no". Though her brain injury produced the freedom to begin doing things for herself, this privilege had been bought at a great price and Inez lacked the feeling of competence that had been hers before her injury.

Barb was also going through a transition in her life. For years she had sacrificed herself in order to provide for the needs and comfort of others but now she was wanting to stand up for herself. She said, "I want my own space, I want my own time, but I don't know how to do it comfortably without offending the other person". At the time of the interviews Barb was going through a stressful period with her woman partner but she said, "With this one I am staying.... I need to get past this issue [of losing my self in a relationship]".

Anna, the widow who began dating a man after fifteen years of lesbian relationships, was perhaps more successful in confronting gender ideologies though even for her it did not come easy. After being widowed Anna used recreation and political activism to help establish a new network of friends, and she easily moved into (and then out of) relationships with women and with men. However, Anna felt estranged in both the heterosexual and the lesbian communities; she described herself as a 'round peg in a square hole'. But she had a measure of self confidence that allowed her to make friends and she was able to take a stand on controversial issues and work for what she believed in. Those traits carried her through times of transition and helped Anna negotiate an accepted place for herself in a variety of social situations.

Understanding negotiation

In trying to understand why some of these women were more effective than others at negotiating gendered expectations, we came to understand that negotiation is not possible in all facets of our lives. Broad cultural beliefs — those hegemonic structures that are deeply embedded in society and internalized by individuals — are not easily amenable to negotiation or compromise. When confronted with gendered expectations at that level these women were more likely to accommodate — that is, to quietly go along without raising a challenge — rather than to negotiate for acceptance. We saw this in the lesbians who attempted to hide their identity in public and in the women with brain injuries who felt like they no longer could be a friend, wife, or mother. Accommodation is different from negotiation because it quietly hides a stigmatized condition rather than asking for or demanding changed attitudes and acceptance.

On the other hand, some women truly negotiated an accepted place for themselves in their social worlds. These women were aware of how they differed from the gendered ideal but asked for, and received, acceptance and affirmation in spite of that difference. Denzin (1970) referred to this as "self-lodging" or negotiating an understanding in which one's identity is accepted and affirmed by others. Once this acceptance has been achieved, negotiation itself is no longer necessary.

Since this type of negotiation occurs through direct interaction with others it happens most often within the more private networks of family and friends. It cannot happen unless both parties are willing to compromise, therefore it is unlikely to occur among strangers or against institutionalized forms of discrimination. Those of you familiar with literature on the ecological perspective (cf. Brofenbrenner, 1979; Germain, 1992) might realize that we are differentiating here between the macro and micro layers of the social environment. Gender negotiation requires direct interaction and is most likely to be achieved in the inner circles of our lives.

We see this best in the old lesbians who established networks of supportive friends, most often with other lesbians in the community. In the company of these women the old lesbians found support and acceptance, and gender, age, and sexual orientation were no longer problematic. The old lesbians can be contrasted with Mary whose husband and daughter wanted nothing less than the wife and mother that Mary had been before her accident. With her cognitive limitations and a family who was unwilling to compromise, Mary was not able to negotiate a comfortable place where her new, disabled self was accepted and affirmed.

We differentiate between accommodation and negotiation in order to emphasize that negotiation creates new meaning in relation to broader cultural discourse, but women's responses are more complex than this dualistic discussion implies. Accommodation does not mean submissiveness, and the old lesbians often accommodated in selective environments because that was the best strategy for that situation. In addition, negotiation might be most evident when it occurs between people but it also happens internally as women struggle against their own beliefs about what a woman should do or be. We don't imply that these are the only responses available to women, but we do emphasize that negotiation is a more stable solution because it replaces stigma with acceptance.

What does it take to negotiate gender? It appears from these women's stories that gender negotiation requires an understanding that there are many different ways to be a woman. In fact, gender itself must be stripped from its dichotomous framework and relegated to the background, with emphasis placed instead on the qualities that each individual possesses. This attitude must exist not only in the individual woman but also in others with whom she interacts. Also, as was clear for several women in these studies, gender negotiation requires the mental capacity and self confidence to stand up for one's self and willingness to work for acceptance in the face of stigma.

And what about leisure?

As we wrote this paper we kept trying to focus the above discussion on gendered aspects of leisure for we knew our ultimate goal was to make a statement of interest to leisure scholars. However, it was difficult to isolate leisure from other aspects of these women's lives. We have come to realize that leisure can be understood only in relation to the broad cultural discourses that create meaning in a person's life. For the women in these studies, gender ideology shaped what it meant to be an old lesbian or a woman with a brain injury, and without understanding that it would be impossible to understand anything about their leisure. So perhaps our first remark to leisure scholars is to reiterate the importance of studying leisure in context.

The most obvious and perhaps least interesting insight is to note that gendered expectations were present in leisure. Similar to the findings of many other studies, these women serviced their families' leisure in traditional ways when involved in heterosexual marriages or before acquiring brain injuries. More interesting, perhaps, is to note that this role was not always perceived as restrictive or confining. Mary, the consummate wife and mother, would find her life immensely enhanced if she could return to her roles as soccer mom and the woman who managed a campsite as efficiently as she ran her home. It is imperative that we respect women like Mary for whom traditional gender roles carry significant meaning, even when they do not portray our ideal of what leisure should be.

Of more interest to us was the way these stories enhanced our understanding of freedom. Freedom itself must be understood in relation to those things which potentially constrain it (Sartre, 1956). In leisure, the ideology of freedom comes into direct conflict with the ideologies of gender, sexuality, (dis)ability, age and many other forms of cultural discourse which shape the meanings and judgments that we assign to ourselves. The intersection of these conflicting ideologies made us believe that leisure would be an ideal site to view the processes of gender negotiation.

We were at least partially wrong. For the women in these studies, gender negotiation was most visible outside of leisure as these women struggled with the stigma of being lesbian or being unable to perform the activities normatively associated with womanhood. More remarkably, leisure was sometimes characterized by the absence of visible conflict or negotiation. In retrospect this should not have been surprising. Though negotiation was apparent in those women who were still trying to achieve acceptance and an element of freedom in their leisure, it was not salient for women who had already established affirming friendships and safe, rewarding leisure contexts. For those women, successful negotiation of gendered expectations had produced leisure settings where negotiation itself was no longer necessary.

Though we have never believed in freedom as an absolute condition of leisure, this analysis of negotiation has given us added insight into how freedom is made possible. In effect, freedom can be seen as the consequence of successfully negotiating the cultural discourses that assign meaning to our selves and our activities. Being free does not require that a woman resist cultural discourses, only that she is comfortably situated in relation to the meanings that those discourses create. Some women attain this freedom through their ability to meet the gendered ideal, while other women find it by negotiating acceptance of their divergence from that ideal. We had originally expected to study gender negotiation as it occurs within leisure but we reached a much more complex and interesting awareness of gender negotiation as way to understand leisure.

Before closing we have one more important point to make. Our initial thinking about leisure and gender negotiation was strongly influenced by discussions of leisure and resistance, particularly Betsy Wearing's (1990, 1991) work. However, we had trouble imposing the label "resistance" in analysis of these women's stories. For example, Jacobson's study included a lesbian woman who had worn men's pants in the 1940s even though that action subjected her to police harassment. Asked if this was an act of resistance this woman said no, men's pants were simply more comfortable. That study also included Anna who was an activist for environmental, feminist, and lesbian concerns because she wanted to initiate change in the world. We may be academically justified in calling both of those actions "resistance" but doing so hides important differences in what those activities meant to the individual women.

We were much more comfortable approaching our analysis from the framework of negotiation. Both terms, resistance and negotiation, refer to processes whereby women attempt to situate themselves in relation to the cultural discourses that surround them. Some acts of negotiation are definitely acts of resistance, and the cumulative effect of negotiation may be to erode or change dominant ideologies that are restrictive. But for us, negotiation is a more comprehensive term that better captures the processes of interaction whereby resistance is made evident, and a more inclusive term that better captures women whose goals are simple acceptance rather than social change.

This emphasis on negotiation parallels earlier symbolic interactionist discussions of leisure (cf. Kelly, 1983; Samdahl, 1988) but better situates leisure within broad cultural discourses that shape and define our lives. In line with poststructural ideology (cf. Ussher, 1997), negotiation adds emphasis to the interactive processes that mediate between agency and structure (see Rojek, 1989) and highlights the ways that leisure is embedded in our lives. Many of the attributes that have been linked to leisure (e.g. self-expression, self-determination, flow) come about when the self has been comfortably situated and hegemonic expectations are no longer problematic. We are excited about this approach to the study of women's leisure because it provides a more dynamic and integrative view of leisure than traditional feminist or leisure theory.

References

Brofenbrenner, U. (1979) The ecology of human development: Experiments by nature and design. *Cambridge, MA: Harvard University Press*

Denzin, N. K. (1970) 'Symbolic interactionism and ethnomethodology', in J. Douglas (ed) Understanding everyday life: Toward the reconstruction of sociological knowledge. *Chicago: Aldine Pub. Co.*

Hutchinson, S. (1996) An exploration of the processes of self-identity reconstruction by people who acquire a brain injury. Unpublished masters thesis, Dalhausie University, Halifax, Nova Scotia.

Germain, C. B. (1992) Human behavior in the social environment: An ecological view. *NY: Columbia University Press.*

Jacobson, S. A. (1996) An examination of leisure in the lives of old lesbians from an ecological perspective. *Unpublished doctoral dissertation, University of Georgia, Athens, GA.*

Kelly, J. R. (1983) Leisure identities and interactions. *London: Allen and Unwin.*

McCall, G. J. & Simmons, J. L. (1966) Identities and interactions. *NY: The Free Press.*

Mead, G. H. (1962 [1934]) Mind, self, and society, C. W. Morris (ed). *Chicago: University of Chicago Press.*

Samdahl, D. M. (1988) 'A symbolic interactionist model of leisure: Theory and empirical support', Leisure Sciences, Vol. 10, pp. 27–39.

Sartre, J. P. (1956) Being and nothingness: An essay in phenomenological ontology, H. E. Barnes (trans). *Secaucus, NJ: Citadel Press.*

Thomas, W. I. (1937) The unadjusted girl. *Boston: Little Brown.*

Ussher, J. M. (1997) 'Towards a material-discursive analysis of madness sexuality and reproduction', in J. M. Ussher (ed) Body talk: The material and discursive regulation of sexuality, madness and reproduction. *NY: Routledge.*

Wearing, B. (1990) 'Beyond the ideology of motherhood: Leisure as resistance', Australia and New Zealand Journal of Sociology, Vol. 26, pp. 36-58.

Wearing, B. (1991) 'Leisure and women's identity: Conformity or new individuality?', Loisir et Societe/Society and Leisure, Vol. 14, pp. 575-586.

Being Cool as a Social Imperative: Young Women's Resistance to Health Promotion Messages about Physical Exercise

Eleanor Peters
The Children's Society, Stafford

Diana Woodward
Graduate School, Cheltenham and Gloucester College of Higher Education

Introduction

Its concern to promote healthy lifestyles was expressed by the previous Conservative Government in *The Health of the Nation White Paper*, published in 1992. It identified the major causes of premature mortality and avoidable morbidity, and set public health targets for the year 2000 to be achieved through educating individuals about health-threatening behaviours, such as smoking and excessive alcohol consumption, and encouraging health-promoting activities such as exercise and improved diet. A qualitative study of young women[1] in two West Midlands towns explored the prospects of certain relevant targets being achieved for this group within the population, and provided the basis for a feminist critique of recent Government health promotion initiatives.

The material presented here concerns the young women's experiences and practices in relation to participation in physical activity. It is argued that the cult of femininity and the desire for acceptance by peers militate against participation in physical activity other than recreational dancing, and promote smoking and even disordered eating habits as weight control measures. In discussing young women's engagement in physical exercise, the work of Scraton in particular has been utilised (Scraton, 1986; 1987; 1990; 1992; 1994; 1995). She argues that the cult of femininity encourages young women to view physical activity as masculine, uncool, and at odds with their self-image. The issues discussed in this paper have numerous implications for health promotion professionals, as it highlights the continual failings of health promotion campaigns to target young women effectively. The research also suggests that the role of teachers, 'youth workers' and parents as informal health promoters is limited. This study contributes to the small but growing literature on young women's lives, with particular emphasis on the often neglected topic of the place physical activity plays in the everyday lives of some young women.

In this paper we begin with an account of *The Health of the Nation* targets, and provide a feminist critique of them and of past health promotion campaigns. We then give details of the empirical study whose results this paper reports, going on to review feminist ethnographies of young women, including discussion of the cult of femininity. We then present the study's findings concerning physical activity and exercise, exploring the reasons for young women's reluctance to embrace the healthy lifestyle message. The paper concludes with some recommendations for future health promotion initiatives.

The Health of the Nation

The Health of the Nation: A strategy for health in England, produced by the previous (Conservative) Government, set objectives and targets relating to health status to be met by the year 2000. (There were similar separate documents for both Wales and Scotland.) The objective of this White Paper was to focus attention on key aspects of the nation's health, to guide campaigns and interventions by agencies and individuals. It identified five key areas: coronary heart disease and stroke; cancers; mental illness; HIV/AIDS and sexual health; and accidents. Risk factors associated with each of the five key areas were identified to provide a basis for intervention. For example, within Coronary Heart Disease some of the risk factors identified were smoking, diet and obesity, and lack of exercise. The majority of the targets were directed at the general population with only one smoking target and one sexual health target specifically directed at young people. Although the document suggested that success in meeting the targets could be achieved through public policies geared to promoting a healthy environment and healthy lifestyles, and the provision of high quality health services, the focus was clearly on the individual and modification of their behaviour.

Feminist critique of The Health of the Nation and health promotion campaigns

Many of *The Health of the Nation* targets were set at different levels for men and women, for example the projected decrease in smoking prevalence and reduction in obesity levels. However, there was little discussion or explanation of gender differences in health status within the document, and scant recognition that women and men may require different health promotion interventions if the targets were to be achieved. The key areas in the document were linked to a number of important groups within the wider population such as women, people from ethnic minorities, elderly people and people with disabilities, giving rise to the implicit assumption in The Health of the Nation that the normal person is white, male and middle-class (Sidell et al., 1997).

Women's smoking has been a major preoccupation of health educators for many years. Women, particularly pregnant women, are heavily exposed to health promotion campaigns designed to encourage them to quit. However, all too often these campaigns seek to frighten women smokers by highlighting the medical problems associated with smoking rather than on seeking to address the social and personal conditions which promote women's propensity to smoke:

> In view of the connection between social deprivation and stress on the one hand, and women's smoking on the other, the argument that health is a matter of individual choice ignores the social determinants of choice if it ignores the fact that health itself is a social product. (Oakley, 1993: p. 104)

Health promotion, as practised by the previous Conservative administration, rarely engaged with the social elements that may render women's lives unhealthy, assuming that to arm consumers with knowledge about health-damaging behaviours will of itself result in changes in those behaviours. Women smokers have been targeted by health promotion campaigns because of the harm their own practices can do to others, most notably their children. However, these campaigns do little to empower women to make the changes within their lives to enable them to make healthy choices, nor do they address the structural and cultural issues that underpin the allegedly personal choice to smoke.

Women are the principal providers of health-care both, within the home and outside it (Doyal, 1995; Oakley, 1993). However, *The Health of the Nation* does not analyse or address women's particular needs, firstly as women, and secondly as the main providers of care for children and adults within families. Oakley suggests that the education of mothers, particularly in the developing world, is emerging as an important factor in reducing infant mortality rates, but this could be seen as yet another example of a cultural imperative which ignores women's individual identities and circumstances, in favour of concentrating on their social roles in relation to others (Oakley, 1993: p. 106).

The study

The study reported in this paper was conducted in youth clubs and schools in two towns, one in a conurbation and one located in a rural area, with about fifty young women aged between 13 and 16 years of age. Two youth clubs in Wolverhampton were studied, which we shall call Poolside and Parkside, together with Hillside (all proper names are pseudonyms) school and youth club in Hereford and Worcester (now Herefordshire and Worcestershire). The main method of enquiry was participant observation, supplemented by interviews. In order to gain an insight into young women's family lives and the extent to which parental opinions and actions influence young women's health-related behaviours, teachers, youth workers and the mothers of some young women involved in the study were also interviewed. Notes were made while attending the youth clubs and schools, which were written up and subsequently analysed. All interviews were tape-recorded and then transcribed and analysed. A grounded-theory (Glaser and Strauss, 1967) approach was used to analyse the data, which allowed fieldwork to inform theory, which in turn informs further fieldwork.

The research problem identified was to examine the place of some health-related beliefs and behaviours within the context of the everyday lives of young women. The approach was chosen in order to ascertain to what extent improvements in the health of young women, such as those proposed by *The Health of the Nation*, were likely to be achieved taking into account the social, economic and cultural influences and constraints young women may face. Young women in their mid-teens are neither children nor adults; they are financially dependent on their parents, and almost all still live at home, yet their parents and teachers are beginning to accord them some of the licence and autonomy associated with adult status. The adults' own ambivalence about what constitutes an appropriate mix of regulation and control, on the one hand, or freedom, on the other, is a recurrent theme in this study. It has major implications for health promotion work with young people, by both state or local agencies and parents, as coercion, control and direction are likely to be resisted by young people. The eating, sleeping and recreational habits of young people cannot be monitored or regulated to the same extent as the lives of primary school age children are, and yet the adults responsible for their care or education acknowledge that they are still too young to be accorded complete autonomy. Their concern about their own effectiveness as health educators or health promoters is an issue which professionals within the field of health promotion need to address. An interest in young people's health is demonstrated in *The Health of the Nation* and in more recent policy documents such as *Our Healthier Nation* and also in the media, and in academic and health promotion literature. This interest is derived from the belief that health-damaging forms of behaviour in adulthood often commence during the teenage years and therefore the establishment of a healthy lifestyle at this age is crucial for long-term health. There is also a widespread romantic notion that childhood should be a time of innocence, far from the reality of a society in which young people and children take drugs, eat junk food, smoke, consume alcohol and have sex. The belief that young people need protecting from themselves and from certain temptations has a long history dating back to at least the 1800s (Pearson, 1983).

Growing up female — Feminist ethnographic studies of young women

It is possible to trace a line of ethnographic enquiry into young women's lives from the 1970s to the present day, and to identify both consistencies and shifts in their findings. The early studies focused on young women's experiences at school (Fuller, 1982) or their daily lives (McRobbie, 1977), and their transition from school to work (Griffin, 1985). All these studies explore both relationships between young women and the processes of growing up female. The earlier studies, such as those of McRobbie (1977), McCabe (1981) and Griffin (1985), assert that young women's close friendships with each other tend to decline when they begin to form steady relationships with young men, in puberty. However, a shift in focus can be traced since those early studies, with more recent feminist studies on young women's lives and friendships portraying female friendship as a mechanism for support and resistance (Griffiths, 1988a, 1995; Wulff, 1988; and Morris, 1997). Earlier studies were rooted in the structuralist idiom of the time, which emphasised social constraints based on class and race divisions. Perhaps influenced by the postmodern focus on flexible identities and lifestyles, later studies appear more upbeat and optimistic, with more attention paid to the mechanisms young women use to resist societal pressure than to their relative powerlessness.

The cult of femininity

Since these earliest ethnographies of young women's lives, feminist researchers have analysed the influence of the cult of femininity on young women. In the 1970s, McRobbie (1977) published some ground-breaking research about young women's lives in which she analysed popular magazines aimed at them, such as *Jackie*. She discusses the culture of romance pervasive in these magazines, whereby the general tone of the magazine, especially its photo-stories, encourages young women to see themselves as successful only if they have a boyfriend. Her study of working-class young women attending a youth club in Birmingham revealed that they saw their destiny as marriage and children:

> Although the working-class girl may have few illusions about marriage it does still remain her destiny and being left single is an unambiguous sign of failure. (McRobbie, 1991: p. 54)

These romance magazines tapped into the perceived failure of unattached single young women, and advised them on how to attract a male partner, and also stressed the importance of not trusting other girls because they might steal your boyfriend. Magazines aimed at young women today, such as *Just 17*, do not focus so much on the culture of romance. Although they still contain a large number of articles on fashion and make-up, their emphasis is now on looking good for yourself, and not just in order to get a man.

The use of the tools of femininity such as an overtly sexualised appearance has been seen as a form of young women's resistance to the rules of school, teachers, parents and other adults. Nava suggests:

> In a context in which sexuality is considered appropriate for adults only, girls' expressions of it amount to a form of subversive behaviour which, unlike other forms of adolescent resistance, does not jeopardise femininity. However, as a strategy for resistance it is limited in its effectivity for precisely this reason. Although constituting a challenge to parental and school authority it does not free girls from the regulation of boys (unless of course it is lesbian sexuality). Ultimately and paradoxically, girls' most common form of rebellion serves only to bind them more tightly to their subordination as women. (Nava, 1992: p. 82)

Exercise and physical activity

While *The Health of the Nation* did not set a specific target concerning the British population's exercise levels, it is seen as an important contributory factor in the reduction of Coronary Heart Disease (CHD), a key target area in the document. Exercise protects against CHD by reducing blood pressure and obesity, and can also facilitate smoking cessation (Dargie and Grant, 1991: p. 154). Numerous health promotion campaigns have extolled the virtues of physical activity (such as the *Look After Your Heart* and *Active For Life* campaigns), and the Health Education Authority asserts that exercise as well can produce general improvements in health, as reducing the likelihood of CHD (Health Education Authority, 1995).

Exercise is viewed by health professionals as an extremely positive activity for both adults and young people. Their desire to promote regular physical activity for young people is seen as helping them to grow into healthy adults:

> The health benefits of regular physical activity have been demonstrated primarily for adults. Yet many people firmly believe that regular exercise during adolescence establishes a pattern that lasts into adulthood, promotes generalizable health-protective behaviours, inhibits health-compromising behaviours and leads to improve health status. (Millstein and Litt, 1990: p. 445)

The head of the physical education department in Hillside secondary school, Ms Powers, backed up her assertion that many young people were not very fit by referring to some fitness tests the school had conducted on students in years ten and eleven:

> Having done one or two of the Euro-fit tests with them, then we know on the whole they're not very fit, so I think perception is backed up by some research, not major research but something like the multi-stage fitness test which is a test for cardiovascular endurance. Most of them struggle on that, which is not always a good sign, because they're only young.

However, some evidence in this study points to young women being interested in physical activity, but not in the kinds of activities currently available to them. Questionnaires circulated to young women at youth clubs in Wolverhampton and Hillside established that many young women were interested in activities such as basketball, skateboarding, horse riding and ice-skating. Predictably, they also expressed a keen interest in dancing, an issue to which we return later.

Within the participant observation phase of the study, Sally and Eliza were shadowed for a week at school, during which time they had two physical education (PE) lessons in their timetable. In the first lesson, Sally said she was not participating as she had a letter from her mother excusing her because of asthma. Eliza was also not planning to participate. When asked why not, she said "I told the teacher I forgot my kit, but I haven't, though". Sally, Eliza, and the other non-participators (about five other young women out of about 30 in the class) were instructed to walk around the outside of the running track. At first, it seemed that Eliza's lack of enthusiasm was attributable to not wanting to take part without her best friend, Sally. However, later that day, during lunch time, when walking past the tennis courts where some young women were playing, Sally said the young women were squares [uncool] for playing sport in their lunch hour, although she conceded she "quite enjoys tennis". The day before Sports Day, Sally asked a young man whether he was taking part and when he said yes, she called him a 'keeno' for doing so. The young man himself said "Its better than sitting in the hall doing nothing or doing the lessons". Sally said she preferred doing lessons to taking part in sports day. For Sally, being seen as cool was extremely important. She felt that even participating in an activity which she enjoyed, such as tennis, would ruin her credibility as a sophisticated rebel.

The second time Sally and Eliza had PE, again they both joined the line of non-participants outside the PE block. Both of them were given a detention for 'forgetting' their kit twice. During the session the rest of the mixed-sex group played either rounders or tennis, while they stood on the tennis courts watching the others. Eliza expected to be called into the Head of Year's office the following day, and resolved to start doing PE again because her mother grounded[2] her if she got any detentions. When asked why they dislike PE so much, Eliza said, "I really hate PE", and Sally also said "I hate it". Further attempts to elicit their reasons for feeling this way brought no further explanation. When asked about the reluctance of some young women's to participate in PE, Ms Powers, the Head of PE, replied:

> There's a hard core, if you like. It's not a massive group, There's certainly a handful and they're the ones who come with some reason for not doing it on a regular basis ... though since you came down the last time with Eliza, she's done it every time since then, because I pointed out to her that she wasn't fulfilling the National Curriculum and none of them are stupid. They realise they have to, and she's now suddenly rediscovered the fact that she can take part. I think the biggest problem for young girls is they don't like changing in front of others, and as a result they don't like doing the activity because they see the activity has this horrible bit at the beginning and the horrible bit at the end and in the end it ends up that the middle bit, the PE bit, is the horrible bit as well because it entails a lot of problems for them and I think adolescent girls really struggle with it.... Although I totally agree with the fact that people should have showers, we've actually gone against the forcing of shower rule in this school for girls because we found we had more problems by saying you must have a shower [and] people were actually bringing notes to be excused PE because they didn't want a shower. I thought that was a retrograde step, so we encourage them and don't say you must, we do go into the healthy aspects of 'you start to smell if you don't

wash', et cetera, and 'you must change out of your clothes and must bring a change', but we don't actually force them in the showers, and we've had less problems since we've done that than when we stood there and made them go through the showers, which I felt was a barbaric way, I'm afraid, of enforcing health and healthy aspects.

This underlying reason for young women's aversion to PE has already been identified by researchers such as Pennycook (1987), Measor (1989) and Scraton (1995). They assert that many young women, as they go through puberty, are often embarrassed about their changing bodies. Scraton suggests that young women are loath to show their bodies because they feel they do not conform to the stereotypical acceptable physique of womanhood.

> Adult women are not expected to expose their bodies and are encouraged to dislike their body shape unless it conforms to the ideal feminine stereotype. During adolescence the PE changing room or shower area is an exposed situation where young women's developing bodies are put on view. (Scraton, 1995: p. 125)

When the young women were shadowed at school, none of them voluntarily took a shower after PE lessons, and they all changed from their PE kit to their school uniform using ways which did not expose their bodies.

Physical activity and femininity

When considering why Eliza and Sally had been so opposed to taking part in physical activities within the school curriculum, we considered that, in addition to being considered uncool, this was also due to the constraints of teenage femininity. Obviously there are people who dislike physical activities. It would therefore be reasonable to expect to find some young men in Eliza and Sally's school year who, like them, disliked PE lessons, but from personal observation, this phenomenon certainly applied more to young women than young men. Many young women observed during lessons at Hillside school carried make-up bags around with them, Sally and Eliza being no exception. Frequently they applied make-up in class, and Eliza was often instructed by teachers to remove her make-up as wearing it contravened school rules. The young women were very interested in their appearance, as was Alison (another young woman shadowed), and all three regularly talked about clothes, challenging the boundaries of school uniform with fashionable clothes, and they wore make-up and jewelry to school. These young women were engaging in the 'rituals of femininity' where looking good is a priority; running around getting sweaty and dirty is not glamorous and contravenes their norms of femininity.

> Young women are not expected to run around, get dirty or indeed sweat. The old adage that young ladies glow as opposed to sweat remains firm in today's thinking. (Scraton, 1995: p. 119)

At Hillside school, many young women attempted to stretch the boundaries of school uniform, like Alison and her friends, but usually with little success. They were allowed a small amount of jewelry, one ring and stud earrings, although most preferred to see how many rings they could wear without detection by teachers. In discussing her participant observation study of young working-class women in Birmingham, McRobbie points out how important it is for young women to look fashionable and up-to-date:

> By managing to make the uniform at least compatible with, if not indistinguishable from, what was currently fashionable, the girls could register their femininity in the classroom ... Underpinning this was a clearly articulated demand that they be taken seriously not as children but as women. (McRobbie, 1991: p. 43)

As McRobbie's quote illustrates, young women are attempting to reconcile a childish uniform with adult fashions. Scraton (1995: p. 124) suggests that the regulation school PE uniform is even more of an anathema to young women's burgeoning adult sexuality. At Hillside school young women could wear track-suit trousers for PE, which was probably more acceptable to them than the short skirts previously specified. Ms Powers noted that many young women do not like messing up their hair in PE lessons, and linked this to the perceived need young people have in looking just right if they are to be popular. She felt that young women's opposition to physical activities was firmly anchored in their conceptions of femininity:

> The one they always throw at me is 'I don't want muscles', you know? I don't know what sort of muscles they think they're going to get from what they're doing. They get this vision that they're going to get great big whopping muscles. Well actually, you won't. You don't do enough to get whopping muscles, but they're very concerned about the way they look, their self-image which goes hand in hand, I suppose with self esteem. They think they've got to look glamorous and look good for anybody to like them. The media image is that you're glamorous without doing a lot, at times.

A great deal of work is involved in achieving a glamorous appearance but for young women this is time spent shopping for clothes and experimenting with make-up and perfecting their 'look'. While experimenting with make-up may be a pleasurable activity for young women (Morris, 1997), and young women's magazines such as *Just 17* stress the importance of looking good for yourself, not just to 'get a man', these rituals of femininity are time-consuming and expensive. Although being slim may be important in young women's constructions of femininity, being slim through physical activity is in opposition to popular ideas of passive femininity. This is linked to the issues of erratic eating habits and using food control to stay slim, rather than exercise.

As Ms Powers observed, many young women have internalised the messages that they should look glamorous without investing too much physical effort. Representations of the female body in women's magazines (and men's magazines such as *Loaded*, even more so) rarely portray women in the many sizes and shapes that exist in real life. The image of the athletic woman who looks fit through exercise, not dieting, is becoming more prevalent in some magazines (such as health publications), but is still almost as absent from general magazines as is the averagely proportioned woman, the preference being for skinny models with boyish figures (which has been called heroin chic).

Dance

However, as indicated earlier, not all forms of physical activity are deemed uncool or unfeminine. Dancing is extremely popular among young women and in this section we explore why dancing can be reconciled with young women's self-image in a way that other physical activities apparently cannot. Social and formal dancing are both very popular with young women. Although a few of the young women studied did take part in formal dancing, this discussion focuses upon dancing as an informal social activity.

The youth club staff at Hillside found that when a new under-18s night was introduced at a local club, Tuesday evening attendance was severely depleted, especially affecting the young women. In the following few days the young women discussed with relish the clothes they had chosen to wear that evening, and what happened on the dance-floor. It was very obvious that for many of them, this was the highlight of their week. Similarly, in her study of young women in West Yorkshire, Griffiths noted the popularity of dancing and its accompanying rituals.

> Whether through schools of dancing, youth clubs or discos, dancing forms an important part of many young women's lives. Although it is sometimes directed at men, girls enjoy dancing first and foremost for its own sake, as a pleasurable, sensual experience which gives them some control over their bodies. (Griffiths, 1988b: 123)

One of us (EP) has many years experience as a youth worker. In every youth club, young women can be seen occupying floor space to learn dance routines, either copied from their favourite bands, or choreographed by themselves. Boys were usually excluded from this activity, and on occasions were quite violently removed from the space the young women had claimed as their own. Occasionally young men were allowed to participate in this activity for a short time, but only on the basis that they were good dancers, who enjoyed dancing and would not tease the young women about their dancing prowess. Young women for whom the suggestion of other youth club activities was met with sighs of derision would work hard at getting their dance steps right, and relished the achievement of a dance routine well learnt.

Thornton suggests that the feelings of liberation from the routine rules of school, work, parents, teachers and employers which social dancing engenders in young women have been "over-politicised in the field of leisure" (Thornton, 1993: p. 31). However, we would suggest that the importance of dance for young women cannot be over-emphasised. The ability to use their bodies in an expression of physicality, and to occupy space in a socially approved environment, represent choices often lacking for young women who do not have the same freedom of movement as young men. Sport, as we have seen, is a more socially acceptable activity for boys than for girls. McRobbie, in her study of young women in Birmingham in the 1970s found that dancing allowed young women some licence to loosen their self-control.

> With a virtual absence of boys, except for those three or four who hung about the coffee bar, the girls had no need to compete with each other. They did not feel self-conscious about dancing, nor did they need to adopt their more usual defensive strategies. In fact this was the one occasion when all the barriers were down. The girls were immersed in what was a thoroughly enjoyable activity. Much time and effort was spent in learning different routines to go with different records and the girls had perfected a number of styles to fit the different kinds of music the DJ played. (McRobbie, 1991: p. 56)

Conclusion

In this paper we have examined data from a recent empirical study of young women in two Midland communities in relation to exercise. We have suggested that *The Health of the Nation* and numerous health promotion campaigns ignore young women's motivations and experiences, seeing them instead as a target group for exhortation and admonition, rather than trying to adapt their health promotion messages to fit young women's lives and circumstances. Those studies which do record with any authenticity the realities of young women's lives (such as McRobbie, Griffin and Scraton) have rarely been used to inform health promotion strategies. This paper has examined the cult of femininity and its influence on young women's capacity to 'choose' a healthy lifestyle, and it explored the powerlessness felt by mothers and teachers in seeking to intervene effectively to encourage health-promoting behaviours.

Turning to recommendations for improved health promotion strategies concerning young women, young women should not be viewed as passive targets for Government intervention, or as the objects of health promotion campaigns. Rather, they are growing up in what at times can be a confusing, contradictory, complex social world. They are capable not only of responding to changing circumstances, but also of shaping their own destinies. Many health promotion initiatives have been unsuccessful because health professionals have failed to acknowledge any discrepancy between what they (as professionals) have identified as problematic health issues for young people, and those issues which the young people themselves believe to be important. (The provision of contraceptive and sexual advice is an obvious example, which is still called family planning by some professionals.) There appears to be a mis-match between this and what professionals think young people need to know

Health professionals must work in partnership with young women in identifying their own health priorities and devising effective strategies. Health projects at youth clubs and schools which genuinely work *with*, not *on*, young women, and where they have some input and ownership, will be more successful than those initiatives imposed on young women by socially remote health professionals. Health professionals have evidently devised their own programmes for action, derived in recent times from the political concerns of central government, an example of which is their emphasis on reducing the annual number of under-age pregnancies, which is higher in Britain than in other European countries. Successful health promotion initiatives will need to accept young people's view of the world and work with it, not against it.

As the proponents of feminist research have argued for many years, the most effective and illuminating qualitative research involves informants as equal participants in the research process. Health promotion specialists, youth workers, teachers and parents seeking to improve the health of young people have much to learn from this approach.

Notes

1   Although the young women involved in this study were all teenagers at the time, aged between 13 and 16 years, the term 'teenager' often has implications of deviance, as do the terms 'youth' and 'adolescent'. We refer throughout to 'young women' both as a term of respect to them and in recognition of their impending social and biological adulthood.

2   Being 'grounded' refers to parents forbidding their children to leave the house to spend time with their friends.

References

Dargie, H. and Grant, S. *(1991) The role of exercise, in R. Smith (ed)* The health of the nation: The British Medical Journal view. *London: British Medical Journal.*

Department of Health *(1992)* The health of the nation: A strategy for health in England. *London: HMSO.*

—— *(1997)* The health of the nation briefing pack second edition. *London: HMSO.*

Doyal, L. *(1995)* What makes women sick: Gender and the political economy of health. *Basingstoke: Macmillan Press.*

—— *(1997) Gendering health: Men, women and wellbeing, in Sidell, M., Jones, L., Katz, J. and Perberdy, A.* Debates and dilemmas in promoting health. *London: Macmillan, pp. 333–343.*

Fuller, M. *(1982) 'Young black and female', in E. Cashmore and B. Troyna (eds)* Black youth in crisis. *London: Allen and Unwin, pp. 87–99.*

Glaser, B. and Strauss, A. *(1967)* The discovery of grounded theory: Strategies for qualitative research. *Chicago: Aldine.*

Griffin, C. *(1985)* Typical girls?. *London: Routledge and Kegan Paul.*

Griffiths, V. *(1995)* Adolescent girls and their friends. *Aldershot: Avebury.*

—— *(1988a) 'From 'playing out' to 'dossing out': Young women and leisure', in Wimbush, E. and Talbot, M. (eds)* Relative freedoms: Women and leisure. *Milton Keynes: Open University Press, pp. 48–59.*

—— *(1988b) 'Stepping out: the importance of dancing for young women', in Wimbush, E. and Talbot, M. (eds)* Relative freedoms: Women and leisure. *Milton Keynes: Open University Press, pp. 115–125.*

Health Education Authority *(1995)* Health update 5: Physical activity. *London: HEA.*

McCabe, T. *(1981) / (1995 [new edition]) 'Girls and leisure', in A. Tomlinson (ed)* Leisure and social control *(LSA Publication No. 19). Eastbourne: Leisure Studies Association, pp. 125–133 (new edition).*

McRobbie, A. *(1977)* Working-class girls and the culture of femininity. *University of Birmingham. Unpublished MA thesis.*

—— *(1991)* Feminism and youth culture. *London: Macmillan.*

—— *(1994)* Postmodernism and popular culture. *London: Routledge.*

Measor, L. *(1989) '"Are you coming to see some dirty films today?" Sex education and adolescent sexuality', in L. Holly (ed)* Girls and sexuality. *Milton Keynes: Open University Press, pp. 25–51.*

Millstein, S. G. and Litt, I. F. *(1990) 'Adolescent health', in Feldman, S. S. and Elliott, G. R. (eds)* At the threshold: The developing adolescent. *Cambridge: Harvard University Press, pp. 431–456.*

Morris, K. *(1997)* Girl power. *University of Bristol, Unpublished PhD.*

Nava, M. *(1992)* Changing cultures: Feminism youth and consumerism. *London: Sage.*

Oakley, A. *(1993)* Essays on women, medicine and health. *Edinburgh: Edinburgh University Press.*

Pearson, G. *(1983)* Hooligan: A history of respectable fears. *Basingstoke: Macmillan.*

Pennycook, W. *(1987) 'Anorexia and adolescence', in M. Lawrence (ed)* Fed up and hungry: Women, oppression and food. *London: Women's Press, pp. 74–85.*

Scraton, S. (1986) 'Images of femininity in the teaching of girls' physical education', in J. Evans (ed) Physical education, sport and schooling: Studies in the sociology of physical education. *Lewes: Falmer, pp. 71–94.*

———— *(1987) Gender and physical education: Ideologies of the physical and the politics of sexuality, in Walker, S. and Barton, L. (eds)* Changing policies, changing teachers: New directions for schooling? *Milton Keynes: Open University Press, pp. 169–189.*

———— *(1990)* Gender and physical education. *Victoria: Deakin University.*

———— *(1992)* Shaping up to womanhood: Gender and girls physical education. *Buckingham: Open University Press.*

———— *(1994) 'The changing world of women and leisure: Feminism, postfeminism and leisure',* Leisure Studies *Vol. 13, No 4: pp. 249-61.*

———— *(1995) 'Boys muscle in where angels fear to tread: Girls' sub-cultures and physical activities',* in C. Critcher, P. Bramham and A. Tomlinson (eds) Sociology of leisure: A reader. *London: E. and F.N. Spon, pp. 117–129 [first published 1985 in* Leisure and Youth, *ed. Ken Roberts, LSA Publication No. 17. Eastbourne: Leisure Studies Association].*

Sidell, M., Jones, L., Katz, J. and Perberdy, A. *(1997)* Debates and dilemmas in promoting health. *London: Macmillan.*

Thornton, S. *(1993)* Record hops to raves: Authenticity and subcultural capital in music and media cultures. *Strathclyde University. Unpublished PhD Thesis.*

Wulff, H. *(1988)* Twenty girls growing up: Ethnicity and excitement in a South London micro culture. *Stockholm: Department of Social Anthropology.*

Developing Bodies: The Negotiation of Femininities and Physicalities by Girls in Physical Education

Laura A. Hills

Sport, Health and Exercise, University of Durham (UK)

Introduction

Girls' and women's physicality has been the subject of much discussion, particularly with regard to relationships between physicality and gender ideologies. Central to this study is an exploration of the tension between feminist discourses of the body that focus on social practices that produce 'docile female bodies' and discourses which highlight the potential for physical activity experiences to challenge traditional ideas of femininity. Physical Education represents one context where girls learn about and develop their bodies. This paper looks the relationship between at how girls' experience their bodies in relation to the gender discourses and social practices. Of particular interest is an exploration of the dichotomous representation of female bodies as either 'feminine' or resistant, as well as the interplay between physicality and gender.

Physical Education, gender and schooling

Physical Education, and more broadly, schooling have been identified as significant spaces where students learn about social ideologies of gender (Scraton, 1992; Stanworth, 1981; Thorne, 1993). Gendering practices in schools often serve to emphasise differences between boys and girls and support traditional ideas of masculinity and femininity in line with the current patriarchal social order. Much of the work on girls and schooling has focused on comparisons between boys and girls behaviours and experiences, looking at how education supports gender inequities in ways that limit girls' experiences and expectations (Measor and Sykes, 1992; Stanworth, 1981).

Physical Education accentuates gender difference in part through segregating girls and boys in lessons and with regard to the curriculum. Boys may do rugby while girls do field hockey. Scraton's (1992) work with Physical Education teachers highlights the existence and promotion of stereotypical ideas of masculinity and femininity. Acceptable female physicality includes compliance to heterosexual norms such as "heterosexual appeal, desire, objectivity, and subordination" and emphasises control, appearance and presentation (p. 118). She found that these ideologies and policies can serve to limit and restrict girls' experiences and opportunities for girls. Chepyator-Thomson and Ennis' (1997) work on masculinity and femininity reveals that boys and girls in Physical Education behave and experience Physical Education in ways that are consistent with traditional conceptualisations of masculinity and femininity. They conclude that while most students behave according to stereotypical gender norms, the traditional cultures of masculinity and femininity were resisted through oppositional behaviours. Teachers' tendencies to allow students to behave in stereotypical ways were found to perpetuate gender inequities and negatively influence girls' perceptions of their competencies, strength, and capabilities in Physical Education. The focus of this study has been girls' subjective experiences of Physical Education and their own physicality with reference to ways that they conform to, negotiate, resist and transform the ideologies of 'femininity' that pervade practices in school PE. Post-structural theorists have critiqued dualistic approaches to understanding gender and have encouraged a more complex under-standing of how we conceptualise 'femininity'.

Feminist post-structuralism

Feminist post-structural theories have been employed to explore the relationship between social discourses and practices of the body that occur in school PE in the context of gendered power relations. Bordo (1993) suggests that a "major paradigm shift" has occurred which entails moving from conceptions of the body as "a fixed, unitary, primarily physiological reality" to a view of the body as a "historical, plural, culturally mediated form" (p. 288). Within this framework, understandings of bodies are con-structed in relation to particular social contexts. Because meaning is socially constructed rather than 'natural' or 'essential' there may be multiple 'discourses' that conflict, change, and co-exist.

These discourses, however, are positioned differently in relations to power. Weedon (1987: p. 105), drawing from Foucault's work on bodies and power, writes that "Neither the body nor thoughts and feelings have meaning outside of their discourse arti-culation, but the ways in which discourses constitute the minds and bodies of indivi-duals is always part of the wider network of power relations, often with institutional bases". For Foucault, power does not exist as something one group has over another, but as a "network of practices, institutions, and technologies that sustain positions of dominance and subordination within a particular domain" (Bordo, 1993: p. 15). Situ-ating female physicality as a social discourse rather than a 'natural' quality creates the possibility for changes in meaning due to the multiple, competing and historically specific characteristics of discourse. Some discourses may predominate in society, but their dominance is never absolute.

Post-structural theorists, among others, have critiqued the idea that there is a monolithic 'femininity' that represents female experience. However, they recognise a discourse of femininity that Connell (1987) describes as 'emphasised femininity'. Idealized female bodies are slim and slight, not muscular or powerful, moving in a con-trolled and sexualized fashion where skin, hair, and clothing are cared for and presented as a heterosexual female body for the male gaze. Iris Young's phenomenological work suggests that "the more a girl assumes her status as feminine, the more she takes herself to be fragile and immobile and the more she enacts her own body inhibition" (Young, 1990: p. 154). The use of the term 'femininity' proves problematic as it is so clearly associated with 'emphasised femininity', and there is a question as to whether it can realistically be re-claimed or expanded to include alternative femininities. Davis (1997), Connell (1987), Moore (1994) and others assert that there are multiple femininities that exist and are created, altered, and discarded, in relation to other individuals, other social locations, and available social discourses and institutions. Within the constraints of gender power relations, however, individuals resist, challenge, and transform meanings around femininity and physicality to account more clearly for changing meaning, and the somewhat under-appreciated diversity of girls' and women's experiences of physicality. Kenway *et al.* (1994) suggest that Physical Education may be an arena where girls can learn alternative ways of experiencing their bodies, however, they provide little theoretical support for how this would work. There has been some work, however, in gaining understanding of how physical activity may be a site for resistance and even empowerment.

Physical activity

Physical activity has been presented as a way of challenging "the self-estrangement which lies close to the heart of the feminine condition" (Wright and Dewar, 1997: p. 82). To a certain extent, female physicality has been associated with fragility, weakness and passivity. On the other hand, masculinity, particularly hegemonic masculinity, is thought to be consistent with physical activity performance as it is associated with qualities of strength, power, and skill. Participation in sports is seen as more appropriate for men, leading to the devaluing and trivilization of women's sporting activities. Gatens' (1992: p. 130) assertion that the "female Olympic athlete may have more in common with a male Olympic athlete then with a wife/mother" illustrates the tendency to define sports performance as outside women's experience. The physically capable female has often been portrayed as an anomaly or as 'unfeminine'. She also fails to acknowledge that the female athlete has attributes beyond her 'sport' self. Post-structural theories acknowledge the potential of oppositional discourses, but also suggest that there should be the possibility that 'femininity' could actually be inclusive of the spectrum of female physicalities. From this perspective the female athlete would still be circumscribed within the bounds of 'femininity'.

Recognizing the contextual, social, and historical meanings of physicality, and subsequently the potential of alternative meanings, may be a way to reconceptualise 'femininity'. Inherent in many discussions of physicality found in the sport and leisure literature is a belief that physical activity participation can provide a path towards an alternative female physicality that will be empowering to the individual and that has the potential to challenge gendered power relations. McDermott (1996) identifies a need to move away from masculinist definitions of women's physicality which connect them to practices which sexualise, objectify and commodify a 'particular way of looking female' towards a construction that relies more heavily on women's experiences.

Theberge (1987, pp. 201-202) and others have portrayed physical activity participation as means through which women can provide alternative scriptings of femininity, resist masculine hegemony, and experience personal liberation:

> The potential for sport to act as an agent of women's liberation, rather than their oppression, stems mainly from the opportunity that women's sporting activity affords them to experience their bodies as strong, powerful and free from domination. If sexuality is the linchpin of gender inequality, then women's sporting practice can challenge gender inequality by challenging sexual stereotypes and patriarchal control of women's bodies.

Sports, Physical Education, and physical activities have the potential to disrupt as well as conform to traditional understandings of femininity and masculinity by providing alternative understandings of female physicality. Contrary to the presentation of 'docile bodies' featured in much post-structural feminist work (Bartky, 1988; Bordo, 1993), theorists in sport and leisure have highlighted ways that physical activity may allow women and girls to experience their bodies in empowering ways. Within this paper there is no attempt to define experiences as 'empowering'. The analysis focuses on girls' experiences of their own physicality and their responses to schooling practices that differentiate males and females based on traditional conceptions of gender.

Methods

The participants in this study included all of the girls in year eight (thirty-five 12-13 year olds) from a mixed comprehensive school in the North of England. The school is an inner city school which is characterised by its low income and ethnically diverse student population. Each girl had one double lesson of Physical Education each week. Some of their lessons were mixed gender and others were girl only. The girls from this school have little access or opportunity for participation in organised sports. In fact, at the time of the study only one girl participated in an organised sports program (Tae Kwan Do), and a second girl joined a football team towards the end of the study. Most work on physicality and gender has focused on adult women reflecting back on their experiences or on children and youths who are involved in organised sports programs (Hill and Brackenridge, 1989; Wright and Dewar, 1997). In this study, I sought to explore a population of girls whose experiences are often excluded from the literature.

The data for this study are drawn from observations and interviews conducted during a larger ethnographic study of girls' Physical Education. During the year, I observed 45 double lessons of Physical Education, in addition to observations in other classes, during breaks, lunch or after school. In addition, 28 of the girls were interviewed individually and all girls were included in one or more of 9 focus groups. The individual interviews ranged in length from approximately 25– 55 minutes. The data from my field notes and from the individual interviews have provided the basis for this analysis.

A thematic analysis was employed to generate themes relating to girls' Physical Education experiences. Extracts from the transcripts relating to broad areas, such as gender and self-perceptions, were grouped in addition to more specific areas generated from the interview topics, such as attitudes towards specific activities, mixed PE, beliefs about the importance of PE, and thoughts about physical activity participation after school. Using broad categories allowed me to extend my analysis beyond the specific content of the interview guide and to explore more general themes relating to gender and physicality. In relation to post-structural theory, when analysing the data I tried to be sensitive to both the diversity and commonality of girls' experiences. In addition, I tried to provide a broad enough framework to incorporate inconsistent and contradictory subject positions. The original transcripts were still used in the analysis in order to maintain an holistic sense of individual girls' narratives.

Girls and Physical Education

The discussion is divided into two main sections. The first section highlights the subject positions that girls occupy in relation to 'emphasised femininity' as exemplified through their perceptions of physical activity, the curriculum and their own physical self-perceptions. This is a starting point for exploring post-structural theorists' assertions that multiple femininities exist. Although the focus of this paper is 'gender', the diversity of girls extends to other social categories such as class, race, ability, etc. Diversity may occur both among and between girls who occupy different social locations.

The second section of the paper explores how girls experience gendering practices that differentiate between male and female bodies. The focus in this section is on how girls, who may occupy a range of subject positions or 'femininities' and 'physicalities', negotiate, conform to and resist more traditional discourses of gendered physicalities. The aim in this study is to explore girls' interpretations of these practices. Together these sections represent an attempt to look at girls' physicality at an individual level and then move to looking at how these individual subject positions relate to the common experience of institutional differentiating practices. Gender, difference, and power affect all girls, however, they do not affect all girls in the same way nor do they mean the same thing to all girls.

Perceptions of PE

Rather than dividing into groups who either liked or disliked Physical Education, most girls were represented in a broad middle ground of both liking and disliking various elements of Physical Education. Some girls described Physical Education as their 'best lesson' although no one characterised PE as their least favorite lesson. The majority of girls fell into a middle ground, responding to my general question about what they thought of their PE lesson with mixed responses such as 'I like it, but I don't like it', 'Sometimes it's OK, but sometimes you can get really boring lessons', or 'It's not like my best lesson but I'm not saying I completely hate it either'. These girls like some aspects of Physical Education but don't find the experience entirely positive. Within this paper, there is no attempt to explore the reasons girls provided to explain their attitudes towards Physical Education, but rather to simply establish that in this study it was difficult to portray a simple picture of girls who like PE and girls who dislike PE. Most girls fell somewhere between these two extremes, both liking and disliking aspects of the lesson.

Similarly, discussions of particular sports generated a range of responses. The sports discussed are confined to those that the girls experienced during their two years in secondary school. No girls disliked or liked every activity offered, and each girl had a unique profile of likes and dislikes with regard to the curriculum.

Shameen: "Netball is my favourite sport. And badminton. Them kinds of sports, You know, balls and bats. But rounders is my favourite game ever, and netball."

LH: "What do you like best?"

Jennifer "Swimming. This year none of them really, they're boring — badminton's OK, it's better than netball and basketball, nobody likes netball."

Alice "I liked doing aerobics, but I don't think I'll like doing gymnastics. I hate rounders, I don't like doing things where you bat things."

Theresa "I like everything in PE except swimming, I don't like it."

Girls' responses to the curriculum reveal a range of attitudes and valuing of different activities. One girl loves netball while another insists that 'no one likes netball'. Their feelings about activities varied in relation to time and context. One girl started out hating badminton, and as her skills developed began to love playing. Basketball was cited most often by girls as one of their favourite lessons. However, only eleven out of 28 mentioned basketball. Some of those eleven girls cited other 'favourites' and 17 others failed to mention basketball and chose other activities. There was no clear agreement among the girls about which activities were most enjoyable. Girls were able to highlight qualities of Physical Education experiences that shaped their attitudes towards activities. Many of the issues raised relate to elements of 'empowerment' (as described by Gilroy, 1996; Theberge, 1987; Wright and Dewar, 1997). Although this paper does not focus on empowerment, nor on explanations for why girls chose particular activities, the array of characteristics, including social location, feelings of competence, bodily confidence, agency and ideologies of gender, that girls describe as shaping their experiences do indicate a relationship between qualities of empowerment and girls' experiences that may lead to alternative 'femininities'. In describing their favourite activities girls express a range of attitudes and experiences. These attitudes relate in part to girls' feelings about their own physicality.

Girls' self-perceptions

Again, in order to explore girls' self-perceptions of physicality, I have chosen to highlight the diversity of ways that girls experience their bodies. Within the feminist literature described above there is a tendency to cluster girls' subjective experiences of physicality as either conforming to notions of emphasised femininity which produces 'docile' bodies, self-disciplined bodies, or more extreme resistant bodies. It is important here to look both at the continuum of individual girls' subjective bodily experiences and to look more closely at characteristics of positive and negative feelings of subjectivity.

In asking girls about their physical activity experiences, I was surprised by the detail with which some of the girls discussed and described their own physicality. Haug (1987) has described how girls and women learn to 'dissect' their bodies, labelling qualities of individual body parts such as 'I like my eyes', 'my hips are too wide', 'my stomach is flat but my ears stick out'. When placed in the context of physical activity, the discussions of bodies related closely to feelings of competence. The girls reported information about what their bodies could or could not do, and how that made them feel. One girl discussed her feelings about catching: "I feel dumb when I can't catch a ball because most of the girls can catch. My body goes all stiff. I feel like a fool" (Kiranjit). Her description is reminiscent of Young's (1990) portrayals of female physicality, although Kiranjit's perception that girls in general can catch well may be contradictory. In contrast, April, a girl known by her classmates as being good at football says, "I like shooting. People are scared of me. People say to me I kick the ball too hard. I don't kick the ball hard. Like on Sunday I was playing and I hit it high and it went straight to Johnny and he headed it in. And everybody said, 'Wow, she's got a big foot'". April's physical sense of self seems to present an oppositional subject position that disrupts traditional notions of femininity.

While April and Kiranjit may represent ends of a continuum, most of the girls place themselves somewhere along the middle. Amy says, "I like basketball and I like rounders. But one thing, I'm not a very good catcher. I like bowling, I'm good at bowling. I'm not a very good catcher, it was coming right to me and I went 'oh' [she claps her hands together] and missed it". Another girl describes her basketball experience: "My skill was getting the ball to people, I wasn't that good actually at shooting" (Shameen). These self-assessments illustrate both the reflection that girls undertake regarding their physicality as well as the diversity of subjective experiences among and even within individual girls. Even in a single activity girls may feel both competent and clumsy.

The capacity for girls who do not identify themselves as 'sporty' to self-analyse their abilities seems to suggests a real interest in bodily physical skills that may not be evident in writings on girls and physical activity. I have chosen to highlight the diversity of girls' experiences of their bodies in physical activity. Some girls seem to be experiencing the 'docile' body, others a more oppositional physicality, and still others inhabit less clearly definable forms of gendered physicality.

This discussion of diversity, evidenced through the range of attitudes towards given sports as well as the continuum of physical self-perceptions provided by the girls, indicates that understandings of girls' physicality need to move away from dualistic frameworks that position girls as embodying a particular form of femininity. There is no single, monolithic depiction of girls' experience that equates with 'emphasised femininity'. And, oppositional, resistant and alternative discourses vary in their relations to 'emphasised femininity'. As Haug (1987), Young (1990) and others have observed, however, subjective experiences of physicality do relate to gender ideologies. The diversity of subject positions occupied by girls supports McDermott's (1996) assertion that physicality needs to be defined through gaining understanding of individual subjectivity. Rather than defining girls' physicality in relation to traditional notions of 'femininity' there needs to be expanded conceptualisations of physicality grounded in experience. The following section of the paper explores how girls' subjectivity relates to the gender ideologies encountered in Physical Education practices.

Gender discourses and physicality

As described in the literature review, Physical Education has been shown to promote the gender binary, through practices that differentiate between girls and boys, a privileging of male sports experience, and the promotion, through the overt and 'hidden' curriculum, of ideologies of gender that support traditional understandings of 'femininity'. Scraton (1993) and Chepyator-Thomas and Ennis (1997) found that schools reproduce traditional cultures of femininity. These messages, however, are not seamlessly presented nor are they received unquestioningly by students; gender messages are negotiated, resisted, and conformed to. In this section, I want to look at how the girls negotiated the gendering practices engaged in by schools.

Differentiating by gender: the case of football

Within this study, football provides a useful case study for exploring girls' gender related perceptions of physicality. Football was offered for boys, but not for girls. A number of examples are given because the case of football usefully illustrates the variety of subject positions occupied by girls in response to a single differentiating practice. Theresa, and April, two self-described and peer acknowledged 'sporty girls', served as examples to other girls of girls who are highly skilled at sports. As in Thorne's (1994) discussion of girls who cross gender boundaries, these girls provided examples of girls' strength and skill. Their existence provided an alternative discourse of femininity for others, however, their experiences were still discussed within the context of broader social discourses of what 'girls' are like. The challenge was often a partial challenge as exemplified by Cindy and Kathy's descriptions: "I don't like football though, it's just for lads. You know April? She loves football". April is not a lad, so Cindy's gender logic fragments or at least appears inconsistent.

Kathy:	"I like aerobics and I like basketball and netball. I don't like football though."
LH:	"Why not?"
Kathy:	"It's just for lads. You know April? She loves football, always plays football at home she goes onto the five-a-side, she plays with all the lads."
LH:	"But you think it's just for boys?"
Kathy:	"I wouldn't like to play. I play it at home when my cousins come down. I play it with them and I play volleyball."

Similarly, Kathy maintains that football is for 'lads' even though she acknowledges April as a girl who loves football. Again, the argument relies on traditional gender dualisms of masculinity and femininity that recognise female participation as oppositional rather than part of a broader definition of femininity. Even April herself says, "None of the (other) girls like playing football." Within these discourses, football is perceived as a 'lads' game and school practices support this ideology.

Some girls identified their exclusion from football, however, as sexist or exclusionary:

Theresa:	"I think school's a bit sexist as well. 'Cause they just let the boys do football and not the girls."
LH:	"Why do you think they do it like that?"
Theresa:	"I don't know, 'cause of TV, it's just men isn't it doing football. I think there should be a girls' team. 'Cause I enjoy football. They just don't let us do it."

For Theresa, acknowledged throughout her year as a 'sporty' girl by students and staff, the denial of football lessons for girls was identified as a 'sexist' practice related to the exclusion of girls and women in the media. She, however, maintains her belief that girls should be able to play football and that she 'enjoys it'. Rachel, a girl who dislikes much of Physical Education, addressed the issue of girls' football as well:

| LH: | "So do you wish girls did football and things like that?" |
| Rachel: | "No, 'cause I don't like it, but for April and them I wish we did, 'cause it's not fair on them, is it? I don't mind doing it as long as it's just girls. Or even girls and boys. At least girls are getting a chance aren't they?" |

Her response indicates an ability to differentiate between her preferences and a broader sense of social justice. She would rather participate in football rather than have girls excluded. For her the exclusion links to limitations on girls' experience. Again, the exclusion of girls from football situates discussions of physicality in terms of a gender binary where appropriate forms of physicality are linked to traditional norms of masculinity and femininity which limits the range of available discourses in favour of an 'emphasised femininity' approach. Some girls believe that football is for lads, however, an even larger number of girls felt that girls can do 'anything' and that the gendering practices engaged in by the school served to unfairly limit girls' opportunities.

Other differentiating practices

Beyond football, girls experienced other gender differentiating practices. As in the case of football, these practices served to exclude, limit, or devalue girls' abilities. Rachel describes a differentiating experience from Physical Education.

Rachel: "And also, right, one time, when we were doing rounders or something there was like the big bats and the little bats and Mr. Martin says the girls have to have the little bats and the boys can have the big bats and we were saying "why, why" and he just said because the boys are used to doing things like that and I didn't think that were fair 'cause we could manage a big bat as well couldn't we? I mean we should like get a choice whether we wanted a big bat or a little bat but we weren't allowed a big bat because we were girls. They think that girls are like weaker than boys and boys stronger. There's some boys that can't do it like Steve and all them lot. Sorry if I had to mention his name. He can't do it and he still got to use the big bat just because he was a boy, didn't he. I didn't think that were fair."

In this story, the teacher differentiates by gender, rather than ability or student choice to distribute equipment. In so doing, he demonstrates a practice that privileges male experiences and ability. Rachel interpreted his actions as evidence of the teacher's belief that boys are stronger then girls. She, however, rejects his gender logic, drawing again on both the concept of fairness and the presence of girls whose physicality disrupts traditional gender ideologies.

Linda reflects on the implications of designating particular activities as male or female appropriate. She recognises that the sports the boys are involved in are 'big' or higher status. She rejects the separation of sports by gender drawing on boxing, one of the most recent male bastions to be opened to women.

Linda: "They [boys] probably think 'Well we're better than them so just let them ... do netball, we want to do basketball'. They do the big sports and only girls do the small sports. Well, you can do it either way, like with girls boxing now.

Again, she defines the practice of differentiating sports as a reflection of the beliefs of the teaching staff and the boys. She rejects the practice, drawing on the example of women who box, another discourse that can be defined as oppositional to traditional femininity. Differentiating sports, for her has implications for student attitudes as well, it reinforces the idea that boys' sports are 'big'. Differentiating practices serve to present traditional views of masculinity and femininity. For some girls these practices are perceived as 'sexist' and as promoting a view of physicality that privileges male experience. This binary gender logic is challenged by some girls who refer to examples of alternative physicalities.

Conclusion

This paper has illustrated that girls' experiences of physical activity differ, and that from girls' perspectives the gender differentiation practised in school Physical Education fails, in many cases, to correspond to their experiences, beliefs, and gender sensibilities. The girls in this year group occupied a spectrum of physical self-perceptions and attitudes rather than separate, definable categories of physicality. No clear monolithic 'girl' emerged from the data. Although physicalities that could be defined as 'oppositional' did appear, the experiences of the 'sporty girls' were still complex and situation specific. Griffin's (1983) work on girls' experiences in Physical Education also indicated the presence of a range of subject positions. Within the environment of gymnastics she found that girls' participation could be described as either serious, exploratory or reluctant. The findings from the present study suggest that these patterns could be broken down and explored even more thoroughly to look across activities and within categories. Girls who are exploratory in gymnastics may be serious in basketball. One girl said, "I'm not a sporty girl, I'm just a normal girl". 'Normal girls' experiences in physical activity need to be conceptualised in a way that does not rely on dualisms of 'sporty' or 'not sporty', 'feminine' or 'not feminine'. If the term 'femininity' is to continue to be used, it must be recognised to encompass a diverse and complex spectrum of experiences.

Within this study, a tension existed between girls' experiences, beliefs, and attitudes and the gender differentiating practices that they experienced in Physical Education. Practices that rely on traditional notions of gender fail to recognise the reality of girls' experience, and serve to limit, de-value and demean girls' participation. Girls themselves experience these practices as 'unfair' and 'sexist'. In many cases, girls' understandings of their own physicality did not correspond with the differentiating practices engaged in by the school. Research that explores, challenges, and disrupts the 'binary' gender logic that permeates society through the documentation of personal experience may assist in creating new understandings of female physicality (Johnston, 1998). One of the most rewarding aspects of this study was the reflective capabilities of girls in relation to their sports experience that it revealed. The depth with which some girls were able to discuss and describe their experiences indicates the possibilities for work with this age. Post-structural frameworks are useful for analysis as they provide a starting point for understanding gender as a process rather than a 'natural' quality. Applying post-structural theories to the context of physical activity, physicality, and 'femininity' may allow us to re-think our understandings of female physicality in ways that correspond more closely to girls' experiences.

References

Bartky, S. (1988) 'Foucault, femininity and the modernization of patriarchal power', in Irene Diamond and Lee Quinby (eds) Feminism and Foucault: Reflections on resistance. Northeastern Boston: University Press, pp. 61–86.

Bordo, S. (1993) Unbearable weight: Feminism, western culture, and the body. Berkeley, CA: University of California Press.

Chepyator-Thomson, J.R., and Ennis, C. (1997) 'Reproduction and resistance to the culture of femininity and masculinity in secondary school physical education', Research Quarterly for Exercise and Sport, 68(1): pp. 89–99.

Connell, R. (1987) Gender and power. Stanford University Press: Stanford, CA.

Davis, K. (1997) Embodied practices: Feminist perspectives on the body. Sage Publication: London.

Gatens, M. (1992) 'Power, bodies and difference', in M.Barrett and A. Phillips (eds) Destabilizing theory: Contemporary feminist debates. Cambridge: Polity Press, pp. 120–137.

Gilroy, S. (1996) The embody-ment of power?: Women and physical activity. Unpublished Ph.D.

Griffin, P. (1983) 'Gymnastics is a girl's thing: Student participation and interaction patterns in a middle school gymnastics unit', in T. Templin and J. Olson (eds) Teaching physical education. Champaign, IL: Human Kinetics, pp. 71–85.

Haug, F. (1987) Female sexualization: A collective work of memory. London: Verso.

Hill, J. and Brackenridge, C. (Autumn, 1989) '"My body's a complete wreck": the contribution of PE to physical confidence', Physical Education Review; *12(2): pp.147–157.*

Johnston, L. (1998) 'Reading the sexed bodies and spaces of gyms', in H. Nast and S. Pile (eds) Places through the body. London: Routledge.

Kenway, J.; Willis, S.; Blackmore, J.; and Rennie, L. (1994) 'Making 'hope practical' rather than 'despair convincing': Feminist post-structuralism, gender reform and educational change', British Journal of Sociology of Education, *15 (2): pp. 187–210.*

McDermott, L. (1996) 'Toward a feminist understanding of physicality within the context of women's physically active and sporting lives', Sociology of Sport Journal, *13: pp. 20–30.*

Measor, L. and Sykes, P. (1992) Gender and schools. London: Cassell.

Moore, H. (1994) A passion for difference. Cambridge: Polity Press.

Scraton, S. (1992) Shaping up to womanhood: Gender and girls' physical education. Buckingham: Open University Press.

Stanworth, M. (1981) Gender and schooling: A study of sexual divisions in the classroom. London: Hutchinson.

Theberge, N. (1987) 'Sport and women's empowerment', Women's Studies International Forum *10(4): pp. 387–393.*

Thorne, B. (1993) Gender play: Girls and boys in school. Rutgers, NJ: Rutgers University Press.

Weedon, C. (1987) Feminist practice and poststructuralist theory. Oxford: Basil Blackwell.

Wright, J. and Dewar, A. (1997) 'On pleasure and pain: Women speak out about physical activity', in G. Clarke and B. Humberstone (eds) Researching women and sport. London: Macmillan Press, pp. 80–95.

Leisure Studies Association
LSA Publications

An extensive list of publications on a wide range of leisure studies topics, produced by the Leisure Studies Association since the late 1970s, is available from LSA Publications.

Some recently published volumes are detailed on the following pages, and full information may be obtained on newer and forthcoming LSA volumes from:

LSA Publications, c/o M. McFee
email: mcfee@solutions-inc.co.uk
The Chelsea School, University of Brighton
Eastbourne BN20 7SP (UK)
fax: (+44) (0)1323 644641

Among other benefits, members of the Leisure Studies Association may purchase LSA Publications at highly preferential rates.

Please contact LSA at the above address for information regarding membership of the Association, LSA Conferences, and LSA Newsletters.

LEISURE CULTURES, CONSUMPTION AND COMMODIFICATION

LSA Publication No. 74. ISBN: 0 906337 84 4 [2001] pp. 171
ed. John Horne

Contents

LEISURE AND SOCIAL INCLUSION: NEW CHALLENGES FOR POLICY AND PROVISION

LSA Publication No. 73. ISBN: 0 906337 84 4 [2001] pp. 204
eds. Gayle McPherson and Malcolm Reid

Contents

JUST LEISURE: EQUITY, SOCIAL EXCLUSION AND IDENTITY

LSA Publication No 72. ISBN: 0 906337 83 6 [2000] pp. 195+xiv
Edited by Celia Brackenridge, David Howe and Fiona Jordan

Contents

JUST LEISURE: POLICY, ETHICS AND PROFESSIONALISM

LSA Publication No 71. ISBN: 0 906337 81 X [2000] pp. 257+xiv
Edited by Celia Brackenridge, David Howe and Fiona Jordan

Contents

MASCULINITIES: LEISURE CULTURES, IDENTITIES AND CONSUMPTION

LSA Publication No. 69. ISBN: 0 906337 77 1 [2000] pp. 163
Edited by John Horne and Scott Fleming

Contents

GENDER ISSUES IN WORK AND LEISURE

LSA Publication No. 68. ISBN 0 906337 78 X
Edited by Jenny Anderson and Lesley Lawrence [pp. 173]

Contents

SPORT, LEISURE IDENTITIES AND GENDERED SPACES

LSA Publication No. 67. ISBN: 0 906337 79 8
[1999] pp. 196
Edited by Sheila Scraton and Becky Watson

HER OUTDOORS: RISK, CHALLENGE AND ADVENTURE IN GENDERED OPEN SPACES

LSA Publication No. 66 [1999] ISBN: 0 906337 76 3; pp. 131
Edited by Barbara Humberstone

Contents

POLICY AND PUBLICS

LSA Publication No. 65. ISBN: 0 906337 75 5 [1999] pp. 167
Edited by Peter Bramham and Wilf Murphy

Contents

CONSUMPTION AND PARTICIPATION: LEISURE, CULTURE AND COMMERCE

LSA Publication No. 64. ISBN: 0 906337 74 7 [2000]
Edited by Garry Whannel

Contents

GENDER, SPACE AND IDENTITY: LEISURE, CULTURE AND COMMERCE

LSA Publication No. 63. ISBN: 0 906337 73 9 [1998] pp. 191
Edited by Cara Aitchison and Fiona Jordan

Contents

THE PRODUCTION AND CONSUMPTION
OF SPORT CULTURES:
LEISURE, CULTURE AND COMMERCE

LSA Publication No. 62. ISBN: 0 906337 72 0 [1998] pp. 178
Edited by Udo Merkel, Gill Lines, Ian McDonald

Contents

TOURISM AND VISITOR ATTRACTIONS: LEISURE, CULTURE AND COMMERCE

LSA Publication No 61. ISBN: 0 906337 71 2 [1998] pp. 211
Edited by Neil Ravenscroft, Deborah Philips and Marion Bennett

Contents

LEISURE PLANNING IN TRANSITORY SOCIETIES

LSA Publication No. 58. ISBN: 0 906337 70 4
Edited by Mike Collins; pp 218

Contents

LEISURE, TIME AND SPACE: MEANINGS AND VALUES IN PEOPLE'S LIVES

LSA Publication No. 57. ISBN: 0 906337 68 2 [1998] pp. 198 + IV
Edited by Sheila Scraton

Contents

LEISURE, TOURISM AND ENVIRONMENT (I) SUSTAINABILITY AND ENVIRONMENTAL POLICIES

LSA Publication No. 50 Part I;
Edited by Malcolm Foley, David McGillivray and Gayle McPherson (1999);
ISBN 0 906337 64 X

Contents

LEISURE, TOURISM AND ENVIRONMENT (II) PARTICIPATION, PERCEPTIONS AND PREFERENCES

LSA Publication No. 50 (Part II)
Edited by Malcolm Foley, Matt Frew and Gayle McPherson
ISBN: 0 906337 69 0; pp. 177+xii

Contents